Arthur Symons
Critic of the Seven Arts

Studies in the Fine Arts: Criticism, No. 25

Donald B. Kuspit, Series Editor

Professor of Art History
State University of New York at Stony Brook

Other Titles in This Series

Arthur Symons
Critic of the Seven Arts

by
Lawrence W. Markert

UMI Research
Press

Ann Arbor / London

NX
640.5
.S96
M37
1988

Produced and distributed by
UMI Research Press
an imprint of
University Microfilms Inc.
Ann Arbor, Michigan 48106

Library of Congress Cataloging in Publication Data

Markert, Lawrence W. (Lawrence Wayne), 1946-
Arthur Symons : critic of the seven arts.

(Studies in the fine arts. Criticism ; no. 25)
Bibliography: p.
Includes index.
1. Symons, Arthur, 1865-1945—Criticism and
interpretation. 2. Arts. I. Title. II. Series.
NX640.5.S96M37   1988   700'.92'4   87-22802
ISBN 0-8357-1845-X (alk. paper)

British Library CIP data is available.

To Carol and Brooke Peirce

Arthur Symons, 1891
(*Photograph courtesy Princeton University Library*)

Contents

Preface

In their anthology, *Strangeness and Beauty*, Eric Warner and Graham Hough state that "Arthur William Symons has long been one of the ghosts of literary history" (II:210). Indeed, Symons has remained a curious, shadowy figure who was important to many phases of the literary world during the late nineteenth and early twentieth centuries. He deserves to be much better known than he is, for as it stands he is known primarily as the author of *The Symbolist Movement in Literature* (1899).

A sense of Symons's importance in literary history can be easily established, as Warner shows in his excellent introduction to the section from Symons's work. Symons was one of Yeats's closest friends. Yeats also acknowledged Symons's influence on the theory and practice of his poetry and mentioned that Symons had become "the best critic of his generation" (letter from W. B. Yeats to Rhoda Symons, October 13, 1908). T. S. Eliot and Ezra Pound also paid tribute to Symons's influence. Both claimed that the knowledge of contemporary French literature Symons provided changed their poetry. Symons helped the young James Joyce find a publisher for his poems and defended the work of Conrad and Hardy during the early decades of this century. Despite such achievements, Symons has virtually dropped from consideration as an important literary figure.

Only a few important studies of Symons's work have appeared. Most are superficial accounts. W. G. Blaikie-Murdock wrote an early study, *Arthur Symons*, in 1907, and T. Earle Welby offered a more extensive view with *Arthur Symons* in 1925. But it was not until Frank Kermode published *Romantic Image* (1957) that Symons's aesthetic was given serious consideration, particularly in relation to the literary traditions which he synthesized. John Munro's *Arthur Symons* (1969) is the most substantive critical evaluation available, and Tom Gibbons's *Rooms in the Darwin Hotel* (1973) places Symons in the transition from Victorian to modern.

More recent critical activity on Symons indicates a renewed interest in his work, which may result in some adjustment of his reputation. Warner and Hough's anthology, *Strangeness and Beauty* (1983), includes a significant amount of Symons's critical writing. Warner's introduction also sets the stage for a reevaluation of his position in literary history. Another recent text which has also contributed to a resurgence of interest in Symons's work is Karl Beckson's *The*

Memoirs of Arthur Symons (1977), a collection of Symons's previously unpublished essays, which form part of the Symons Collection in the Princeton University Library. There are, as well, several texts just published or forthcoming. Karl Beckson's biography, which will replace the flawed biography by Roger Lhombreaud, will be published this year by Oxford University Press. The definitive bibliography, edited by Karl Beckson, Ian Fletcher, John Stokes, and me, is forthcoming from the Garland Press. Finally, the University of Iowa Press will publish soon a selection of Symons's letters, edited by Karl Beckson and John Munro.

Part of the problem with Symons's reputation stems from the fact that in the late summer of 1908 he suffered a mental breakdown from which he never fully recovered. A picture of this period is clearly drawn in Karl Beckson's short article, "The Critic and the Actress: The Troubled Lives of Arthur and Rhoda Symons," which is based upon letters exchanged between Arthur and Rhoda recently acquired by the Butler Library, University of Columbia. During this period, Yeats helped secure for Symons a government pension once it was clear that Symons was never going to fully regain his intellectual powers. Symons continued, once he was released from medical care in 1910, to write and publish his work, but what he now published proved only to undermine his reputation as a writer. He cannibalized previously published essays and combined these extracts with prose dominated by personal obsessions.

Prior to his breakdown, however, Symons was regarded as one of the most important critics of his generation. He produced an astounding number of books, articles, and reviews, including not only literary criticism but also poetry, fiction, drama, and travel sketches. Indeed, it is the breadth of his interests and commentary that is one of the most fascinating aspects of Symons's work as a literary figure during the late nineteenth and early twentieth centuries.

In 1906, when he published *Studies in Seven Arts*, Symons defined the scope of his interests as they had evolved. He had been well known as a literary critic and as a poet. In 1903, however, he published *Plays, Acting, and Music*, which showed his expanding interest in all aspects of art and culture. In *Studies in Seven Arts*, though, he offers a fuller and more clearly focused evaluation of the various arts: "With the art of poetry, or literature in general, I am not here concerned: that is my main concern in most of my other books of criticism. In this book I have tried to deal with the other arts, as I know or recognize them; and I find seven: painting, sculpture, architecture, music, handicraft, the stage (in which I include drama, acting, pantomime, scenery, costume, and lighting), and, separate from these, dancing" (v–vi). He goes on to say that he has tried to study each of these arts from its own point of view and in its contemporary aspect.

What I have tried to accomplish in this study is to deal directly with some of the more important aspects of Symons as a critic of the seven arts. Most studies thus far deal only with Symons's work on other arts as it informs his literary criticism. The chapters which follow focus on his criticism of these separate arts.

I have begun with a brief chapter on elements of Symons's literary background. His work as a literary figure has been fully dealt with by several critics. The first chapter, then, deals with some aspects of his literary background that relate most directly with his criticism of the other arts. "The Art of the Theatre," the second chapter, within which is included some consideration of the art of dance, begins the fuller description of Symons's work as a critic of the various arts. The next chapter concerns Symons's travel writings, his interest in the aesthetics of the spirit of place. Living life as art became especially important to the aesthetic traveller during this period. "Art and Artists" deals with Symons's theory of the visual arts, including handicraft, and his evaluation of various individual artists. The final chapter describes Symons as a music critic, evaluating his ideals in music and the art of musical performance. These chapters deal not with each of the seven arts, but with Symons's role as a critic of these arts.

In addition, I have described and evaluated some of the major influences on Symons's criticism of the various arts. By organizing this work into chapters on the individual arts, I am better able give a clear picture of the traditions from which Symons draws. He was very much a man of his time, a representative figure, and he read and synthesized much. As a drama and dance critic Symons read Charles Lamb and Gordon Craig, among others. Symons was an avid traveler and wrote with sensitivity about the spirit of place. He read widely in travel writing, including articles and books by George Borrow, John Addington Symonds, and Vernon Lee. As an art critic, he read the work of James McNeil Whistler and George Moore, as well as the more obvious figures, John Ruskin and Walter Pater. Symons as a music critic has to be understood in the context of the literate composers to whom he looked for artistic guidance, including Richard Wagner and Robert Schumann, whose critical writing he read in order to better appreciate the aesthetic qualities of music.

This study is based upon an evaluation of all of Symons's articles and reviews, as well as the various texts he published. The full bibliography will be published by the Garland Press, but in order to fully evaluate Symons's work as a critic of the various arts it is necessary to consider his many uncollected reviews and articles. For example, Symons's commentaries on Claude Debussy's work are found only in the 1928 edition of *Plays, Acting, and Music* and in several uncollected reviews. His work as a critic of the visual arts is not only shown in his texts on painting, but also in many of the reviews he wrote as an art critic for various periodicals.

Acknowledgments

Many friends and scholars have read through this manuscript and offered advice throughout its development. Professor Karl Beckson, Brooklyn College of the City University of New York, has been especially generous with his time and knowledge. Ian Fletcher, Arizona State University, and John Stokes, University of Warwick, have been very helpful in tracking down various articles and texts by Symons. Mrs. Dorothy Bednarowska, St. Anne's College, the University of Oxford, read this study in draft form through final revisions. All that is good in this book is due to her dedication to its completion. Mr. Christopher Butler, Christ Church, the University of Oxford, has been an intellectual inspiration for many years. My wife, Diane, and children, Gillian and Andrew, put up with long hours of quiet in the house, or as much as they could tolerate. My wife also spent many hours in front of the word processor typing most of the manuscript.

Finally, I would like to offer my thanks to Carol and Brooke Peirce, to whom this book is dedicated. They have been the most important intellectual forces in my life.

1

The Literary Background

Born on February 21, 1865, at Milford Haven, Wales, to Mark Symons (an itinerant Wesleyan preacher) and Lydia Symons, the young Arthur Symons grew up in an atmosphere he found personally and artistically oppressive. As he says in "A Prelude to Life," which he published in *Spiritual Adventures* (1905), "My parents were deeply religious; we all went to church, a nonconformist church, twice on Sundays; I was not allowed to read any but pious books or play anything but hymns or oratorios on Sunday; I was taught that this life, which seemed so real and so permanent to me, was but an episode in existence, a little finite part of eternity" (*Works* 5:12). This autobiographical story, written in the tradition of Walter Pater's "The Child in the House," describes fully the unimaginative, middle-class world against which Symons rebelled. Literature and the other arts served as a form of escape, and Symons's literary life always seemed to be lived in opposition to the limitations of his background.

Symons established early that he wanted to be a literary man, and he took seriously all that prepared him for this future life. Charles Churchill Osborne (1825–1900) was one of Symons's teachers and served as an intellectual guide to Symons as his curiosity led him from author to author. Osborne was also the editor of *The Salisbury and Winchester Journal*, in which Symons published some early reviews. The letters between Osborne and Symons, now in the Princeton University Library Collection, describe the artistic growth of Symons as a young man. Osborne answered questions Symons posed about various writers and supplied him with texts, magazines, and other items of literary and artistic interest. It becomes clear from these letters that the literary figures most important to Symons were Walter Pater, Robert Browning, George Meredith, and Algernon Swinburne.

Symons's first major work, *An Introduction to the Study of Browning* (1886), written while he was still living in rural England with his parents, manifests the influence of a number of these literary heroes. He sent copies to Meredith, to whom the book is dedicated, as well as to Browning and Pater. Indeed, all the works of this period, including his editing of the *Shakespeare Quarto Facsimiles* under the direction of Frederick Furnivall, bear the mark of these literary figures.

His early work as a literary journalist is also evidence of his early literary interests. He wrote admiring reviews of Browning's work, compared Browning to Meredith at a lecture for the Browning Society, and defined many of his own artistic ideals in his various reviews of Pater's work.

Pater's *Imaginary Portraits* depict essential aspects of an individual's personality. Symons admires Pater's portraits for their unique quality of character. As he says in his review, "Walter Pater's 'Imaginary Portraits,'" each represents "the study of a soul" (160). Allied with this aspect of the narratives is another important element, sincerity in terms of one's own feelings; these portraits are provocative because they are based upon the process of "looking within, and projecting now this now that side of oneself on an external plane" (160). Interestingly, the personalities, the consciousnesses described, have an essential temperament in common:

> I only mean that the attitude of mind, the outlook, in the most general sense, is always limited and directed in a certain way, giving one always the picture of a delicate, subtle, aspiring, unsatisfied personality, open to all impressions, living chiefly by sensations, little anxious to reap any or much of the rich harvest of its intangible but keenly possessed gains; a personality withdrawn from action, which it despises or dreads, solitary with its ideals, in the circle of its "exquisite moments," in the Palace of Art, where it is never quite at rest. (160)

When Symons wrote his own imaginary portraits, *Spiritual Adventures*, the same type of personality became central to his work. Indeed, the autobiographical persona he developed for "A Prelude to Life" is a mirror image of "the Paterian temperament" Symons describes in his review. As John Munro has shown, Symons "became saturated in his early years with Pater, attempting to reproduce the involutions of his prose style and laying himself open to 'all impressions,' and doing what he could to bring about 'a more intimate sympathy with some of the subtler aspects of art'" (21).

In his review of Pater's *Imaginary Portraits*, Symons also compares Pater's depiction of the soul with Browning's in *Sordello*, which shows further how Symons's aesthetic was developing as an integration of literary forces: "It is somewhat such a soul, I have thought, as that which Browning has traced in 'Sordello;' indeed, when reading 'Marius the Epicurean,' I was struck with a certain resemblance between those two exquisite books, and a little of the same feeling comes up again when reading some of the 'Imaginary Portraits' (160). The connection Symons sees between Browning's and Pater's aesthetics is further elaborated in *An Introduction to the Study of Browning* (1886).

In the Browning study, Symons also alludes to Matthew Arnold to give weight to his argument that the soul becomes apparent when character is placed "in some situation where its vital essence may become apparent—in some crisis of conflict or opportunity" (9). Arnold had made a similar observation in the preface to *Poems* (1853): "How unspeakably superior is the effect of the one moral impression left by a great action treated as a whole, to the effect produced by the most striking single thought or by the happiest image'' (6). Earlier in his preface, Arnold had commented on the type of action with which the poet must deal, ''those, certainly, which most powerfully appeal to the great primary human affections: to those elementary feelings which subsist permanently in the race, and which are independent of time'' (4). Symons, in relation to Browning, intensifies this same idea by quoting from Pater: ''To realise such a situation, to define in a chill and empty atmosphere the focus where rays, in themselves pale and impotent, unite and begin to burn, the artist has to employ the most cunning detail, to complicate and refine upon thought and passion a thousand fold. . . . Yet, in spite of this intricacy . . . we receive from it the impression of one imaginative tone, of a single creative act'' (qtd. in *Browning* 9–10). As Munro says about this passage, ''both Pater and Browning were concerned with the same thing: to isolate the significant moment; and, by contemplating it, to penetrate to the very essence of a character or situation'' (23). Symons's admiration for ''the Paterian temperament,'' which he found equally in Browning's dramatic situations, is evident throughout his work.

Symons's letters to Osborne also speak often of Swinburne's work, alluding to artistic ideals which are in line with those derived from Pater and Browning. In 1883, after Osborne had asked for Symons's thoughts on *Circe's Lovers*, a novel Osborne had written, Symons uses Swinburne as a means of focusing on a central artistic tenet: ''Art, to be anything, should be true, natural; the highest art, the only truly admirable art, is that which unites ideality and reality, in what Swinburne calls *imaginative realism*'' (letter, July 14, 1883).

Symons moved to London in 1889, taking up residence in Fountain Court, the Temple, where he remained for ten years. He also periodically maintained residence in London after his marriage in 1901 to Rhoda Bowser. In 1891 he joined the Rhymers' Club, where he first met W. B. Yeats. And it was also at this time that he began to write music-hall reviews for the London *Star*. Symons's literary life was beginning to expand rapidly. By the end of 1891 he had already published articles on music, art, literature, and drama. And in 1893 he published ''The Decadent Movement in Literature'' in *Harper's*, an essay which caused considerable stir in the artistic community and established Symons as a major figure in the *avant garde*.

But Symons's artistic theories developed out of his early literary influences. They form the base upon which he builds his criticism of all the arts. His essay on decadence broadens the scope by including a wealth of French authors, whose influence is further elaborated and refined in *The Symbolist Movement in Literature* (1899). These same influences and trends figure significantly in his writing about drama, travel and the spirit of place, art and artists, and music. Some of his most significant single works, ''The Decadent Movement in Literature'' (1893), *The Symbolist Movement in Literature* (1899), *William Blake* (1907), and *The Romantic Movement in English Poetry* (1909), written at the height of his career, show especially well some of his relevant literary ideals and offer a base from which his writings about the other arts may be better understood.

As Munro has observed, the years between the publication of *Days and Nights* (1889) and *London Nights* (1895) may properly be referred to as Symons's decadent period (40). To use Symons's own definition of the concept, he was attracted to a literature characterized by ''an intense self-consciousness, a restless curiosity in research, an over-subtilizing refinement upon refinement, a spiritual and moral perversity'' (858–59). A long entry in his notebook of ideas during this period gives additional insight into the poetic qualities he admired: ''Make a volume of poems on a common theme—the character of a modern man, modern in even the decadent sense.'' His character will be depicted to show decadent characteristics: ''The vagueness of his character (internally represented as unstable, a mere creature of moods)—his varying impressions, desires, passions or fancies (love, aesthetic delights—form and colors, art) give him a fine scope.'' The decadent credo that he evolves at this time seems oriented towards a debased Epicureanism which Pater's writings appeared to sanction. He says in this notebook, in fact, that the poems could finally be ''arranged in some sort of spiritual sequence'' to produce ''a book—like *Marius*—of 'Sensations and Ideas,' or 'Impressions and Sensations.''' The subtitle of Pater's *Marius the Epicurean* is ''His Sensations and Ideas.'' But Symons identifies other influences as well, noting that he himself should study various writers (especially Huysmans, Mallarmé, and Verlaine), restudy the *Fleurs du Mal*, and perhaps get Goncourts' *Idées et Sensations* (notebook).

''The Decadent Movement in Literature'' sets out to define decadence, as well as two other terms which had become current, impressionism and symbolism. Aspects of the decadent movement were consistent with ideas Symons developed earlier, including his interest in the human document, in works such as autobiography which draw directly on human experience. The decadent writers tried to restore man as a central topic by concentrating attention on his emotions and sensations, those aspects of man which made him unique. But in many ways this essay is a preliminary study in preparation for *The Symbolist Movement in Literature*. In the earlier study he deals primarily with Verlaine, Mallarmé, Maeterlinck, Huysmans, and the Goncourts. But the essay contains much more than just a decadent credo; it contains many of the ideas Symons develops in *The Symbolist Movement in Literature*, as well as many of the aesthetic ideals he uses in his other writings.

Symons begins ''The Decadent Movement in Literature'' by showing that the artistic ideals of classicism are outmoded; they no longer adequately reflect the world: ''simplicity, sanity, proportion—the classic qualities—how much do we possess them in our life, our surroundings, that we should look to find them in our literature—so evidently the literature of a decadence?'' (859). He then sets out to establish decadence as the movement of the modern era. The movement, in turn, has two main branches, impressionism and symbolism: ''What both seek is not general truth merely, but *la vérité vraie*, the very essence of truth—the truth of appearances to the senses, of the visible world to the eyes that see it; and the truth of spiritual things to the spiritual vision'' (859). Symons tries to equate these two concepts because he believes that there is a necessity for visual impression in order to achieve a recognition of the soul or the spirit that animates the world. The impressionist looks for the ''soul of the landscape'' (859). This aspect of the world is apprehended through the visible. The symbolist flashes ''upon you the 'soul' of that which can be apprehended only by the soul—the finer sense of things unseen, the deeper meaning of things evident'' (859). There is some confusion in Symons's definitions, but it seems clear that he sees all these artistic developments working together. At this stage he considers the decadent ideal as the most important.

The writings of the Goncourts helped Symons focus on the development of new ways of seeing. The new aesthetic of decadence demanded a revolt against the old forms, against ready-made impressions and language. The Goncourts in prose and Verlaine in verse invented a style that molded the new aesthetic: ''No one has ever tried so deliberately to do something new as the Goncourts; and the final word in the summing up which the survivor has placed at the head of the *Préfaces et Manifestes* is a word which speaks of 'tentatives, enfin, où les deux frères ont cherché *à faire du neuf*, ont fait leurs efforts pour doter les diverses branches de la littérature de quelque chose que n'avaient point songé à trouver leurs prédécesseurs''' (859). Later in this essay Symons speaks of the opera-glass image which the Goncourts used to define the fact that they had developed a new way of seeing. In the preface to *Chérie*, which Symons quotes, Edmond de Goncourt comments that his aim is that of having ''une langue rendant nos idées, nos sensations, nos figurations des hommes et des choses, d'une façon distincte de celui-ci ou de celui-là, une langue personnelle, une langue portant notre signature'' (qtd. 860). This new language was set in opposition to the journalistic news item. Verlaine's verse also accomplished this level of expression. As Symons says, ''To be a disembodied voice, and yet the voice of a human soul: that is the ideal of decadence, and it is what Paul Verlaine has achieved'' (862). And Huysmans, especially in *A Rebours*, figures significantly: ''His work, like that of the Goncourts, is largely determined by the *maladie fin de siècle*—the diseased nerves that, in his case, have given a curious personal quality of pessimism to his outlook on the world, his view on life'' (865). In ''Huysmans as Mystic'' in *Studies in Two Literatures*, Symons comments that *A Rebours* ''is the one real, the one quintessential, book which has been produced by the literature vaguely called decadent'' (300). He goes on to state: ''And, in giving final expression to this theory of the charm of what is diseased, unnaturally beautiful, to this lust of strange sensations, it ends with an even more hopeless cry of dissatisfaction'' (300).

Symons accomplished quite a bit through his exploration and artistic definitions of the decadent movement in literature. In many ways the *fin de siècle* spirit is, indeed, defined by his various pieces of literary and cultural criticism. He also mixed in the artistic ambitions of various important French writers, especially after 1899, when he made his first trip to Paris, accompanied by Havelock Ellis. But it is undoubtedly true, as Munro and others have observed, that Symons carried the decadent credo as far as it could go. He explored all the possibilities but was left dissatisfied. Symons, instead of turning to the church, as many had done, fell under the influence of W. B. Yeats, who introduced him to his own version of the spiritual world. He found, through Yeats, a fuller definition of symbolism and, therefore, a new aesthetic. Symons, however, had maintained an uncertain belief in the spiritual world; he was not a complete disciple of Yeats's spiritualism. He characterized himself in "A Prelude to Life" as being obsessed with two thoughts: "the uncertainty of life, and the uncertainty of what might be life after death" (*Works* 5:11).

The relationship between Symons and Yeats, however, seems to have allowed Symons to refine his understanding of the accomplishments of the authors he wrote of as decadent. Throughout his writings he had spoken of moments of intensity of feeling and emotion. He had in "The Decadent Movement in Literature" written that these moments contain "*la vérité vraie*, the very essence of truth." It was not a big step to state that during these moments communication with or the evocation of the "Divine Essence" becomes possible. The association with Yeats prompted Symons to look again at his decadent writers. He began to see them not simply as writers whose primary concern was to explore abnormal behavior and momentary impression, but as writers who sought transcendence through their art. Equally important, this literary association allowed Symons to produce a book which, as Richard Ellmann observes, "gave a name to the preoccupation with modes of half-uttered or half-glimpsed meaning which, as we can see clearly enough now sixty years have passed, was a principal direction in modern thought" (xiii).

The short introduction Symons wrote for his collection of essays on symbolist writers is revealing, for it includes his justification for refining his perspective from decadent to symbolist, and it shows the continuity between his earlier work and his most important single text. In relation to decadence, for example, he now suggests that the term has significance only as a definition of stylistic qualities: "As a matter of fact, the term is in its place only when applied to style; to that ingenious deformation of the language, in Mallarmé, for instance, which can be compared with what we are accustomed to call the Greek and Latin of the Decadence" (4). But if we look at Symons's essay on Mallarmé, he offers a different perspective on the use of language:

> It is the distinction of Mallarmé to have aspired after an impossible liberation of the soul of literature from what is fretting and constraining in "the body of that death," which is the mere literature of words. Words, he has realised, are of value only as a notation of the free breath of the spirit; words, therefore, must be employed with an extreme care, in their choice and adjustment, in setting them to reflect and chime upon one another; yet least of all for their own sake, for what they can never, except by suggestion, express. (70)

The stylistic innovations of the Goncourts were motivated by their recognition of the limitations of conventional French. They altered the language to make it more expressive, to give it a broader scope of expressive possibilities. Mallarmé, finally, alters language in order to evoke the reality beyond the visible: "The word, chosen as he chooses it, is for him a liberating principle, by which the spirit is extracted from matter; takes form, perhaps assumes immortality" (70). Symons's discussion of the Goncourts, which he included in the 1919 edition of *The Symbolist Movement*, does, however, have a primarily decadent orientation: "The Goncourts' vision of reality might almost be called an exaggerated sense of the truth of things; such a sense as diseased nerves inflict upon one, sharpening the acuteness of every sensation. . . . It is a world which is extraordinarily real; but there is choice, there is curiosity, in the aspect of reality which it presents" (149–50).

In line with his evaluation of the Goncourts' sense of reality, Symons deals significantly with the relationship between the visible and the spiritual. For authority on this issue, Symons now draws on Thomas Carlyle: "In the Symbol proper, what we can call a Symbol, there is ever, more or less distinctly and directly, some embodiment and revelation of the Infinite; the Infinite is made to blend itself with the Finite, to stand visible, and as it were, attainable there" (qtd. 2). The soul, which had been Symons's concern before, figures significantly, as does his opposition to the material world defined by science, which is a world of "everything that visibly exist[s], exactly as it exist[s]" (3). Now the world has more to offer: "After the world has starved its soul long enough in the contemplation and the rearrangement of material things, comes the turn of the soul; and with it comes the literature of which I write in this volume, a literature in which the visible world is no longer a reality, and the unseen world no longer a dream" (2–3). The final paragraph in the introduction carries the point further; he describes the movement as Arnold had described art, as a religion:

> Here, then, in this revolt against exteriority, against rhetoric, against a materialistic tradition; in this endeavour to disengage the ultimate essence, the soul, of whatever exists and can be realised by the consciousness; in this dutiful waiting upon every symbol by which the soul of things can be made visible; literature, bowed down by so many burdens, may at last attain liberty, and its authentic speech. In attaining this liberty, it accepts the heavier burden; for in speaking to us so intimately, so solemnly, as only religion had hitherto spoken to us, it becomes itself a kind of religion, with all the duties and responsibilities of the sacred ritual. (5)

These, then, are the ideals of the symbolist movement as Symons defines them. It is necessary, in fact, for Symons to use the term rather loosely in order to show how various writers function within the movement, for the relationship between the world of appearances and the world beyond is both dynamic and individual. Ellmann objects to the looseness of Symons's definition on these grounds:

> In the essays on Nerval and Villiers symbolism is primarily the perception of a reality which is opposite to the world of appearance; in the essays on Mallarmé and Maeterlinck this reality is not opposed to appearance, but is just barely over its borders; with Rimbaud and Verlaine, on the other hand, symbolism is the perception of the world of appearance with a visionary intensity; with Huysmans symbolism is the understanding of the organic unity of the world of appearance. Symons includes among the symbolists those who reject the world, those who accept it so totally as to see it with new eyes, and those who regard it under the aspect of eternity. (viii)

Ellmann's evaluations of Symons's view of each writer are correct, but the fault, it seems, is not in Symons. Indeed, there is no real fault. As in "The Decadent Movement in Literature," Symons is dealing with many writers who are at their core members of a movement—they seek the same end—but they approach their art differently.

If we had to identify Symons's own artistic practice, we would have to focus on his description of Verlaine, who sees the world of appearances with a visionary intensity: "To him, physical sight and spiritual vision, by some strange alchemical operation of the brain, were one" (43). He seeks in the world manifestations of a world which is beyond our senses. His conclusion ties this ambition to day to day existence: "Allowing ourselves, for the most part, to be but vaguely conscious of that great suspense in which we live, we find our escape from its sterile, annihilating reality in many dreams, in religion, passion, art; each a forgetfulness, each a symbol of creation; religion being the creation of a new heaven, passion the creation of a new earth, and art, in its mingling of heaven and earth, the creation of heaven out of earth" (94). The integration of heaven and earth is a form of proof "that there is something which makes it worth while to go on living, in what seems to us our best way, at our finest intensity . . ." (95).

Symons's description of the symbolist's marriage of heaven and hell makes his appreciation of Blake very evident. His interest in the visionary poet was long-lived. He wrote in 1884 some admiring verses to him, which he later included in an essay, "Notes on Romani Rai." As Munro says, Symons's poems to Blake show "his youthful enthusiasm for the poet, and, particularly, his desire to transcend the forms of external circumstance, which was evidently rooted in him at an early age" (100). The connection between Blake and the French symbolist writers dates from an earlier time as well. He had published in 1890 "A French Blake: Odilon Redon" in *Art Review*. In his preface to the original edition of *William Blake* (1905) Symons states that he began to read Blake's poetry as a child and that Blake has remained one of his favorite poets. He adds that he learned a great deal from Yeats, especially because of the 1899 edition of the *Works of William Blake* which Yeats and Edwin Ellis edited. Symons was also familiar with other critics of Blake, especially Rossetti and Swinburne.

Blake, it seems, embodied many of Symons's artistic ideals and was, as Symons saw it, an English equivalent to and predecessor of symbolism. It was fitting that, following the publication of *The Symbolist Movement in Literature*, he should go back to Blake. Indeed, Symons's critical text, *William Blake*, as well as *The Romantic Movement in English Poetry*, begin to establish or identify the symbolist movement in English literature, with Yeats as the current exponent. The sense of tradition that Symons wants to establish is given in the first paragraph of his study: "When Blake spoke the first word of the nineteenth century there was no one to hear it, and now that his message, the message of emancipation from reality through the 'shaping spirit of imagination,' has penetrated the world, and is slowly remaking it, few are conscious of the first utterance, in modern times, of the message with which all are familiar" (*Works* 4:1). As we have seen, the belief in revolt against established conventions and the necessity of developing new ways of seeing, as did Verlaine and the Goncourts, is important to Symons. He begins his study of Blake, therefore, by showing him as breaking down barriers. Later he observes that "Blake wrote when the eighteenth century was coming to an end; he announced the new dispensation which was to come, Swedenborg had said, with the year (which was the year of Blake's birth) 1757" (*Works* 4:106).

In line with his discussion of the symbolists, Symons felt that Blake's dispensation involved the escape from literalists of the imagination. Indeed, he describes Blake's artistic ambition in relation to a world which was still very much Symons's own:

> The rationalist's denial of everything beyond the evidence of his senses seemed to him a criminal blindness. . . . To Blake the literal meaning of things seemed to be of less than no importance. . . . Religion was asleep, with Art and Literature in its arms: Blake's was the voice of the awakening angel. What he cried was that only eternal and invisible things were true, and that visible temporal things were a veil and a delusion. (*Works* 4:107)

Blake's visionary approach to the world coincides with the symbolist doctrine Symons elaborated in *The Symbolist Movement in Literature,* and Blake's belief in art seems to have influenced Symons as well: " 'There are three powers in man of conversing with Paradise,' said Blake, and he defined them as the three sons of Noah who survived the flood, and who are Poetry, Painting, and Music" (*Works* 4:6). As with other writers, Symons tries to identify the quality of Blake's work by identifying his vision with that of a newly born child. Blake sees the world, in Symons's view, as unhampered by earthly convention: "It is like the voice of wisdom in a child, who has not yet forgotten the world out of which the soul came" (*Works* 4:50). Indeed, Symons suggests that to define the poetry of Blake requires new definitions.

Symons continues his evaluation of Blake by quoting the letter to Dr. Trusler in which Blake evaluates his own writing and painting. He has been asked to make his work understandable. Blake comments in relation to the authors and the great books as he defines them, those that show the greatest imagination: "What is it sets Homer, Virgil, and Milton in so high a rank of Art? Why is the Bible more Entertaining and Instructive than any other book? Is it not because they are addressed to the Imagination, which is Spiritual Sensation, and but mediately to the Understanding or Reason?" (qtd. in *Works* 4:77). What Blake seeks, what Symons, too, seeks, is the source or soul beyond reason and beyond appearance: "He knows, like Krishna, in the *Bhagavad Gita*, that 'above this visible nature there exists another, unseen and eternal, which, when all created things perish, does not perish'; and he sees the soul's birth in that 'inward spiritual world,' from which it falls to mortal life and body, as into death" (*Works* 4:105).

Finally, Blake, too, distinguishes between the various ways in which artists use language. Language which creates symbols is in itself "vision or inspiration."

Prose writers, on the other hand, use allegory, "which is but realism's excuse for existence" (*Works* 4:80–81). Symons quotes from Blake on the same issue: "Vision or imagination is a representation of what actually exists, really and unchangeably. Fable and allegory are formed by the daughters of Memory" (*Works* 4:81).

In a letter to Edmund Gosse on April 5, 1908, approximately five months before his breakdown, Symons comments on *The Romantic Movement in English Poetry* (1909), which he is just completing: "I am putting the very last touches to my 'Romantic Movement,' which I hope will be the best prose book that I have done (I have been working at it for 10 or 12 years)." He also mentions in this letter that fewer and fewer magazines are interested in having him write for them. He was, in fact, having many of his articles rejected. What seems to be happening at this point in Symons's career is that he is slowly losing step with the trends of twentieth-century literature. *The Symbolist Movement in Literature* helped significantly to usher in the new century and modernism, but Symons, once he had written that text, lagged behind. This sense of no longer being in step with the literary world, along with his growing concern over money and financial stability, certainly contributed to the breakdown he had in the late summer of 1908.

Symons hoped that *The Romantic Movement in English Poetry* would be the best prose book he had written. It is not, but it is clear that he saw this text as a sort of English equivalent to *The Symbolist Movement in Literature*. As with most of his essays on Blake, Symons was trying to give the artistic ideals he abstracted from various European authors a British context. He was establishing a symbolist tradition in Britain. Blake was an essential progenitor; other romantic poets offered additional support. In his introduction to this volume, he elaborates on a number of his artistic concerns in order to describe what Symons calls, borrowing the phrase, "the Renaissance of Wonder," from Watts-Dunton, "that 'great revived movement of the soul of man, after a long period of prosaic acceptance in all things, including literature and art,' which can be roughly indicated as the romantic movement" (17).

Symons begins his discussions, however, with an evaluation of the differences between prose and poetry. He is concerned with differentiating between the use of prose in our daily lives and the creative power of poetry, which transcends our bondage to the earth. Often Symons draws on French writers and critics in his discussion. He uses Joubert, for example, in his definition of poetry's power, magically transformed from the prose words of which it is composed, and of poetry's ability to transport the reader: "Call it atmosphere, call it magic; say, again with Joubert: 'Fine verses are those that exhale like sounds or perfumes'; we shall never explain, though we may do something to distinguish, that transformation by which prose is changed miraculously into poetry" (6). As Symons observes, Joubert said, "Nothing is poetry which does not transport: the lyre is in a certain sense a winged instrument" (6). To Symons, prose is the language of real life and holds us to the ground.

Those prose genres that do seem to speak more freely and evocatively, the novel and the prose play, to be most effective should deal with the personal. Symons gives very little defense for this view, but he does show, again, his interest in the "human document" as perhaps the most intense form of writing. Autobiography, Symons says, is perhaps of all forms of fiction the most convincing because "we see prose at work directly on life" (8). Indeed, "all the best fiction, narrative or dramatic, is a form of confession, personal or vicarious; and, in a sense, it is all personal; for no novelist or dramatist ever rendered vitally a single sensation which he had not observed in himself or which he had not tested by himself" (8). Even though he concedes some ground here, Symons goes on to draw on Baudelaire: "Prose listens at the door of all the senses, and repeats their speech almost in their own tones. But poetry (it is again Baudelaire who says it) 'is akin to music through a prosody whose roots plunge deeper in the human soul than any classical theory has indicated' " (9).

This preliminary argument about the nature of poetry is given in order to establish a background for his consideration of the nature of romantic poetry. The connection between this book and *The Symbolist Movement* becomes increasingly apparent. Curiously, however, Symons now describes British poetry in terms of the geography of the British Isles. The quality which distinguishes the poetry of the beginning of the nineteenth century is the quality of its imagination, and this quality is seen chiefly as a kind of atmosphere, which adds strangeness to beauty. The English poet "transforms the bare outlines of practical reality, clothing them with an atmosphere which is the actual atmosphere of England" (14–15). He states that this transformation of reality can be found in all English poetry, especially during the romantic period. But what is essential here is the liberating aspect of the imagination, the awakening of the imagination in romantic poetry. Like the symbolists, these poets united in the aim of emancipating the world and the mind "from the bondage of fact, opinion, formality, and tradition; and when fact, opinion, formality and tradition go out, imagination comes in" (18). The claims he makes for this period bring together his own essential artistic concerns. The final sentences to his introduction sum up his position well:

> Nature was accepted, yet strangeness was sought rather than refused, that salt which gives savour to life; and there was an arduous and discrete cultivation of that "continual slight novelty" without which poetry cannot go on in any satisfactory way. Imagination was realized as being, what only Blake quite clearly said, reality; and the beauty of imagination the natural element of that which it glorifies. Poetry was realised as a personal confession, or as an evocation, or as "an instant made eternity." It was realised that the end of poetry was to be poetry; and that no story-telling or virtue or learning, or any fine purpose, could make amends for the lack of that one necessity. (20)

2

The Art of the Theatre

The evaluation of Shakespeare's artistic development in Symons's introduction to *Cymbeline* (1906) invokes the inevitable conflict between art and life: "As his art tired, we may think, of the playhouse, so his nature, which had been content with cities, cried out for something which was not in cities. The open air, the sea, the fields, the hills, came to mean to him something which they had never meant" (xvii). Symons often makes highly personal judgments; he brings his own life to bear on his evaluations of other artists. "Amends to Nature," published in 1905, is written in the same spirit as his introduction to *Cymbeline*. It describes a similar change in attitude in Symons's own life. The opposition of a natural world with the artificial urban environment anticipates his view of Shakespeare's life and work. This aspect of Symons's work is more fundamentally exposed within the context of dramatic literature and theory. We see real people in imaginary lives, or to use Marianne Moore's useful expression, we see real toads in imaginary gardens.

Symons's interest in drama and dramatic theory began as a part of his early experiments as a writer. In "Notes on My Poems" he explains that he started to write, in 1878, a tragedy entitled *Almansor*, and that in 1880 he had written the "opening of 'Cassandra: a Tragedy' in blank verse with chorus in long rhymed lines" (111). Symons was already interested in what he was later to refer to as the "great stories." They contained the quality and suggestion of universal tragedies: "The great plays of the past were made out of great stories, and the great stories are repeated in our days and can be heard whenever an old man tells us a little of what has come to him in living" (*Plays, Acting, and Music* 1909, 211). His later interest in gypsies and the ancient secrets he felt they possessed is prefigured by these early dramatic experiments. Additionally, Symons increases what he learned from his early play writing through critical evaluations of Elizabethan and pre-Elizabethan drama. His first major project as a literary scholar and critic was to edit several of the *Shakespeare Quarto Facsimiles* for a series of publications supervised by Frederick Furnivall. His unpublished essay, "The Miracle Plays and the Puritan's Attack," written in 1913, shows a continued interest in pre-Elizabethan and Elizabethan dramatic literature. When Sidney Lee, the Elizabethan scholar, wrote to Symons asking whether he would be interested in editing and writing an introduction for *Cymbeline*, Symons commented, "I am glad of the chance of going back to the first subject I ever wrote about. I believe I was about 19 when I began to edit Shakespeare Quarto Facsimiles!" (letter to Sidney Lee, March 7, 1902). He actually never stopped going back to this first subject, for he wrote an essay on *Romeo and Juliet* in 1903 for *Harper's*, and in 1907 he wrote an essay on *Troilus and Cressida*, also for *Harper's*.

Symons's interest in drama ranged even more widely and included a rather profound fascination with performance as an art in itself. He, properly, did not see drama as a purely literary event. Early aspects of his fascination with various sorts of performance were the result of his interest in fairs, an interest which he also shared with Pater. Some of his early poems, such as "The Knife-Thrower" in *Days and Nights* (1889) and "To a Rope Dancer," published in the March, 1890, *Art Review*, evoke the sense of intrigue these performers manifest for him. In 1889 he wrote to James Dykes Campbell that he was going to review for the *Athenaeum* a forthcoming book on acrobatics, *Acrobats and Mountebanks* by Hughes Le Roux and Jules Garnier. Acrobatics, Symons says, is a subject "in which I consider myself rather a specialist" (letter, November 1, 1889). Additionally, in the early 1890s Symons joined the staff of the London *Star* as their music-hall critic. His reviews describe the more usual music-hall acts, such as Charles Chevalier's singing and numerous ballets, and they also deal interestingly with acrobatics of various sorts. Acrobatics is alluded to throughout Symons's work as an analogue for artistic technique. Finally, allied with these early interests is the even more sophisticated fascination with dance and acting.

Symons's writings, then, on drama and performance, including dance, are extensive and various. In the tradition of such nineteenth-century essayists as Charles Lamb and Leigh Hunt, he evolves his aesthetic slowly, based upon the appreciation and observation of individual performances. Percy Fitzgerald's comment on Lamb is a case in point, especially since Lamb is the figure Symons most often appeals to in his dramatic writing: "Lamb touches all departments of the stage: acting, scenery, writing, in succession, and though there is no strict method in his treatment, we find his system perfectly homogeneous. The same principle is at the bottom of all his speculations—viz., that a literal transcript of what we have with us in life, is no gain, and offers no genuine interest" (*The Art of the Stage* 225). This statement applies significantly to Symons's critical methods and to the beliefs that he evolves. Drawing on Lamb, he develops a theory of the stage which is anti-realistic and aesthetic. Implicit in his writings is the opposition of life and art he saw manifested in Shakespeare, and, additionally, his arguments merge theories of aestheticism with theories of symbolism. These aspects of his writing on drama are particularly evident in two areas of interest alluded to thus far: dramatic criticism (including dramatic theory) and performance in general.

Dramatic Theory

Very little has been written about Symons's dramatic theory, no doubt because at first glance he seems to have produced very little overt theory. It is clear, however, that Symons felt that he was developing an aesthetic of the stage which took into account the literary qualities of drama but which was also performance oriented. As he says in "Literary Drama," a work of art has to "answer the purpose of its existence." We must, therefore, consider drama within the context of its purpose: "Now, a play is written to be acted, and it will not be literature merely because its sentences are nicely written. It will be literature, dramatic literature, if in addition to being nicely written, it has qualities which make a stage-play a good stage-play" (*Plays, Acting, and Music* 1903, 94).

As with all Symons's theories, his discussions of drama are empirically based. In the foreword to *Plays, Acting, and Music* (1903)—the text in which he begins to develop his theory of the stage—he announces his intention of elaborating an overall aesthetic and also suggests that it is an aesthetic derived from observation: "I am gradually working my way towards the concrete expression of a theory, or system of aesthetics, of all the arts" (preface). Ruth Z. Temple rightly questions whether this book is rather "an *a posteriori* classification for groups of essays which had been written" (178), but Symons's method, as always, is to evolve theory rather than to write essays to illustrate certain preconceived ideas. The evolution of *Plays, Acting, and Music* is an example of Symons's methodology and begins to answer some of the objections to his lack of theoretical coherence. The first edition, published in 1903, is very poorly organized and is, as Temple suggests, merely a collection of essays that had already been written. It is not divided into sections in order to distinguish topics actually treated, and the order of the included essays seems arbitrary. The fact that he does announce in this volume his intention of developing an overall aesthetic seems completely unjustified by the text. He says, however, in the forward that he is concerned with presenting "a particular thing, immediately under my eyes" (preface).

The second, revised, edition (published in 1909) is completely remodelled and does represent a reasonably clear statement of theory abstracted from the essays that made up the first edition. The text is now divided into three sections, "Plays and Acting," "Drama," and "Music." The overall introduction, in the form of "An Apology for Puppets," focuses the argument of the text on the essential artificiality of art as opposed to the natural world, which, in this case, is identified with the physical presence of an actor; and the conclusion, "A Paradox of Art," focuses on the same issue more generally: "Art has to do only with the creation of beauty, whether it be in words, or sounds, or colour, or outline, or rhythmical moment . . ." (322). These are some of the aspects of art with which the text has dealt. Now, as Symons says in the new preface, the book makes more sense as a statement of aesthetics: "It is now more what it ought to have been from the first; what I saw, from the moment of its publication, that it ought to have been: a book of theory. The rather formal announcement of my intentions which I made in my preface is reprinted here, because, at all events, the programme was carried out" (vii). Appropriately, he had written to Edmund Gosse on October 28, 1901, saying that he found himself "getting fonder and fonder of abstract thought."

The abstract theory of drama that Symons evolves in *Plays, Acting, and Music*, as well as in *Studies in Seven Arts*, is revealingly based upon his reading of Lamb. Additionally, the dramatic theory he draws from Lamb, as well as from some of Percy Fitzgerald's commentary on Lamb, focuses for Symons what he admires in the work of Maurice Maeterlinck, W. B. Yeats, and Edward Gordon Craig.

The influence of Lamb on Symons is due in part to Pater's prior appreciation of him. Symons, for example, at various times in his letters to Dykes Campbell mentions looking for and obtaining Pater's essay on Lamb, which had originally appeared in the *Fortnightly Review* for October 1878. It is also at this time that he mentions to Campbell that "next to Browning and Meredith, he [Pater] is perhaps the living English writer whom I most admire" (letter to Dykes Campbell, January 28, 1901). He undoubtedly learned from Pater's essay to appreciate Lamb as an early elaborator of aestheticism and impressionism: "In the making of prose he realizes the principle of art for its own sake, as completely as Keats in the making of verse. And, working ever close to the concrete, to the details, great or small, of actual things, books, persons, and with no part of them blurred to his vision by the intervention of mere abstract theories, he has reached an enduring moral effect, in a sort of boundless sympathy" (*Appreciations* 109–10). In other words, Lamb is perfectly suited to the role of Pater's aesthetic critic. He discriminates the details of his own experience and incorporates a moral dimension by the cultivation of a "boundless sympathy."

Symons continues this same line of thinking in his own appreciation of Lamb as an aesthetic critic. Throughout his essays on drama, acting, and dramatic theory, he alludes to Lamb in order to focus his arguments, particularly in relation to his own concern with the creation of beauty. He abstracts from Lamb a number of traits appropriate to aestheticism. In "The Sicilian Actors," for example, he refers to Lamb's famous essay, "On the Tragedies of Shakespeare, Considered with Reference to their Fitness for Stage Representation," in order to evolve a discussion of whether the beauty of a play, associated with the imaginative world its language is able to evoke, is not lost in the stage production. Lamb states that with some of Shakespeare's plays this is the case: "But the Lear of Shakespeare cannot be acted. The contemptible machinery by which they mimic the storm which he goes out in, is not more inadequate to represent the horrors of the real elements, than any actor can be to represent Lear" (*Miscellaneous Prose* 124). And later in the essay he goes on to say that Shakespeare's characters who are of nature still have something in them which "appeals too exclusively to the imagination, to admit of their being made objects to the senses without suffering a change and a diminution" (126). From one point of view, Lamb is objecting to the way Shakespeare has been presented. Percy Fitzgerald, who, as we shall see, seems to be responsible for focusing Lamb's aesthetics of drama for Symons, comments that "Lamb is really condemning the established system of stage effect of his day" (*The Art of the Stage* 176). Realistic imitation is, for Lamb, the lowest form of art, if art at all. Whether a play of Shakespeare's can be adequately performed depends on whether the quality of the production is dominated by the "corporal dimension" rather than the imaginative.

In "The Price of Realism" Symons elaborates much the same point, criticizing the modern and inartistic endeavor to be real: "This costly and inartistic aim at reality, then, is the vice of the modern stage, and, at its best or worst, can it be said that it is really even what it pretends to be: a perfectly deceptive imitation of the real thing?" (*Plays, Acting, and Music* 1909, 164–65). The spectator should, instead, abandon himself to the magic of the play. The magic of the play is what Lamb also feels is lost. And, as Symons further says, the illusion created by the play should not be of a world like our own: "The true actor walks in a world as real in its unreality as that which surrounds the poet or the enthusiast" (163).

The nature and art of staging a play during the Victorian period had much to do with the quality of the theatrical experience. As John Stokes points out in *Resistible Theatres*, "staging, like organization, plays a vital role in shaping the theatrical experience, and its techniques and principles received an increasing amount of attention in England in the eighties and nineties" (33). During the first three quarters of the century, play production became dominated by commercial realism. An elaborate realistic setting was developed in order to increase the spectacle of the standard melodrama. As has often been pointed out, the spectacle of realism became so extensive as to include actual hansom cabs on stage, or, as Symons comments on adversely, boats on real Thames water.

In contrast to this trend, Symons begins to develop a more self-conscious art of the theatre founded on the principles of aestheticism. The plays that were interesting were those that tended to break down traditional staging conventions, plays which were self-consciously artificial and required a more imaginative approach in staging. Shakespeare's later plays, he felt, employ this ideal: "That spirit, I think, we see in the later plays of Shakespeare, in which not only does metre dissolve and reform, in some new, fluctuant way of its own, but the whole structure becomes vaporous, and floats out through the solid walls of the theatre" (*Cymbeline* x). This observation recalls Lamb's similar pronouncement and offers a framework for the promotion of Symons's idea of poetic drama. The focus, as in Lamb's essays, is on the imaginative, verbal qualities of the drama and what they are able to elicit in the reader and spectator. Symons says, for example, in "Algernon Charles Swinburne," that poetic drama, as in Shakespeare's *The Tempest*,

creates a new world: "But, as it seems to me, the aim of the poetic drama is to create a new world in a new atmosphere, where the laws of human existence are no
longer recognized. The aim of poetic drama is beauty, not truth . . ." (*Figures*
189). The fact that this kind of drama is to be solely based upon the creation of
beauty ties it to late-nineteenth-century aestheticism. The laws of human existence
are now irrelevant.

Symons always seems to lean in the direction of aestheticism, but he often tries
to balance aestheticism with an equal interest in reality. There is a sense in which
a purely disembodied voice would become too "dehumanized" (Gordon 429). In
"Literary Drama" Symons describes a less aloof aestheticism, one more aptly defined as aestheticized reality. Henrik Ibsen, therefore, figures significantly: "The
poetic drama, if it is to become a genuine thing, must be conceived as drama, and
must hold us, as a play of Ibsen's holds us, by the sheer interest of its representation of life" (*Plays, Acting, and Music* 1903, 97). The paradox implicit in art
described in this passage, which is also significant in relation to dance as an image
of artistic perfection, is inevitable. As Jan B. Gordon says about dance, Symons's
ideal is to "aestheticize the randomness of human existence, to transmute life into
artifice without losing the qualities of either" (429).

Symons's discussions of poetic drama raise a number of issues which evolve
naturally out of Lamb's concern with the imaginative and poetic qualities of the
theatrical experience. The conflict between poetry and prose, for example, as
well as all the associations that accompany the use of those two words, becomes
important. For the most part, Symons takes a fairly simplistic view, assuming, first
of all, that there is a distinct difference and, secondly, that prose is necessarily more
referential, more reality-oriented and narrowly scientific. The most elaborate argument, in relation to its literary implications, is developed in the *Romantic Movement in English Poetry* (1909). Literary or poetic language transforms and extends
our perception of the world. Charles Baudelaire's aesthetic theories lend support
to his claim: "Prose listens at the doors of all the senses, and repeats their speech
almost in their own tones. But poetry (it is again Baudelaire who says it) 'is akin
to music through a prosody whose roots plunge deeper in the human soul than any
classical theory has indicated'" (9). Edgar Allan Poe also helps to advance the argument that rhythm in poetry has a psychological and aesthetic value beyond the
capability of prose. The inclusion of both Poe and Baudelaire begins to show how
Symons mixes an interest in aestheticism with an equal interest in symbolism. The
creation of beauty is allied with a further correspondence to the mysteries of existence. But what Symons is mostly interested in pursuing, in line with Lamb's
thinking, is the nature of the romantic movement. He wants to contrast it with his
own increasingly prosaic time: "What is really meant by all these phrases, and by
the name of the romantic movement, is simply the reawakening of the imagination,
a reawakening to a sense of beauty and strangeness in natural things, and in all the
impulses of the mind and the senses" (17). He goes on to see the movement as an
emancipation from the poetic and spiritual limitations of the eighteenth century.

The same positive characteristics of poetry, which define the spirit and artistic temperament of an ideal age, apply to poetic drama, which Symons often contrasts with the prose play. The poetic drama, like poetry, involves absolute truth. The aesthetic qualities lend themselves to ultimate expression: "The dramatist must bring speech nearer to that obscure thing of which speech is but a suggestion; the poetic dramatist, who speaks in a finer, more expressive, and therefore truer, language, may come much nearer to the truth, to the real meaning of words, than the dramatist who writes in prose can ever come" (*Prose and Verse* 253). In "A Theory of the Stage," written several years later, he elaborates the same belief, although now he is unsure of his aim. He has the work of Yeats as a dramatist, as well as that of Maeterlinck, to back up his argument. Their symbolist dramas add a sense of validity to the aestheticism he derives from Lamb. Again, he is concerned with accenting the imaginative and aesthetic nature of poetic drama in contrast to the reductive qualities of prose: "Verse lends itself to the lifting and adequate treatment of the primary emotions, because it can render them more as they are in the soul, not being tied down to probable words, as prose talk is" (*Plays, Acting, and Music* 1909, 211).

The concept of primary emotions is partially drawn from his reading of Nietzsche's *The Birth of Tragedy*. In "Nietzsche on Tragedy" he elaborates an interest in tragedy as "a manifestation and objectification of Dionysiac states" (*Plays, Acting, and Music* 1909, 14). The primary emotions, essential expressions of the soul, are identified with these states. There is, additionally, in the contrast of Apollonian and Dionysian an analogue for Symons's own contrast of art and life. His appreciation of the molded Dionysian quality of art, then, is used as a sort of definition of works that manifest the important essential qualities of life. Tolstoy's play, *The Power of Darkness*, is a prose-play which contains poetry because of the language the peasants speak: "They speak as Russians speak, with a certain childishness, in which they are more primitive than our more civilized peasants. But the speech comes from deeper than they are aware, it stumbles into a revelation of the soul" (*Plays, Acting, and Music* 1909, 210–11). This admiration for the Russian peasantry is obviously due somewhat to Yeats's influence and recalls Symons's statement about the "great stories." The scientific and nonemotive qualities of language are underplayed because they do not create a correspondence with "a revelation of the soul" implicit within these people. Appropriately, then, John Synge is tied in with Yeats; they are "two notable writers, each wholly individual, one a poet in verse, the other a poet in prose" (*Plays, Acting, and Music* 1909, 209). If, as he says, he is living in an age dominated by prose forms, then what that form can express does not necessarily have to be reduced and confined.

Although these elaborations on poetic language and primary emotions seem somewhat unrelated to Lamb's more purely aesthetic approach, Symons brings his argument back around to Lamb. In relation to Tolstoy's play, *The Powers of Darkness*, he again alludes to Lamb's discussion of poetic language: "Yet, though it is by its poetry that, as Lamb pointed out, a play of Shakespeare differs from a play of Banks or Lillo, the poetry is not more essential to its making than the living sub-stance, the melodrama'' (*Plays, Acting, and Music* 1909, 203). Curiously, Symons uses melodrama as a term to define life in its raw form. Melodrama was the dominant dramatic mode of this time, and Symons's various reviews for the *Star* and the *Academy* deal with it as such; but it appears that Symons takes the rather inartistic and overly sentimental qualities of melodrama as one extreme in order to introduce the more artistic approach offered by Lamb. He qualifies Lamb's aestheticism, stating that in his overall theory of the stage, both life and art, poetry and melodrama, must be present. He is, however, striking a blow for a renewed interest in the aesthetic principles of Lamb. Thus, in the revised *Plays, Acting, and Music* (1909) he evaluates contemporary dramatists according to these criteria. Ibsen has ''a firm hold on structural melodrama,'' on the substance, ''but ask him for beauty and he will give you . . . the cliches of a minor poet'' (205). Maeter-linck ''brought back mystery to the stage'' (206). D'Annunzio, however, is all out-line with no real substance (206). The true aim of drama, then, as Symons outlines it, is a correspondence between life and art:

> Life and beauty are the body and soul of great drama. Mix the two as you will, so long as both are there, resolved into a single substance. But let there be, in the making, two ingredients, and while one is poetry, and comes bringing beauty, the other is a violent thing which has been scorn-fully called melodrama, and is the emphasis of action. The greatest plays are melodrama by their skeleton, and poetry by the flesh which clothes that skeleton. (200)

Other aspects of Lamb's theories find their way into Symons's discussion of an overall art of the theatre. Lamb, as we have seen, centers his argument on a con-trast between imagination and the limiting characteristics of stage presentation. The same issue arises in his essay, ''Barrenness of the Imaginative Faculty in the Productions of Modern Art.'' For the most part, this essay deals with modern painting, but the artistic ideals apply generally as well. Throughout the essay, in fact, Lamb draws analogies with other art forms. Often, therefore, he involves the stage in his discussion. In relation to what Symons says about the transforming and magical quality of art, Lamb's observations seem especially appropriate. The es-sential aspects of life cannot be discovered through surface imitation. As Lamb says, ''not all that is optically possible to be seen, is to be shown in every picture'' (II:261). Symons's concern over distinguishing between description and impres-sion, in his travel writing in particular, follows this same line of thought. Further on in this essay, sounding like a predecessor of Whistler, Lamb comments: ''Art-ists again err in the confounding of *poetic* with *pictorial subjects*. In the latter, the exterior accidents are nearly everything, the unseen qualities nothing'' (II:264). Lamb connects this last statement to drama by referring to Othello's color and Fal-staff's corpulence. In reading these plays such physical characteristics recede and the poetic elements increase. We cannot help but recall the same observation in ''The Tragedies of Shakespeare'': ''What we see upon a stage is body and bodily action; what we are conscious of in reading is almost exclusively the mind, and its movements: and this I think may sufficiently account for the very different sort of delight with which the same play so often affects us in the reading and the seeing" (I:126).

Again, the objection Lamb makes seems to be less an either/or proposition than a question of balance. How much body, how much surface reality, should be mixed with what is the imaginative essence of the work? Reading is a form of experience which allows for an almost ideal appreciation of literature, whereas viewing a play seems too harshly to tie us down to the surface characteristics of reality. He continues this observation in "Barrenness of the Imaginative Faculty": "By a wise falsification, the great masters of painting got at their true conclusion; by not showing the actual appearances, that is, all that was to be seen at any given moment by an indifferent eye, but only what the eye might be supposed to see in the doing or suffering of some portentous action" (II:261). The artist creates the ideal circumstances so that the spectator may experience the essential action of the work. In other words, the spectator is, as Pater would certainly have it, transported by the work. The same process should apply to the stage as well.

Symons's ideas on drama, and art in general, derived in part from Lamb, seem to have been sharpened by the work and analysis of Percy Fitzgerald. Fitzgerald, a minor literary figure during the late nineteenth and early twentieth centuries, published a large number of books on a variety of topics, and he was particularly interested in drama. In 1868 he published a two-volume life of David Garrick; in 1870, *Principles of Comedy and Dramatic Effect*; and in 1871 he published the two-volume study, *The Kembles*. He also wrote and published a considerable amount on Lamb, including *Charles Lamb: His Friends, His Haunts and His Books* and *The Life, Letters and Writings of Charles Lamb*. Although Symons does not refer directly to Fitzgerald, he undoubtedly would have been aware of these works on Lamb, as well as the book, *Music-Hall Land* (1890), which Fitzgerald published on music-hall acts. But the works of Fitzgerald which seem to have particularly influenced Symons and which focus on the aesthetic theories of Lamb are *The Art of the Stage* (1885), a collection of Lamb's essays on the theatre with a commentary by Fitzgerald, and *The Art of Acting* (1892), the printed version of a series of lectures on acting which are, for the most part, based upon Lamb's essays on the same subject.

The connections between these two texts and Symons's own theories as they are derived from Lamb are too strong to be merely coincidental. Fitzgerald's lectures on acting, for example, deal with the establishment of drama as a unified art. He objects to the practice of letting the style of acting overwhelm the play. This characteristic of stage productions was partially due to the changes in the physical nature of the theatre; larger audiences required an exaggerated acting style. The desire for spectacle obviously also supported an exaggeration of gesture and voice, as did melodrama as a theatrical mode. It is the imbalance in the theatrical art, then, that Fitzgerald finds objectionable, as did Lamb before him. In relation to this problem, he focuses on 'crossings' as emblematic of the failure in current dramatic techniques. "Crossings," the stage instruction that required the actor to move from one side of the stage to the other, seem to dominate unnecessarily the stage productions of Fitzgerald's time. Every aspect of a drama should contribute to its overall effect and meaning. Certain portions of contemporary stage productions, however, are extraneous to the overall impact: "And so it is the the 'crossings,' which we find marked in the prompter's copy; these are usually set down with a view to please the eye—capriciously enough—or to break up the monotony of the action" (*The Art of Acting* 62).

Symons, interestingly enough, writes an essay on exactly this same point and arrives at the same conclusion. The final recommendation of "On Crossing Stage to Right" is that the individual aspects of a dramatic performance should be designed and controlled so as to effect a unified experience. In fact, he speaks of the production as if it were a musical composition and a painting; finally, all should harmonize: "If we take drama with any seriousness, as an art as well as an improvisation, we shall realize that one of its main requirements is that it should make pictures. That is the lesson of Bayreuth, and when one comes away, the impression which remains, almost longer than the impression of the music itself, is that grave, regulated motion of the actors . . ." (*Plays, Acting, and Music* 1909, 167–68). This statement corresponds with Fitzgerald's observations. But the English mind, according to Symons, does not aspire to this type of artistic unity. Whenever there is a lull in the action, in the spectacle, the actor is instructed to move to stage right:

> If you look into the actor's prompt-books, the most frequent direction which you will find is this: "Cross stage to right." It is not a mere direction, it is a formula; it is not a formula only, but a universal remedy. Whenever the action seems to flag, or the dialogue to become weak or wordy, you must "cross stage to right"; no matter what is wrong with the play, this will set it right. (*Plays, Acting, and Music* 1909, 167)

Thus, both Fitzgerald and Symons see the stage direction, "cross stage to right," as symptomatic of the failure to distinguish, as Symons says, "between what is dramatic and what is merely theatrical" (*Plays, Acting, and Music* 1909, 170). For the play to be properly dramatic, it must be considered and developed as a whole, not as a collection of individual and unrelated parts.

Elsewhere in *The Art of Acting* Fitzgerald elaborates further what he considers to be the essential nature of the dramatic art, and, as we have already seen in Lamb, he is opposed to the gross realism which had become so popular. The art of the stage requires a greater and more self-conscious selectivity, "for everything on the stage must be prepared and adapted for its peculiarly artificial atmosphere, and duly selected and abstracted" (82). Henry Irving offers an example of one who considers the play from this point of view, for "he brings all into harmony, softening down some portions, and setting others in proper relief, like the conductor of an orchestra" (43). The imagery here, particularly in relation to the musical analogue, is also used by Symons. Mixing the vocabulary of various art forms is a general characteristic of aesthetic criticism, and it is apparent that Fitzgerald abstracts from Lamb a particularly pure form of aestheticism. The allusion to Henry Irving is additionally significant, for it foretells of the progress from the actor-manager to the producer. Gordon Craig, as we shall see, functions significantly in this progress. Symons follows suit in his essay, "Great Acting in English," using the same musical analogue as Fitzgerald: "The business of the manager, who in most cases is also the chief actor, is to produce a concerted action between his separate players, as the conductor does between the instruments in his orchestra" (*Plays, Acting, and Music* 1909, 183).

In line with the need to evolve an aesthetic unity in dramatic performance and with the interest in essentials rather than details, Fitzgerald continues his discussion by drawing on the impressionist painters as emblematic of his ideals. Of course, we cannot help seeing his commentary in the light of Lamb's notion that "not all that is optically possible to be seen, is to be shown in every picture." Like Lamb, the impressionists, as Fitzgerald sees them, are not interested in detail: "Their principle is to record the tone of a scene, not the details; for they tell us that details are not noticed under such conditions" (5).

The essay by Lamb that Fitzgerald seems to draw on most heavily is "Barrenness of the Imaginative Faculty," for it focuses on, in a broader artistic perspective, the same issues raised in "On the Tragedies of Shakespeare." It, more than any other essay, suggests an overall aesthetic approach within the context of various arts; therefore, it is of central importance to Fitzgerald's collection of Lamb's essays on the theatre, *The Art of the Stage*. The title of this book, in fact, anticipates Symons's essay on Gordon Craig, "The New Art of the Stage," and the essays by Lamb and the commentary on them by Fitzgerald elaborate many of the same ideas Symons develops in relation to Craig. Drama, then, according to Fitzgerald, is the world transformed into art. We go to a play, to art for that matter, for what real or ordinary experience does not offer: "We go to the stage to escape from life, to find something that is in a manner spiritual; to be taught the elegant secrets of philosophy" (203). What Fitzgerald derives from and comments on in Lamb is the belief that "it is the essence or quintessence of all things, which must be presented on the stage" (200). He goes on to say that "it is an epitome of life that is going on before our eyes, all that is trivial and unnecessary for the purpose in hand becomes impertinent" (202). Lamb, of course, is the progenitor: "We have been spoiled with a tyrant more pernicious to our pleasures, the exclusive and all-devouring drama of common life, where, instead of the fictitious, half-believed personages of the stage, we recognize ourselves, our brothers, aunts, kinsfolks, allies, partners, enemies, the same as in life" (qtd. in *The Art of Acting* 82).

The aestheticism implicit in Lamb's writings becomes the aestheticism of Fitzgerald and Symons. From it they continue to argue for a theatrical art based upon aesthetic ideals, and these ideals are intended to apply to all aspects of the theatre. "It will be found," Fitzgerald says, "that scenic effect depends on the same principles as dramatic effect. In both it is found, not in details, but in the essence of a number of details'' (208). The form of idealism suggested by Fitzgerald is, in fact, a part of the general tendency during the late nineteenth century to appreciate drama in terms of its essential idealism or realism. Interestingly, Symons focuses on the ghost in *Hamlet* in order to develop an argument for idealism in drama. In his essay, ''On Hamlet and Hamlets,'' he deals with ''the sense of the sublime,'' including the belief that ''revelation has in it more of vision than of reality'' (*Dramatis Personae* 312). The ghost in *Hamlet* represents vision, the absolute for which the dramatist strives. Thus, he quotes Villiers de L'Isle-Adam on the same issue: ''The secret of the Absolute cannot be expressed with syntax, and therefore one cannot ask the ghost to produce more than an *impression*'' (313).

Of course, as Symons also observes, a similar argument was advanced by Lamb. Symons quotes extensively from Lamb here on the possibilities of performing Shakespeare, especially in relation to the presentation of the absolute. About a production in which he has seen two great actors, Lamb says, ''when the novelty is past, we find to our cost that instead of realizing an idea, we have only materialised and brought down a fine vision to the standard of flesh and blood'' (I:114–15). For Lamb, as he says later in the essay and more specifically about the ghosts and spirits in Shakespeare, ''the sight actually destroys the faith'' (II:126). Symons returns to this point again in ''Pantomime and the Poetic Drama.'' He argues with the ghost of Lamb behind him:

> All drama, until one comes to poetic drama, is an imitation of life, as a photograph is an imitation of life; and for this reason it can have, at the best, but a secondary kind of imaginative existence, the appeal of the mere copy. To the poetic drama nature no longer exists; or rather, nature becomes, as it has been truly said nature should become to the painter, a dictionary. Here is choice, selection, combination: the supreme interference of beauty. (*Works* 9:241–42)

It is evident, in fact, that Lamb and Fitzgerald, as well as Symons, develop their aesthetic ideals based upon a belief in the value of the ''supreme interference of beauty.''

Elsewhere in Symons's reading he found support for the aesthetic ideas he derived from Lamb and Fitzgerald. Some of these interests probably predate his reading of Lamb, but it is obvious that Lamb gave a sense of order and perspective to the art of the theatre that Symons did not find in other writers. His admiration of Browning, for example, is extensive, and, as Beckson and Munro have shown in ''Arthur Symons, Browning, and the Development of the Modern Aesthetic,'' Symons owes a great deal to Browning, both in terms of his poetry and overall aesthetic. In terms of dramatic theory, Browning helped Symons evolve an interest in a drama of the supreme moment. ''Browning's example fortified by Pater's precepts did encourage him to value that aesthetic experience which depended for its effect on the isolation of highly charged, profoundly significant moments of intensity'' (695).

In a review for the *Academy*, ''Two Stage Societies,'' Symons states that drama should deal with ''universal human feelings in the light of a vivid individual crisis'' (343). For life as it is presented on the stage, the desire to forge a concrete universal is particularly relevant. Within a more practical framework, this ambition relates to another statement by Symons quoted earlier in the chapter: ''The great plays of the past were made out of great stories, and the great stories are repeated in our days and can be heard wherever an old man tells us a little of what has come to him in living'' (*Plays, Acting, and Music* 1909, 211). The great stories Symons finds so fascinating, such as the story of Tristan and Iseult, embody the universals of human feeling, and their relevance, as well as their reality, continues to manifest itself in contemporary life. They are the myths around which the details of human life cluster. For the generations that followed Symons, including Joyce and Eliot, mythic structure appeared to be the only valid way of organizing art and experience. According to Yeats, the artist follows the impulses of the great memory, which is embodied in all great myths and legends: ''And surely, at whatever risk, we must cry out that imagination is always seeking to remake the world according to the impulses and the patterns in that Great Mind, and that Great Memory?'' (*Essays* 52).

For Symons, of course, the impulses of the Great Memory are also manifest in great aspects of history. One looks to history, however, for its drama rather than for its truth to event. Art and what art projects in terms of the essentials of life are still the supreme value. Thus, we must be aware, according to Symons, that Shakespeare's use of chronicle history only proves ''that he found his way through chronicle to drama'' (''Two Stage Societies'' 343). Symons's interest in the use of history for dramatic purposes is derived from Browning, for he learned from him to seize the ''luminous detail,'' to use Ezra Pound's phrase. As he says in his study of Browning, ''The instinct of the poet seizes on a type of character, the eye of the painter perceives the shades and shapes of line and colour and form required to give it picturesque prominence, and the learning of the scholar then sets up a fragment of the broken past, or re-fashions a portion of the living present, as an appropriate and harmonious scene or background'' (11). Browning, as this combination of elements shows, shapes his drama according to the demands of both the universal and individual consciousness.

''Is Browning Dramatic?''—Symons's first major essay on his poetic hero, which he incorporated in his full-length study, *An Introduction to the Study of Browning* (1886)—also focuses on this aspect of Browning's poetry. In addition, the approach he takes is very clearly allied to a form of aestheticism, that ''supreme interference of beauty.'' Thus, the aspects of history Browning deals with, according to Symons, are not an essential part of the drama: ''Historical fact has nothing to do with poetry: it is mere material, the mere quarry of ideas'' (94). His commentary on *Colombe's Birthday* continues this line of thinking, suggesting, in fact, that it is ''the first play which is mainly concerned with inward rather than outward action'' (65). External events, like external reality, are distinctly of secondary importance. Thus, the new drama, of which Browning is the founder, is subjective rather than objective, and we may assume, emblematic of an aesthetic idealism rather than the reductive characteristics of realism. *The Inn Album*, for example, fails sometimes because it sinks "to the confines of a bastard realism" (169), which Symons identifies with photography. But other parts of the work show its main power, "the higher imaginative realism of the close, yet poetic or creative, treatment of life" (169).

The various dramatic reviews Symons wrote throughout his career, some of which are included in *Plays, Acting, and Music* (1909), are evaluated within this same framework. Arthur Wing Pinero, for example, is criticized for being too concerned with the superficial aspects of reality: "We have seen [in *The Gay Lord Quex*] a picturesque and amusing exterior, and that is all" (110). In his review, "Ben Hur on Stage," he faults the production this time because of the inadequate and misdirected stage conventions used: "The fact is, romance of this remote kind cannot be finely brought before us in the crude way of our modern spectacular theatres" (109). Symons's interest in Alfred Jarry, as well as in the productions of Lugné-Poë, follows the same line of thinking. In "A Symbolist Farce," he describes *Ubu Roi* as a play and as a production: Lugné-Poë's "Symbolist Théâtre de l'Œuvre has so significantly taken the place of the mainly Naturalistic Théâtre Libre" (*Works* 9:236). The progress from naturalism to symbolism, which also determines the nature of Emile Verhaeren's work, leads toward the new art of the theatre Symons wants to identify and promote.

Within this context, Symons's various essays on Ibsen function significantly. At times, he seems unable to make up his mind about the dramatist, which is, in fact, to his credit. During the late nineteenth century there was considerable misunderstanding about Ibsen, and much of this misunderstanding was the result of a confusion of stage convention with dramatic essence. When Symons mentions Ibsen to Dykes Campbell, however, he is full of admiration for the dramatist: "If you want some tremendously serious and startling reading, buy the last 'Camelot' volume and read Ibsen's astonishing plays (introduced by Havelock Ellis, who learnt Norwegian on purpose to read them)" (letter, September 21, 1888). Symons's friendship with Ellis is partially the cause of Symons's enthusiasm. They had recently met, and Symons was very interested in all that Ellis thought and wrote. That Symons's view changed, however, is evident in a letter he wrote to Edmund Gosse when Gosse had sent him his *Ibsen* (1907). Symons's comment on *Brand*, for example, is contrary to Gosse's view: "It seems to be almost a blasphemy to call that tract 'one of the great poems of the world'" (letter to Edmund Gosse, January 9, 1908). Symons's view, appropriately, vacillates somewhere between an outright enthusiasm and the belief that Ibsen was a writer of social and moral tracts.

Symons's first major essay on Ibsen, "Henrik Ibsen," published in 1889 in the *Universal Review*, evaluates the dramatist as more than a social critic. He accents the fact that Ibsen evokes both a truth and a sense of individuality society suppresses: "His fundamental demand is for individual liberty; he would have men live according to nature, and he can conceive of a reasonable society only as an organisation founded on the truth of things, and bound together by sincerity" (570).

These are concerns with which Symons personally identifies in relation to the suppression of life he felt characterized his own middle-class background, which he described in "A Prelude to Life." In 1889 he was still trying to escape what he felt were the limitations of his background, but central to Symons's essay is the observation that Ibsen's style as a dramatist changes: "'Rosmersholm,' the latest and not the least of Ibsen's plays, is, unlike the others, primarily a drama of passion. It has something of the individual intensity of Browning, and like one of Browning's finest works it might have been called 'A Soul's Tragedy.' For a moment society is forgotten in the contemplation of a human soul" (574). That Symons identifies the later Ibsen with the aesthetic values of Browning is appropriate. For Symons to appreciate Ibsen, the naturalism often associated with Ibsen has to be transformed. The issue of whether Ibsen is essentially social and naturalistic or whether he is essentially aesthetic is basic to this period's understanding of his work. When in 1895 Lugné-Poë opened in London with *Rosmersholm* and *The Master Builder*, the realization that Ibsen could be presented in a variety of ways was quite striking. Ibsen, then, can also be seen as transforming from naturalism to symbolism, and the Théâtre de l'Œuvre accented this transformation. Symons foresees these developments in the perception of Ibsen's work, as well as the actual change, in this initial essay on Ibsen.

As Symons evolves as an artist and critic, his criticism of Ibsen continues to center on the prosaic qualities in his work in order to accent the aesthetic and symbolic. When, for example, he reviews the Stage Society's production of *Pillars of Society* in "A Note on Ibsen's Technique" for the *Star* in 1901, he isolates the failure of this drama by saying that as an early play it is limited by traditional dramatic conceptions: "But we do not see the complete dramatist, as we see him in 'Ghosts,' in 'Hedda Gabler.' He has not yet quite found his own form, not yet disentangled human life and human problems from their traditional stage-clothes" (1). Symons identifies the more symbolic and suggestive plays of Ibsen as the ones we should consider the truer works of art. He makes this point again in his longest essay on Ibsen, "Henrik Ibsen," written in 1906 for the *Quarterly Review* and reprinted in *Figures of Several Centuries* (1916). Again, Ibsen's "egoism" is accented, although it is now less courageous than Nietzsche's "pride of individual energy" (223). This issue comes up more importantly as a theme in Symons's own plays. He also now explicitly contrasts the man of science in Ibsen with the artist and, following Coleridge's lead, states that the man of science and research is limited in his perception. He is associated with the fantastic, which is rhetorical, rather than with the imaginative, which is poetic. His plays produce an illusion of reality. In this accomplishment he sets for himself and for his age narrow dramatic limits.

Ibsen's age is, of course, Symons's, and the limits set are those Symons's aesthetic is pitted against: "Ibsen limits himself to that part of the soul which he and science know" (262). He returns to Tolstoy's play, *The Power of Darkness*, as an example of a prose-play that does not limit itself, but rather as Lamb had suggested in "Barrenness of the Imaginative Faculty," it transforms the world. Now, according to Symons, Ibsen's later plays represent the revenge of the imagination, just as the romantic movement did at the end of the eighteenth century: "In these last plays, with their many splendid qualities, not bound together and concentrated as in *Ghosts*, we see the revenge of the imagination upon the realist, who has come to be no longer interested in the action of society upon the individual, but in the individual as a soul to be lost or saved" (254). The change of intention Symons describes in Ibsen also involves a change in artistic technique. Ibsen's drama becomes more imaginatively based and more suggestive.

Maeterlinck, of course, represents the ideal dramatist Symons tries to squeeze out of Ibsen. As Stokes rightly observes, Maeterlinck's essay, "The Tragical in Daily Life," ties together the surfaces of Ibsen with an awareness of "a substratum of meaning" (*Resistible Theatres* 173). Additionally, it is clear that for Symons the drama of Maeterlinck represents a fuller expression of the aesthetic ideals set down by Lamb: "He has realised, after Wagner, that the art of the stage is the art of pictorial beauty, of the correspondence in rhythm between the speakers, their words, and their surroundings. He has seen how, in this way, and in this way alone, the emotion, which it is but a part of the poetic drama to express, can be at once intensified and purified" (*Symbolist Movement* 88). The pictorial allusion, and the suggestion that all parts of the drama should correspond, recalls Lamb, as well as Fitzgerald's elaboration on Lamb. Additionally, Maeterlinck follows very self-consciously in the tradition of Villiers de L'Isle-Adam and, in relation to the production work of Lugné-Poë, represents a renaissance in poetic drama. He combines, for Symons, an interest in aestheticism with an equal interest in symbolism. Symons's description of Villiers in *The Symbolist Movement in Literature*, a book which depicts a new renaissance based upon the symbolist aesthetic, deals with the contrast of idealism with realism. As a literary form, realism is reductive. It employs a language defined by confinement, and the characters are equally mundane: "Villiers, choosing to concern himself only with exceptional characters, and with them only in the absolute, invents for them a more elaborate and a more magnificent speech than they would naturally employ, the speech of their thoughts, of their dreams" (26). Symons finds in the plays of Maeterlinck and Villiers an important corrective to realism.

It is also clear, however, that this stance is a development of Symons's appreciations of Lamb's aesthetic, including some aspects of Browning. The interest in mysticism which Symons expresses in the text involves the same "fight on behalf of the spirit, against that materialism which is always, in one way or another, atheist" (23). And, within this context, the relationship between the drama and the spectator takes on an added significance. For Symons, the truest form of drama involves the spectator so entirely that he becomes one with the ideal activities presented on the stage. *Axël* is a case in point: "But it is in *Axël*, and in *Axël* only, that he has made us also inhabitants of that world. Even in *Elën* we are spectators, watching a tragical fairy play (as if *Fantasio* became suddenly in deadly earnest), watching some one else's dreams. *Axël* envelops us in its own atmosphere; it is as if we found ourselves on a mountaintop, on the other side of the clouds, and without surprise at finding ourselves there" (27). Symons is thinking of the same sort of transportation Pater describes in relation to Leonardo da Vinci's *Mona Lisa*. The visible, sensuous world should correspond with the invisible. In Maeterlinck, "atmosphere, the suggestion of what was not said, was everything" (*Plays, Acting, and Music* 1909, 138).

In his essay, "Maurice Maeterlinck," collected in *Dramatis Personae* (1923), Symons deals, at one point, with Maeterlinck's essay, "The Modern Drama." Part of what interests him in this essay is related to future directions drama might take or, rather, how modern drama "can find that background of beauty and of mystery which was like a natural atmosphere to Sophocles and to Shakespeare" (37). He also states in this essay that with the publication of *Monna Vanna* Maeterlinck began to fall in his estimation. The magic and mystery of his earlier plays seemed to have vanished: "There is logic rather than life" (25).

Increasingly during the early years of the twentieth century, however, Symons began to appreciate the aesthetic qualities of the work of Gordon Craig. In "A New Art of the Theatre," in fact, we have an evaluation of theories of dramatic presentation that draws on Lamb but which finds a sense of fulfillment in Craig's work. Actually, the relationship between Craig and Symons works in both directions; Symons senses the embodiment of his artistic ideals in Craig's productions, and Craig draws upon the theoretical foundation Symons suggests in his various essays for part of his own theories of drama and dramatic presentation.

Craig began his career in the theatre as an actor, following in the footsteps of his mother, Ellen Terry; but he increasingly came to realize an interest in production and set design. His debut as a stage director, in the spring of 1900 when the Purcell Operatic Society staged *Dido and Aeneas*, was received well. Approximately a year later, on March 29, 1901, the Society again staged *Dido and Aeneas*, this time with *The Masque of Love*. Symons reviewed this production favorably for the *Star*, commenting on the overall design of the performance, but it was not until 1902 that he really began to recognize the value of Craig's work.

Yeats undoubtedly helped Symons to focus on Craig. His comment on him in his essay, "At Stratford-on-Avon," shows a very perceptive and immediate response to the 1901 production. As Yeats says, "it was the first beautiful scenery our stage has seen. He created an ideal country where everything was possible, even speaking in verse, or speaking to music, or the expression of the whole of life in a dance" (*Essays* 100–101). The creation of an ideal country, of course, answers Lamb's objections to the various productions of Shakespeare, and Symons, in "The Price of Realism," follows this line of thinking. Craig offers, first of all, an alternative to the "costly and inartistic aim at reality," which is "the vice of the modern stage" (*Plays, Acting, and Music* 1909, l64). Like Yeats, Symons goes on to comment on the design of the production: "Here, for once, we see the stage treated in the proper spirit, as material for art, not as a collection of real objects, or the imitation of real objects. Why should not the visible world be treated in the same spirit as the invisible world of character and temperament?'' (165). The connection between this statement about Craig and the ideals elaborated by Lamb is striking. Craig belonged to that movement in modern art whose chief exponents in England were Whistler and Wilde. The aesthetic ideals of these artists are clearly allied with those of Lamb. Therefore, Symons also becomes interested in the extendability of Craig's concepts: "But there is no doubt that Mr. Craig's method of draping the stage with plain cloths, of lighting it from the top, of doing away with realistic imitations of scenery, and tailor-made imitations of clothes, is a method capable of infinite extension, capable already of giving infinite delight to the eye'' (79).

Much of Symons's evaluation of Craig is based, particularly at this early point, on beliefs about the nature of theatrical presentation that affect the theatre as a whole. His contribution to the theatre involves much more than stage and scene design. In fact, Craig's outline of his intentions in *The Art of the Theatre,* published as a pamphlet in 1905, shows that his antirealistic theatre is part of an overall plan to make the stage art totally unified and distinct. If his early productions were striking because they avoided descriptive detail, as well as elaborate archaeological realism, and appealed self-consciously to the audience's imagination, they are also striking for the unity of production they evidence, as Denis Bablet points out:

> But Craig's great service to the stage lay not so much in his introduction of an entirely new type of scenery, reduced to a few essential elements and fundamental colours, as in his completely original manner of presentation, by which the expressive harmony of the stage picture, composed of colour, line, movement and light, was uninterruptedly maintained. Each scene was built up like a picture, its components inseparably combined, and interpreted the dramatic atmosphere of the moment in association with the music. (41)

Craig's production techniques, which are set in direct opposition to the pretensions of the naturalistic school, aspire to an imaginative unity of artistic effect. The production is considered as an aesthetic whole. In line with this ambition, Bablet uses the same sort of analogues to music and painting that we have seen in Lamb, and which Fitzgerald and Symons elaborate even more fully. Harmony and composition are the operative concepts. Symons, in "A New Art of the Stage," quotes Craig on the lack of artistic balance in the modern theatre: "In the modern theatre a play is no longer 'a balance of actions, words, dance, and scene, but it is either all words or all scene'" (*Works* 9:231). For Symons, this attitude, which he discusses in many of the reviews collected in *Plays, Acting, and Music* (1909), comes as a pleasant relief to the productions, which seem to represent the plays as a separate literary phenomenon. Stephen Phillips fails because "the poetry might be detached from the dramatic framework and the framework would stand exactly as it did before'' (96). And Symons reacts positively to the Shakespeare productions of Julia Marlowe and E. H. Sothern, two American actors who played in London in 1907, for the same reasons; they did not accent one aspect of the drama more than an artistic conception of the whole would allow: "The poetry consumes the rhetoric" (187). Craig, in fact, carries this argument a step further in *On the Art of the Theatre*. The balance he wants to create is based upon the essentials of dramatic production: "The Art of the Theatre is neither acting nor the play, it is not scene nor dance, but it consists of all the elements of which these things are composed: action, which is the very spirit of acting; words, which are the body of the play; line and colour, which are the very heart of the scene; rhythm, which is the very essence of dance" (138).

In *Towards a New Theatre* Craig lists some of the literary figures to whom he feels he is indebted. Included are Blake, Whistler, Pater, and Yeats, figures who were important to Symons as well. It seems equally true, however, that Lamb functions significantly in Craig's thinking, as does Symons. Craig, for example, feels that some of Shakespeare's plays lose too much of their magic when acted, when made into flesh and blood. In "On the Ghosts in the Tragedies of Shakespeare" he returns to the same problem, again recalling Lamb. Here, however, he alludes to Alexander Hevesi, the Hungarian producer and theatre manager who was a follower of Craig. According to Hevesi, the best stage productions evoke the immaterial: "The suggestive shall predominate, for all pictures on the stage pretending to illusionize reality must necessarily fail in their effect or cause a disillusionment" (qtd. in *On the Art of the Theatre* 266). The ghosts in Shakespeare are emblematic of the ultimate poetic quality of his plays; they "raise the action from the merely material to the psychological" (268). As Maeterlinck said, they are "the murmur of eternity on the horizon" (266). This point, as we have seen, was made earlier by both Lamb and Symons.

The connection between Craig and Symons is particularly strongly felt when we consider what each had to say about puppets and marionettes. In both cases, the fascination stems from the belief that art is essentially artificial. As Craig says, "The naturalistic stepped in on the Stage because the artificial had grown finicking, insipid; but do not forget that there is such a thing as *noble* artificiality" (35). Craig continues this argument in relation to the actor in "The Actor and the *Uber-Marionette*," published in *The Mask* in 1908. This essay, along with a few other notable essays, such as "A Note on Marionettes" and "A Note on Masks," deals with Craig's theory of acting, an issue which comes up again in the next section of this chapter. Basically, however, his view of acting is based upon a change in his perspective on the theatre in general. Craig's early appreciation of Henry Irving, for example, changed because Irving's interest in realistic stage productions clashed with Craig's evolving aesthetic idealism. As he says in "The Actor and the *Uber-Marionette*" in *On the Art of the Theatre,* sounding very much like Symons in his aversion to photography: "The actor looks upon life as a photo-machine looks upon life; and he attempts to make a picture to rival a photograph. He never dreams of his art as being an art such for instance as music. He tried to reproduce Nature; he seldom thinks to invent with the aid of Nature; and he never dreams of *creating*" (62).

In line with this tendency in the actor to rely on nature too heavily, Craig feels that he is controlled by his emotions, by what he is trying to represent, rather than controlling his material as a true artist should. The type of drama Craig wants to create, based upon a belief in "noble artificiality," requires a new form of acting, something different than the traditional representation of life: "The painter means something rather different to actuality when he speaks of life in his art, and the other artists generally mean something essentially spiritual" (63). Life to Craig, as to Symons, means something more than what is actual and lifelike. The new style of acting, based upon a standard other than the reproduction of the surface qualities of life, Craig describes in terms of the *über-marionette*: "The *Uber-marionette* is the actor plus fire, minus egoism; the fire of the gods and demons, without the smoke and steam of mortality" (*On the Art of the Theatre* 1925, preface). He is, in fact, interested in an actor who is purified, who does not seem limited by his own physicality. In short, he describes the sort of actor who could, in a tradition established by Lamb, act Lear properly.

Obviously, Craig's ambition is set in contrast to the stage conventions of his day. As he says in "The Russian Ballet," "I am not a believer in the fluttering, bubbling personality of the stage 'Stars,' . . . I am against the emphasis which is laid on the Body in the theatre . . ." (*Gordon Craig on Movement and Dance* 97). He also draws on the observations of Anatole France for further support: "Their talent is too great. It hides everything else! One can see nothing but them" (qtd. in "A Note on Masks" 9–10). This is another way of saying, to quote Lamb, that we "sink Othello's mind in his colour" when we are made to be too conscious of the physical presence of the actors on the stage. And the actors and actresses of the day, particularly Sarah Bernhardt, accented their personality and physicality above any consideration of the play and its overall atmosphere. Thus, Craig, in what appears to be a rather extreme suggestion, calls for the elimination of personality in acting. Of course, France also goes on to speak admiringly about marionettes: "These marionettes are like Egyptian hieroglyph, that is, like something mysterious and pure" (qtd. in *On the Art of the Theatre* 88). A marionette, in fact, could do a far better job because it expresses what is not an accident of his own personality. But, as Bablet observes, what Craig is saying finally is that "The *Uber-marionette* is the actor who has acquired some of the virtues of the marionette and thus releases himself from servitude" (109).

These ideas elaborated by Craig in 1908 were not entirely radical and without precedent, as, in fact, the quotation from France suggests. In 1897 Symons published "An Apology for Puppets" in the *Saturday Review*. He later reprinted the essay as the last part of the first edition of *Plays, Acting, and Music* and as the introduction to the revised edition in 1909. Craig must have read it, as he quotes often from Symons's work in various issues of *The Mask*. Indeed, Stokes owns Craig's signed and annotated copy of *Studies in Seven Arts*. Additionally, the two men became friendly in 1902 and obviously began to influence each other's thinking.

Symons's early essay, then, seems to be part of the basis for the ideas developed by Craig in "The Actor and the *Uber-Marionette*." Symons's thesis, for example, prefigures Craig's later developments:

After seeing a ballet, a farce, and the fragment of an opera performed by the marionettes at the Costanzi Theatre in Rome, I am inclined to ask myself why we require the intervention of any less perfect medium between the meaning of a piece, as the author conceived it, and that other meaning which it derives from our reception of it. The living actor, even when he condescends to subordinate himself to the requirements of pantomime, has always what he is proud to call his temperament; in other words, so much personal caprice, which for the most part means willful misunderstanding; and in seeing his acting you have to consider this intrusive little personality of his as well as the author's. (*Plays, Acting, and Music* 1909, 3)

On one level, Symons is arguing that the actor disrupts the connection between the author and the audience. But this mediation is not all that is implied in Symons's essay. Personal caprice is set in contrast with a more perfect artistic expression, and the essential paradox involved in the question of stage illusion is highlighted. As Lamb had suggested, the theatre should not aim to create the illusion of reality; it should create the illusion of illusion. Marionettes accent the illusory or artificial quality of stage productions and, by extension, of art in general. As Symons says, "It is not nature one looks for on the stage" (5). Symons goes on, as does Craig in "A Note on Masks," to associate marionettes with the Greeks' use of masks: "This is nothing less than a fantastic, yet a direct, return to the masks of the Greeks: that learned artifice by which tragedy and comedy were assisted in speaking to the world with the universal voice, by this deliberately generalizing of emotions" (6). In "A New Art of the Stage," also published in this collection, Symons concedes that, in fact, a play by Ibsen could quite profitably be given using the stage designs of Craig, that is, by the world of marionettes. The nature of the stage production does affect greatly the theatrical experience, and the experience he wants to promote is based on principles allied with aestheticism: "Above all, for we need it above all, let the marionettes remind us that the art of the theatre should be beautiful first, and then indeed what you will afterwards" (7). This last comment actually recalls Swinburne's statement about the art for art's sake movement in *William Blake*: "Art for art's sake first of all, and afterwards we may suppose all the rest shall be added to her" (137–38).

Craig, throughout his work, alludes to Symons. He reprinted, for example, "Pantomime and the Poetic Drama" in *The Mask*, March, 1914, with a note of his own on Symons's essay. The point of Symons's essay is that for the poetic drama nature should cease to exist. He is concerned again with promoting "the supreme interference of beauty" (*Works* 9:242). The language of poetic drama aspires to this level in relation to the other aspects of the production. Craig's comments on this essay follow this line of thinking. He states that "if words were always used in drama 'for their beauty' and 'not for their mere utility' [quotations from

Symons's essay] there would be no fear that the ugliness of interruption would ever mar or spoil our happiness'' (189).

Craig's observations, in fact, involve a compromise that Symons saw as necessary if his procedures were to be most effective. Using Lamb again as a point of reference, Symons points out in "A New Art of the Stage" that Shakespeare loses too much in the acting; Craig, on the other hand, feels that Shakespeare is unsuited for the stage. The stage, according to Craig, is nonverbal in its ultimate appeal. Symons suggests a compromise between "the art of the dramatist" and "the logic of his mechanism" (*Works* 9:234–35). Symons feels that Craig is trying to underplay the value of language in stage productions when actually he is trying to bring all aspects of the drama into proper perspective. Both actually aim to promote the same sort of artistic renaissance. Symons continually associates his work with the spirit and atmosphere of the Elizabethan period. Craig, as he says in the introduction to *The Art of the Theatre*, is motivated by the same spirit: "At present there is too much careless work in every department of the theatre, and even should one man fight free from the old theatre he cannot alone create a renaissance. Such an event develops only after many years of combined efforts. A Wagner, with a great idea, does not *make* the renaissance, he only points the way" (13).

Symons, following in the tradition of Lamb and drawing upon other related writers, sees Craig in this same light: "The whole stage art of Mr. Craig is a protest against realism, and it is to realism that we owe whatever is most conspicuously bad in the mounting of plays at the present day" (*Works* 9:228). Craig's protest forms the new art of the stage Symons seeks, "an art no longer realistic, but conventional, no longer imitative, but symbolical" (*Works* 9:224).

Performance and Acting

Many of the symbolist poets Symons admired also reinforced his fascination with stage performers. Gérard de Nerval found such figures irresistible. As Mallarmé says about the dancer in "Hérodiade," there is a "charm and a curse" wrapped in the character of these people and their art. Nerval, according to Symons, is like a moth charmed by the vision of a flame but destroyed by its heat: "Like so many dreamers of illimitable dreams, it was the fate of Gérard to incarnate his ideal in the person of an actress. The fatal transfiguration of the footlights, in which reality and the artificial change places with so fantastic a regularity, has drawn many moths into its flame, and will draw more, as long as men persist in demanding illusion of what is real, and reality in what is illusion" (*Symbolist Movement* 11). Symons brings into alignment in this statement an interest in the artificial with the symbolist ideal of a world which is significantly transfigured by art. Symons's fascination with actresses and performance in general functions significantly in his overall aesthetics of the theatre.

Performance, further, forces the characteristics of the artistic paradox of life and art more intensely to the surface. Symons's use of footlights, for example, to define the barrier between what is illusion and what is real is recurrent in his work, and it accents the fact that in the theatre the sense of world is as strong as the sense of illusion. In an 1893 review for *The Sketch*, " 'Fidelia,' at the Alhambra," he uses the same analogy more extensively: "I have friends on both sides of the foot-lights who will be asking me presently, 'Well, what do you think of the ballet?'— serious friends, with a serious interest in dancing in the abstract, on this side; and frivolous friends, with a practical interest in dancing in the concrete, on that side" (461). Symons's fascination with dance and the music-hall originates in this aware-ness that it is a world of intense paradox; aesthetic interests mix with sensual ap-peal. If, as has been suggested by a number of critics, including Frank Kermode in *The Romantic Image* and Ian Fletcher in "Explorations and Recoveries II: Symons, Yeats and the Demonic Dance," the symbolist ideal in particular involves a union of these forces, then performance in its various aspects is, as Symons sug-gests in relation to Nerval, the perfect incarnation of what all artists seek. Symons's comment on ballet is a case in point: "A ballet is simply a picture in movement. It is a picture where the imitation of nature is given by nature itself; where the figures of the composition are real, and yet, by a very paradox of travesty, have a delightful, deliberate air of unreality" ("At the Alhambra" 83). The charac-teristics of dance that Symons appreciates are not, however, limited to that type of performance alone, although dance has generated the most discussion by critics. This interest is due, in part, to a related use of the symbolic qualities of dance in Yeats's work. Symons, as we shall see, develops many of the same artistic ideals in his criticism of various actors and actresses, as well as in other aspects of per-formance in general.

Fascination with performance, in fact, is significantly characteristic of the late nineteenth century, as George Rowell points out in his introduction to *Victorian Dramatic Criticism*. Victorian theatre was distinguished by its acting rather than its drama. His selection, therefore, is based on "the play as performance, rather than the play as literature" (xiii). Considerable discussion of dramatic performance as a distinct art, different from the play as literature, also developed during this time. Symons and Craig are two examples. More recently J. L. Styan has observed that "drama, as no other art, uses man's capacity for piecing together vast and varied amounts of sense information with which to build patterns of thinking and acting, just as in life" (27). The multisensuous level clearly distinguishes perfor-mance from a purely literary experience. And, of course, it is on the sensuous level that drama is connected so strongly with life, while the way in which the entire theatrical experience is organized connects it with art and artifice. As Styan also says, "Even in drama at its most realistic, what is seen is there to hint at what is not, and imagination completes the process" (144). Many of the collections of dra-matic criticism published throughout the nineteenth century, such as Leigh Hunt's *Critical Essays on the Performers of the London Theatre* (1807), G. H. Lewes's *On Actors and the Art of Acting* (1875), and Westland Marston's *Our Recent Ac-tors* (1888), to name only a few, focus on performance as well. Lamb, of course, is very much a part of this tradition in a particularly impressionistic way: he tries to recreate the effect the acting has on the observer.

This increased and serious interest in acting as an art is due in part to the changing social position of the actor in Victorian society. When Mrs. Patrick Campbell chose during the 1880s to go into acting in order to help support her family, it was still tantamount to saying she was going to resort to prostitution; but by the end of the century both Henry Irving and Squire Bancroft had been knighted for their service to the theatre. The change in social status in turn allowed for a broadening of artistic interest. Acting styles and the artistic beliefs that informed them became the subject of critical discussion. Sarah Bernhardt, for instance, came to represent one school of thought on the nature of acting and dramatic production. Eleonora Duse, the great Italian actress, however, opposed Bernhardt on a number of artistic grounds. These two figures, as we shall see, focus important artistic questions for Symons and for the period in general. In line with the discussions of acting, George Bernard Shaw supported, particularly in relation to the plays of Ibsen, the notion of the intellectual actress. Janet Achurch and Elizabeth Robins come immediately to mind.

It was not acting alone, however, which received such increased attention. As we have already seen in relation to Symons's dramatic theory, the theatrical experience as a whole came under close scrutiny. In some respects the historically accurate and aesthetically designed productions of Edward William Godwin contrasted with the more mundane domestic realism used to present most drama. Godwin's interest in a harmonious, aesthetic whole, however, was more often than not, for the spectator, buried by the elaborate spectacle of his archaeological realism.

Spectacle was for many theatregoers the most important aspect of any production. This period was, to paraphrase Symons, avid after sensation. As the industrial landscape began to press negatively on the mental state of the population, theatrical spectacle in its various forms came to be a way of dealing with life. The music-hall, the fair, and the circus emerge in part as anodynes to these conditions. It is highly appropriate that in 1890 Chapman and Hall should publish a translation of Hugues Le Roux and Jules Garnier's *Acrobats and Mountebanks*, for this text is significantly the first to deal with the history and artistic quality of gymnasts, equilibrists, and other such performers, as well as to deal with the history of fairs, circuses, and other such organizations.

Symons is very much a part of this world, attuned to the various artistic interests that emerged. When he took up permanent residence in London in the beginning of 1891, he was well prepared for the variety of experiences he would seek. His early interests in fairs and acrobatics broadened as he became associated with the music-hall, particularly as the reviewer for the London *Star*. And, in relation to these early interests, his fascination with dance as a particularly quintessential art evolved.

Since the publication of Frank Kermode's *Romantic Image*, as well as the later essay, ''The Poet and Dancer Before Diaghilev,'' a considerable amount of discussion has centered on dance as embodying for many of the writers during the late nineteenth and early twentieth centuries the ideals of artistic creation. This characteristic of dance seems particularly true if we consider it in the light of the symbolist tradition, which, since the time of Yeats and Eliot, has dominated much of the thinking about modernism in general. Kermode gives Symons credit for initiating much of this interest in dance, but it is probably not adequately recognized how suggestive his essay, "The World as Ballet," really is. On closer examination we sense that many of the elaborations Kermode gives us are clearly derived from Symons's seminal essay. As Kermode says, "The dance, though expressive, is impersonal, like a symbolist poem that comes off" ("Poet and Dancer" 51). It is in this way that the dance becomes for Yeats emblematic of unity of being. Symons, in 1898, offers similar observations: "And something in the particular elegance of the dance, the scenery; the avoidance of emphasis, the evasive, winding turn of things; and, above all, the intellectual as well as sensuous appeal of a living symbol, which can but reach the brain through the eyes, in the visual, concrete, imaginative way; has seemed to make the ballet concentrate in itself a good deal of the modern ideal in matters of artistic expression" (*Works* 9:246). The aesthetic and symbolic ideals which Symons sees embodied in dance are significantly characteristic of this time, particularly as dance manages to mingle the sensuous and aesthetic; dance becomes a "living symbol." In this way, of course, it is consistent with the impressionism Symons had inherited from Pater.

Symons had been interested in dance prior to his meeting with Yeats, whose influence is certainly apparent in the above quotation. He mentions, for example, to Dykes Campbell in 1889 that he was fascinated with the Javanese Dancers when he saw them in Paris, an experience which generated his poem "Javanese Dancers" (letter, October 6, 1889). In 1892 he saw Jane Avril dance at Le Jardin de Paris, and he elaborates his interest in such sensual and enigmatic dancers in "Dancers and Dancing" in *Colour Studies in Paris* (1918). "La Mélinite: Moulin Rouge," in *Silhouettes*, is also based upon this 1892 performance. Many of these early allusions to dance have led critics such as Ian Fletcher to conclude that Symons's early attitude differs from the attitudes that developed in association with Yeats: "The dance, stylized, self-conscious, provocative, came to represent for him the perfect emblem of life in the modern city, for it dramatized his own isolation. Yet through his association with Yeats, the dance later became for Symons not spectacle merely, but participation, and, in some sense, religion" (49). There is some confusion, it seems, in the characteristics of dance Fletcher sees as implicit in Symons's various writings, partially due to a confusion in Symons over the significance of dance. And certainly Symons's appreciation of dance matures, particularly during the years of his association with Yeats. But if we consider a number of his early music-hall reviews, it is apparent that his perceptions are very sophisticated and implicitly contain the elements most often associated with Yeats's influence. It seems that dance, as were other performance arts, was always for Symons more than spectacle and involved a sense of his own participation.

Jan B. Gordon, in "The Dance Macabre of Arthur Symons's *London Nights*," usefully identifies "La Mélinite: Moulin Rouge" with the synthesis of art and life.

In the poem, the dancer dances to herself in the mirror; she is like the decadent poet who has his vision focused upon the mirror of his own imagination. In a very important sense, the correspondence between the dancer and her reflection follows the thinking of Remy de Gourmont. In *Le Livre des Masques* (1896) he describes symbolism using similar imagery: "A writer's work should be not only the reflection, but the magnified reflection of his own personality. The only excuse a man has for writing is to express himself, to reveal to others the world reflected in his individual mirror" (181–82). Symons's interest in personality and temperament, which is clearly associated with a form of hero worship, becomes for him the proper route through which the universal and symbolic can be attained. Ballet is art using nature directly, and La Mélinite's dance shows the artist producing art from her own nature.

From another point of view, of course, the scene in "La Mélinite: Moulin Rouge" is used to show artistic isolation, a characteristic of the symbolist art which Kermode emphasizes in *The Romantic Image*. La Mélinite dancing to herself in the mirror represents the artist lost in his own vision. This idea seems to lead in Symons's work, particularly in relation to dance, to a lack of connection between the artist and his public. Symons, as a spectator of ballet, recognizes simultaneously the ideal beauty implicit in the performance and his essential separation from it. In "To a Dancer" the speaker's appreciation does not seem to contain a sense of involvement. If, however, we consider further some of Symons's reviews of ballets and his descriptions of music-halls, it becomes apparent that the ultimate performance, emblematic of art in general, has to involve the spectator, envelop him, in fact, for that time. He suggests as much, as we have seen, in his essay on Villiers, and, as he says in "Music Halls and Ballet Girls," an essay which Karl Beckson published in *The Memoirs of Arthur Symons*, "only in the music-hall is the audience a part of the performance" (109). He means, of course, that the entire world of the music-hall is an entertainment, not just the activities on the stage. He tries to capture this atmosphere in "At the Alhambra: Impressions and Sensations" by describing the activities behind the scenes, in the audience, and on the stage. But a large part of the impact of this piece is due to the sense of involvement the narrator feels; he becomes tangibly a part of the world of artifice. At one point, for example, Symons shakes hands with the ballet girls as they assemble behind the scenes: "As I shake hands with one after another, my hands get quite white and rough with the chalk-powder they have been rubbing over their skin. Is not even this charming sensation, a sensation in which one seems actually to partake of the beautiful artificiality of the place" (77). The sense of artificiality increases as he becomes more made-up. Indeed, make-up becomes a separate symbol: "As a disguise for age or misfortune, it has no interest for me. But, of all places, on the stage, and of all people, on the cheeks of young people: there, it seems to me that make-up is intensely fascinating, and its recognition is of the essence of my delight in a stage performance" (75).

Throughout his early reviews, particularly those in the *Star* and *The Sketch*, he accents this same aesthetic quality. In an extremely interesting way, for example, Symons projects a sense of his ultimate appreciation of the ballet in "At the Empire," written for the June 7, 1893 issue of *The Sketch*: "It amuses me sometimes to sit at the back of the promenade, and, undistracted by my somewhat too agreeably distracting surroundings, to follow, by the sound of the music, every movement of the ballet on the stage, which I only see in my mind's eye. . . . I see it all, and I see it as in a mirror, with something new and strange in its enticing artificiality" (302). This passage recalls, first of all, Pater's famous phrase, "All art constantly aspires towards the condition of music," for Symons obviously wants to associate his appreciation of ballet as an art of perfect beauty with Pater's theories. The sound of the music, therefore, determines the movement in his mind's eye. The addition of the mirror connects his vision of the ballet to the symbolist vision contained in "La Mélinite: Moulin Rouge." And, there is something new and strange, which also alludes to Pater's definition of romanticism. In " 'Fidelia,' at the Alhambra," he again describes a particularly beautiful tableau and abstracts some aesthetic ideals from it: "A Ballet has so many chances of being a thing of beauty that it has no excuse for not being so, or for abandoning beauty in the search for humor, variety, the grotesque, or anything whatever. The beauty of dancing is so great, and so entirely in itself, that it requires no outside expedients to give it effect, only the due assistance of charming and appropriate scenery and costume" (461). Symons, indeed, identifies ballet in all of his early reviews as, to use Kermode's term, the "romantic image." Symons's observations, therefore, are considerably more suggestive than has been thought, defining, as they do, not only the nature of artistic expression but the relationship that necessarily must develop between the spectator and the spectacle.

Symons's interest in the music-hall and performance in general extends into other areas as well. In "Acrobatics at the Empire," a review written for the *Star* in 1892, he comments that the art of the gymnast has not been properly appreciated. Other reviews for the *Star* deal with similar issues, although often in relation to an appreciation of the sensational aspects of the various acts. Reviews such as "Human Eels" in the *Star* or "The Training of the Contortionist" in the *Pall Mall Gazette* focus on the intense sensations these sorts of entertainments evoke. But, as is evidenced in his 1890 review of *Acrobats and Mountebanks*, Symons sees acrobatics as more important than the source of sensation: "One needs to be something of an artist to understand the whole charm of the fair, the circus, the wandering life of tents and caravans. To the frivolous it is frivolous, to the vulgar it is vulgar, but to the artist it is always attractive" (239).

Symons's sense of the importance of the acrobat is derived in part from observations he discovered in the Goncourts' journal. He quotes them in his review: "There [at the circus] we see clowns, vaulters, men who jump through paper hoops, all following their profession, all doing their duty: in reality the only actors whose talent is incontestable, absolute as mathematics, or, better still, as the *saut périlleux*. For, in that, there is no false show of talent; either one falls or one does not fall" (qtd. 239). This perspective obviously influenced Symons's belief that the circus or music-hall entertainment could be seen as emblematic of significant artistic issues. If the ballet appears to be a concentration of the modern ideal in matters of artistic expression, then acrobatics, too, can be seen as a concentration of technique in relation to artistic expression. First of all, there can be no false show of technical merit, as Symons says in "Technique and the Artist": "Without technique, perfect of its kind, no one is worth consideration in any art. The rope-dancer or the acrobat must be perfect in technique before he appears on the stage at all; in his case, a lapse from perfection brings its own penalty, death perhaps; his art begins when his technique is already perfect" (*Plays, Acting, and Music* 1909, 233).

Symons's ideas clearly relate to Pater's earlier interest in style. Pater quotes Flaubert, who has been dissatisfied with his writing: "I am like a man whose ear is true but who plays falsely on the violin; his fingers refuse to reproduce precisely those sounds of which he has the inward sense" (qtd. in *Appreciations* 33). Flaubert uses the connection between a violinist's technical ability and ultimate artistic expression as an analogue for the writer's use of technique to express the truth of his inward vision. The final issue, as Pater shows, concerns the perfect union of form and content, although Pater opts for suggesting at the conclusion that great art depends on "the greater dignity of its interests" (38). Symons's essay deals with the quality of Eugène Ysaÿe as violinist and Ferruccio Busoni as pianist, using acrobatic technique as the analogue: "Of two acrobats, each equally skilful, one will be individual and an artist, the other will remain consummately skilful and uninteresting; the one having begun where the other leaves off" (*Plays, Acting, and Music* 1909, 233–34).

Symons is very conscious of technique, but he finally chooses to see art in relation to the sense of individuality which, as we have seen, is part of the symbolist ideal. The same issue, derived from his fascination with acrobatics, arises in his dance reviews. The sense of the strange, which he derives from Pater, and the sense of "a continual slight novelty," which he derives from Aristotle, combine to suggest an essential sense of individuality in dance: "The extravagance of the thing was never vulgar, its intricate agility was never incorrect; there was genuine grace in the wildest moment of caprice, there was real science in the pointing of the foot in its most fantastic flights above the head" ("'Cyrene' at the Alhambra" 610). The criterion Symons is using to judge the ballet distills to the science of acrobatic technique and the sense of individual novelty that is its matter.

Yvette Guilbert, more than any other music-hall artist, epitomizes a number of these artistic qualities for Symons; for her art was a unique concentration of forces and, in many ways, embodied the paradox of the symbolist experience. Symons was undoubtedly aware of Guilbert from his early visits to Paris. He first writes about her in 1892, for the *St. James's Gazette*. He was also at this time writing for the *Black and White* on the Paris music-hall. He earlier read Edmund Gosse's article about Aristide Bruant and wrote a review for *Black and White*, "'Au Mirliton': A Visit to Aristide Bruant." It is clear that in relation to these artists, the music-hall for Symons became the source of avant garde theories of art. Certainly the atmosphere in Paris cultivated this belief, as did Toulouse-Lautrec's paintings. Walter Sickert in England showed the same sort of artistic appreciation. Kermode's statement that the music-hall is "a weak descendent of a positive avant garde reaction against commercial theatre in the nineties" should be considered as something of an understatement, for music-halls were, as he says later, "as important in the early history of modern art as folk-music and primitive painting, with which indeed they are obviously associated" ("Poet and Dancer" 54).

Guilbert, within this framework, is considered a supreme artist because of her association with artistic theory. In 1894, for example, *The Sketch* published two pieces about her, "A Reminiscence" and "An Appreciation." At one point in the latter, the author describes her as "an incarnation of the old, old question about the art of morality and the morality of art" and asks whether we should "applaud her for the way in which she sings her songs, or should we hiss her for the impropriety of their character?" (H. N. 137). In other words, there is a radical contrast between the nature of the songs she sings and the art with which she sings them. George Bernard Shaw, when he saw her perform in London, described the character of her songs as wonderfully moral. Her rather grotesque songs, most of which were written by Xenrof (Léon Forneau) and dealt with prostitution, poverty, and the more sordid aspects of life, became the basis of a moral impulse. Shaw, after hearing "La Pierreuse," states that the impact of the song was such that it should move people to action. He is particularly struck by the last verse, which describes the guillotining of the robber. Shaw states that "so hideously exquisite is the singing of this verse that you see the women in the crowd at La Roquette; you hear the half-choked repetition of the familiar signal with which she salutes the wretch as he is hurried out; you positively see his head flying off" (*Music* 226). The intensity with which the scene is communicated, Shaw feels, should cause social reform.

Although Shaw sees Guilbert's dramatic art within a social framework, the same dramatic intensity she is able to create appeals more generally. Her songs are dramas which depend quite literally on her unique mode of presentation. She wanted her visual appearance to work in conjunction with her material. But she chose to accent her art through contrast and irony. As one observer during this period rightly points out, "She had the insight to see that the present age is tickled more by contrast than anything else, and that the more sharp and audacious the contrast the more acute the tickling. Now, the Parisian public admires two things— the *grande dame* of the Faubourg and the intellectual indecency of the Boulevard. If anybody could combine the two, a great triumph was assured" (Guilbert 173).

The same sense of contrast is alluded to by various other commentators, broadening the implications. In *The Song of My Life* Guilbert includes a number of comments on her art by such figures as Octave Mirbeau, Edmond de Goncourt, and others. Most focus on the strange paradox of her art; appearance clashes with the nature of the songs she sings. Paul Hervieu describes her art in relation to tragedy or comedy in her work: "I don't think one should be astonished that Mlle Yvette Guilbert can be so tragic when she is so comic, but, on the contrary, that she can show herself so comic when she is really so tragic" (165). But, as her biographers point out, the first psychological analysis of Guilbert's appeal, and one of the most interesting, was Hugues Le Roux's February 1891 article in *Le Temps*. He, too, centers on the nature of the contrast upon which her art is based:

> In general essence it is the purity, the intact virginity of Diana; in its individual form it is the laugh of the young fauness who knows that she is made to love, who wishes to be loved. And between these two extremes, which are the confines of ingenuousness, lies an exquisite province, a charming Eden, a paradise to lose, around which men revolve, charmed, attracted, ravished; the kingdom of Yvette. (qtd. in Knapp and Chipman 86)

This passage recalls the imagery and atmosphere that surrounded the dancer in the Symons poem, "La Mélinite: Moulin Rouge," and it additionally recalls Mallarmé's "Hérodiade." For Symons, who probably read Le Roux's article, Yvette is also a resolution of forces, and he sees her as importantly emblematic of artistic concerns. He notes, first, her physical charm, an appreciation which he immediately qualifies: "But it is not merely by her personal charm that she thrills you, though that is strange, perverse, unaccountable" (*Plays, Acting, and Music* 1909, 43). He goes on to describe her in terms of the same contrasts that form the basis of Le Roux's essay:

> She is a creature of contrasts, and suggests at once all that is innocent and all that is perverse. She has the pure blue eyes of a child, eyes that are cloudless, that gleam with a wicked ingenuousness, that close in the utter abasement of weariness, that open wide in all the expressionlessness of surprise. Her naivete is perfect, and perfect, too, is that strange, subtle smile of comprehension that closes the period. (*Plays, Acting, and Music* 1909, 45)

The contrasts which are so appealing are self-consciously evoked by the nature of her presentation in relation to the context with which she deals. As the critic for *The Sketch* said at the time, "Her appearance would do credit to a convent, her language would bring a blush to the Boul Miche" (H. N. 174).

This contrast is additionally appealing, however, because it accents the artistry involved and brings into focus the relationship between life and art that the writers of this period found so important. In an interview published in *The Sketch* in 1894 she says that her art is based upon the imposition of art on life: "The song is at the mercy of the singer; in the singer's mouth alone it is coarse or refined. I try to interpret mine in a way that is refined, *même les plus légères*" (qtd. in C. S. C., "A

Reminiscence" 173). Her self-analysis is highly appropriate to the artistic concerns of the period, and many observers, as we have seen, come to similar conclusions about her art. Later in life, when she was writing her memoirs, she felt the need to reach an even fuller understanding of the quality of genius that had tantalized so many audiences. In 1931 she asked Freud for his opinion. He concluded, as one would expect, that "the achievements of artists are conditioned internally by their childhood impressions, vicissitudes, repressions and disappointments" (qtd. in Knapp and Chipman 282).

For Symons, however, Guilbert is the ultimate artistic ideal; she brings life and art together on the stage: "She brings before you the real life-drama of the streets, of the pot-house; she shows you the seamy side of life behind the scenes; she calls things by their right names. But there is not a touch of sensuality about her, she is neither contaminated nor contaminating by what she sings; she is simply a great, impersonal, dramatic artist, who sings realism as others write it" (*Plays, Acting, and Music* 1909, 44). The fact that she appeals on two levels, on the sensual and intellectual, brings her into correspondence with the general appeal of the music-hall for Symons; she brings into focus what is on both sides of the footlights, to use Symons's analogy. When she sings Bruant's songs, she projects the sense of the world they depict, and, yet, "she has transformed the rough material, which had seemed adequately handled until she showed how much more could be done with it, into something artistically fine and distinguished" (*Plays, Acting, and Music* 1909, 47). Symons's review of her performance, after she has been forced to retire for two years because of ill-health, focuses on the same character in her art. She now combines an interest in old French ballads with a lessening interest in the ruder street songs, but the change has not really affected her art. When she sings all becomes drama, and with the "gutter songs" her artistry comes alive in the old way again. What could have been vulgar becomes a masterpiece according to Symons: "Nothing more deliberate, more finished, more completely achieved, is to be seen on our stage; and there is not an effect of which she is not wholly conscious" ("Yvette Guilbert at the Empire" 1).

The appreciation of the artistic quality of Guilbert and other music-hall acts, of course, represents an aspect of Symons's overall interest in performance. References in his letters at this time show both variety and perceptive interest. From Paris he states that he has been to the Moulin Rouge, the Chat Noir, and other famous music-halls (letter to Dykes Campbell, May 25, 1890). In 1890 he comments to Dykes Campbell that he is coming to London to see Bernhardt in various plays, including *Adrienne Lecouvreur, La Dame aux Camélias*, and *La Tosca* (letter, July 3, 1890). He would also brag to Gosse about his music-hall associations. But in many ways, particularly as Symons's artistic ideals matured, his interest in the music-hall gave way to an increasing appreciation of the theatre and acting. Thus, when he published the revised version of *Plays, Acting, and Music* in 1909, Yvette Guilbert is dealt with, along with Sarah Bernhardt, Henry Irving, and Eleonora Duse, in the section entitled "Plays and Acting." In fact, Guilbert appears to have been a part of two worlds. She added a sense of artistic seriousness to the music-hall world, and she, simultaneously, rose above that world to be considered as much an actress as Bernhardt or Duse. Symons, of course, also took the music-hall more seriously than most and found in acting many of the same qualities of art.

John Stokes, in "The Legend of Duse," describes what he takes to be the connections, as well as the distinctions, between the dancer or music-hall performer and the actress, all of which he relates to the artist's relationship with society:

> The solitary dancer aspired to and perhaps achieved a much desired unity of being, and her isolation and self-regard offered an hermetic image that included both artist and work. The actress, conscious of her audience, interpreter of many roles, and contributor to a corporate activity (both of which distinguished her from the *chanteuse* or music-hall performer), offered a more flexible image, a way of keeping social and aesthetic relationships unresolved. (152)

That the image of the actress is more flexible is undoubtedly true. The dancer is immediately more aesthetic, more like (in terms of the relationship between the artist and the work) La Mélinite dancing to herself in the mirror. But Stokes's observations ignore a number of issues. For example, as many reviewers during this period suggest, it often becomes questionable whether the actress is, or appears to be, aware of her audience. This issue is particularly important in relation to Duse, the topic of his essay; for she more than Bernhardt, if we consider her style of acting as emblematic of one important trend, appears to be natural on the stage. This problem occurs again when we compare the two styles in relation to Symons's point of view. Additionally, although, as Stokes says, acting is a corporate activity, as it should be, the more important actors during this period seemed to function almost independently of the rest of the production. Certainly this characteristic of late-nineteenth-century acting comes to be considered a fault, for it destroys the overall appreciation of the theatrical experience, but the fact that the actress did surface as a star, independent of the production and viewed by the audience independently, connects her with the isolated figure of the dancer more than would be normally expected.

The relationship between the actress and the spectator becomes, therefore, equally problematical. Stokes, on one level, is correct in stating that, for the decadent in particular, the spectator cultivated "a voyeuristic position that enabled him to preserve his separateness from both performer and performance" (153).

For Symons the image of the actress is more complex and more suggestive, involving, as it does, words and action in an ideal combination. And the relationship between the spectator and the production, as we have seen, involves more than a voyeuristic appreciation. It is for this reason, for instance, that in "Esther Kahn" in *Spiritual Adventures* Symons tries to bring into correspondence internal and external activities. She sees in gesture more than words can offer: "The gestures of people always meant more to her than their words; they seemed to have a secret meaning of their own, which the words never quite interpreted" (*Works* 5:36). The qualities of Esther Kahn as an actress are identified with a mystical quality within her which she communicates to the audience. An internal validity, due in part to her Jewish heritage, is associated with gesture, which is very much like the movement of the dancer. The same type of figure occurs again in a later essay, "East and West End Silhouettes." Here the girl is more clearly spoken of in terms of her connection with an internal, mystical truth. She appears unconcerned with her environment: "Of what is she thinking, I ask myself, as at last I move on my way, haunted by the clear pallor of that strange, mystic face, those visionary eyes, that immovable attitude" (*Memoirs* 78). This passage ties in clearly with dramatic experience in general, although Symons does not finally say that the spectator should remain so essentially unmoved. As he says in "The Sicilian Actors," "All Art is magnetism. The greatest art is a magnetism through which the soul reaches the soul" (*Plays, Acting, and Music* 1909, 225). And in "The Test of the Actor" he comments on the emotion that, through the actress, affects the spectator: "If the emotion does not seize her in its own grasp, and then seize us through her, it will all go for nothing" (*Plays, Acting, and Music* 1909, 158).

The emotions expressed, although they may appear to, should never overwhelm. Acting as an art involves control of some sort. Symons criticizes Beerbohm Tree, on the other hand, for being nothing but an actor: "Mr. Tree has many arts, but he has not the art of sincerity. His conception of acting is, literally, to act, on every occasion" (*Plays, Acting, and Music* 1909, 121). Lamb is at the back of Symons's observations. In "The Speaking of Verse," in which Symons deals with words in relation to acting, Lamb is cited as having written the most profound essays on acting, and, as with Lamb, Symons is concerned with the quality of the language and how that quality is accented by the presentation. Shakespeare is the particular example: "It is precisely by his speaking of that poetry, which one is accustomed to hear hurried over or turned into mere oratory, that the actor might, if he were conscious of the necessity of doing it, and properly trained to do it, bring before the audience what is essential in Shakespeare" (*Plays, Acting, and Music* 1909, 175). Symons concludes, in keeping with drama as a unified theatrical experience, that the actor should function as a part of the whole. This same issue came up in relation to Lamb and Gordon Craig in the preceding section of this chapter. Here, using similar musical analogues, Symons concerns himself with the essential quality of the play that originates in the author and is transferred to the spectator: "Here, in the rendering of words, is the actor's first duty to his author, if he is to remember that a play is acted, not for the exhibition of the actor, but for the realization of the play. We should think little of the 'dramatic effect' of a symphony, in which every individual note had not been given its precise value by every instrument in the orchestra" (*Plays, Acting, and Music* 1909, 175–76). It is for this reason that Symons finds the theatrical experiments of Yeats, Florence Farr, and Arnold Dolmetsch valuable, for they represent "the only definitive attempt which has been made in our time to regulate the speech of actors in their speaking of verse" (174).

Symons, however, is equally interested in actors and, particularly, actresses as individuals. As he says in "A Paradox on Art," in which he elaborates a concept of beauty independent of artistic medium, acting, as well as other impermanent arts such as dancing, should be taken more seriously: "Art is the creation of beauty in form, visible or audible, and the artist is the creator of beauty in visible or audible form. But beauty is infinitely various, and as truly beauty in the voice of Sarah Bernhardt or the silence of Duse as in a face painted by Leonardo or a poem written by Blake" (*Plays, Acting, and Music* 1909, 318). In relation to acting, in fact, the creation of beauty that is only momentary and which can never be repeated in the same way again seems particularly appealing to Symons. In a sort of Yeatsian paradox, through the process of coming into existence, it is consumed: "That such art should be fragile, evanescent, leaving only a memory which can never be realized again, is as pathetic and as natural as that a beautiful woman should die young" (*Plays, Acting, and Music* 1909, 320). There is, certainly, a quality of decadent consciousness in this observation which associates death with beauty. There are, additionally, aspects of the symbolist's aesthetic apparent. Instead of detaching the art from the observer and creator, which is more probable as a characteristic of aestheticism, symbolism tends to bind together the observer and creator. On the most mystical level, which Symons hints at in *The Symbolist Movement in Literature*, the symbolist's art aspires to evoke occult experiences in the observer. Yeats's poetic ideal, centering on the image as a spiritual and physical vortex, aspires to this level of communication. Great actresses for Symons embody this same aspiration in an art form which accents both the success and impermanence of the experience. The actress, therefore, follows in the ideological footsteps of the dancer.

In his essay, "Sir Henry Irving," Symons contrasts the acting styles of Irving and Eleonora Duse. Irving represents the old school of acting, which is more mechanical in its style. Duse becomes a vortex of physical and spiritual energy. The style of acting Duse embodies, as well as the various suggestions implicit in it for Symons, comes to be the ultimate criterion for judging other actors and actresses. At first, however, there seems to be considerable confusion in Symons's own mind as to the nature of actresses he discusses, what the qualities are he appreciates. Within this context, the issue of whether one actress is better than another comes into play. His 1901 review of Bernhardt for the *Star*, "La Dame aux Camélias," is a case in point: "After all, though Réjane skins emotions alive, and Duse serves them up to you on golden dishes, it is Sarah Bernhardt who prepares the supreme feast" (1). Symons's opinion is due, in part, to the impact of the moment and to his role as a weekly reviewer. But, as his commentary progresses, we begin to see that although Bernhardt "prepares the supreme feast," the menu may not be as rich as it first appears. She is an actress without suggestiveness in her movements. Her style, therefore, is defined as "plastic, a modelling of emotions before you, with every vein visible" (1).

Symons often uses the visual metaphor of sculpting to define the actress' art, for, like the dancer, "the performer is at once creator and interpreter" (*Plays, Acting, and Music* 1909, 317), and, even more particularly, the creator and the material of creation. It is apparent, however, that Symons wishes to qualify his appreciation of Bernhardt's art. She is technically wonderful, as is the acrobat dealt with earlier, but the suggestiveness of Duse and the rowdy attractiveness of Réjane, which are additional, positive qualities, are missing. Symons's comment on Irving seems to apply to his perception of Bernhardt as well: "It is an art wholly of rhetoric, that is to say wholly external" (*Plays, Acting, and Music* 1909, 54).

Symons, in fact, deals most often with the acting styles of Sarah Bernhardt, Réjane, and Eleonora Duse, and, without being too schematic, his interest focuses on distinctive qualities in each. His essay, "Réjane," in fact, lays the groundwork for an analysis of the others, with Duse surfacing as the ultimate artist. The last part of the essay discusses Réjane's acting in *Sappho*: "Here, as elsewhere, she gives you merely the thing itself, without a disturbing atom of self-consciousness; she is grotesque, she is what you will: it is no matter. The emotion she is acting possesses her like a blind force; she is Sappho, and Sappho could only move and speak and think in one way" (*Plays, Acting, and Music* 1909, 41). Réjane, indeed, appeared to be almost overwhelmed by the part she was playing. As Clement Scott says, "some are inclined to think that the spirits of Réjane run away with her in certain scenes" (458). Réjane's own view of her acting contains this same belief; her ambition as an actress, she says, is to literally become the part she is playing: "That is, to interpret, to re-incarnate, if possible, a woman's soul, a woman's individuality" ("Madame Réjane" 520).

In his essay, "Recollections of Réjane," which forms a sort of equivalent to his earlier essay on Duse, "Duse in Some of Her Parts," Symons defines Réjane's appeal in similar terms; she is physical life on the stage, sensual and real: "A real woman lives before one, seems to be overseen on the stage at certain moments of her daily existence" (*Dramatis Personae* 277). In line with the acting style based upon physicality, Symons's response is physical. When he compares the acting of Olga Nethersole, who was also known for her intense and realistic portrayals, he feels, finally, that Réjane is more intense and less self-consciously artistic: "Miss Nethersole forced me to admire her, to accept her; I felt that she was very real, and, as I felt it, I said to myself: 'She is acting splendidly.' With Réjane it was the feeling that possessed me" (*Plays, Acting, and Music* 1903, 128). Although the animalistic appreciation of sensation was very important to him, Symons does not conclude that it is the purpose the observer seeks. As he says in "The Test of the Actor," overwhelming sensation is, rather, the foundation: "The embodying power, the power to throw open one's whole nature to an overwhelming sensation, the power to render this sensation in so inevitable a way that others shall feel it: that is the one thing needful. It is not art, it is not even the beginning of art; but it is the foundation on which alone art can be built" (*Plays, Acting, and Music* 1909, 159).

Bernhardt, on the other hand, is allied with a very sophisticated artistry, style as Pater had described it in relation to Flaubert. In some sense her abilities are particularly Parisian and coincide with the self-conscious artistry of many of the prose stylists of this period, such as Edmond and Jules de Goncourt. Symons, in fact, begins his essay on her in *Plays, Acting, and Music* (1909) suggesting such a stylistic connection, and he opts in *The Symbolist Movement in Literature* to view decadence as a stylistic phenomenon. He looks at Bernhardt in a similar way:

> I am not sure that the best moment to study an artist is not the moment of what is called decadence. The first energy of inspiration is gone; what remains is the method, the mechanism, and it is that which alone one can study, as one can study the mechanism of the body, not the principle of life itself. What is done mechanically, after the heat of the blood has cooled, and the divine accidents have ceased to happen, is precisely all that was consciously skilful in the performance of an art. (17)

Symons is always interested in the self-conscious art of Bernhardt, her mechanically perfect activity on the stage. The divine Sarah is, for Symons, a "divine machine" (29). Symons's distinction between the acrobat who is technically perfect and the true artist comes into play as well. Ultimately, Bernhardt is like the technically perfect acrobat. She embodies a "particular kind of sorcery" (73), especially in relation to the elaborate melodramas and equally exotic life-style, but her art is finally limited by its own self-consciousness, just as for Pater style is finally limited without a proper subject matter.

Eleonora Duse combines the qualities of Réjane and Bernhardt; she appeals on many levels simultaneously. First of all Eleonora Duse was a type of the anti-star. In "Eleonora Duse" Symons states that she is a great actress because she is the opposite of what one expects: "She is an actress through being the antithesis of the actress; not, indeed, by mere reliance upon nature, but by controlling nature into forms of her own desire, as the sculptor controls the clay under his fingers. She is the artist of her own soul, and it is her force of will, her mastery of herself, not her abandonment to it, which make her what she is" (*Works* 9:214). Her appeal, in fact, derives from the uniqueness of her style, which is continually accented during this period by comparison with Bernhardt. In 1893 the reviewer for the *Stage* states in "Duse in *Camille*" that he finds Bernhardt's portrayal of Marguerite to be unconvincing. The death scene in particular showed that her method is "all artifice" (13). What the reviewer finds offensive is the totally sensational and exaggerated acting style. Duse, on the other hand, works through subtlety and suggestion: "When the end comes her arm falls from its place—nothing more; and the effect is deeply impressive. It may also be noted that Signora Duse does not, like Madame Sarah Bernhardt, scan her features in the mirror—she merely looks at her poor wasted hands as she murmurs. 'How changed I am'" (13). These observations are particularly apt, for they show that through suggestion and nuance dramatic effect can be increased. As Symons says, the "external, rhetorical art" that had been taken for acting is replaced by a new method: "Duse's art, in this, is like the art of Verlaine in French poetry; always suggestion, never statement, always a renunciation'' (*Works* 9:223). Her style is a form of synecdoche, a small movement stands for deeper impressions.

Symons's appreciation of Duse was intense; for, like other artists with whom he identified personally, she was an artist who mirrored his own situation. Thus, his comment that she, too, was a wanderer has deeper implications: "Duse, like myself, was incurably restless, a nomad, a wanderer over the sea and the land, one who desires to escape from the thraldom of material things and to disappear. Like Watteau, she was 'always a seeker after something in the world that is there in no satisfying measure or not at all'" (*Duse* 53).

Elsewhere in his study, *Eleonora Duse* (1926), he associates her with gypsies, the figures who are emblematic of the artist and the eternal truth the artist seeks. It becomes apparent, then, that Symons sees in Duse the fulfillment of his symbolist ideals. The allusion to Verlaine lends additional support, and many of his comments on her acting also express this view: "All her acting seems to come from a great depth, and to be only half telling profound secrets" (*Works* 9:221). She is, like the dancer, a symbolist poem. Stokes makes the astute point that, in fact, Symons's description of Duse—"Her face is sad with thought, with the passing over it of all the emotions of the world, which she has felt twice over, in her own flesh and in the creative energy of her spirit" (*Works* 9:215)—has the shadow of Pater's description of the *Mona Lisa* behind it. The many thoughts and experiences of the world have been etched and moulded there (155). The figure that appears to us in the painting embodies the secrets of the grave, just as Duse's acting only half tells "profound secrets" (*Works* 9:221). Thus, the sculpture imagery Symons uses becomes that much more functional: "The face of Duse is like the clay under the fingers of Rodin" (*Works* 9:220).

In line with the sense of her presence, the writing about Duse during the late nineteenth and early twentieth centuries is dominated by the almost mystical belief that she is moved as an actress by spiritual forces. This belief helps to explain the tendency during this period to suggest that great actresses appeared to forget that they were acting on the stage. The acting of Bernhardt, with its sensational appeal which relies on theatrical tricks, is found wanting when compared to such sincerity of action. As Mrs. Patrick Campbell says, "The beauty pulsates, and never for a moment is there a feeling of tricks" (346). In keeping with this notion, Duse's acting seems to be the result of the "sculpture of the soul upon the body" (*Works* 9:221). Gabriele d'Annunzio, whose plays Duse presented and with whom she had an involved love affair, describes her character and her acting using similar imagery: "She is always different, like a cloud that from second to second seems to change before your very eyes without your seeing the change. Every movement of her body destroys a harmony, and creates another more beautiful" (qtd. in Bordeux 78). And later his observations center on her facial expressions which, in effect, seem to transfigure her entire being: "The expression is the life of the eyes, this indefinable something more potent than any word or sound; infinitely profound, yet instantaneous as a flash of lightning, even more rapid than lightning—innumerable, all-powerful: summed up—the expression'' (79). D'Annunzio goes on to state that the expressiveness actually is defused through Duse's body, or actually envelops her body. Although he is known for his exuberant prose style, this passage is truly characteristic of the general observations about Duse. When Eva Le Gallienne, Richard Le Gallienne's daughter who settled in America as an actress and producer, came to write her biography of Duse, based upon many personal reminiscences, she appropriately titled it *The Mystic of the Theatre: Eleonora Duse*. It is Le Gallienne's point that Duse, like the mystic, expresses a universal self. She becomes, in a sense, a medium through which profound truths are expressed. Philip Houghton's review of *Marguerite Gautier* for *The Theatre* in 1894 describes Duse, as does d'Annunzio, as the embodiment of archetypal feelings: ''Mirrored with ineffable tenderness and by innumerable touches of infinite grace and delicacy we have known Love's very self, heard Love's very voice, seen her every gesture'' (303).

Within the context of Duse as a mystic, the discussion of her famous blush becomes somewhat more explicable. Duse was known for her insistence on performing without makeup, and, as we have seen, makeup was an important symbolic part of the late-nineteenth-century world. The use of makeup and cosmetics became emblematic of the barriers between art and life. Symons certainly follows this line of thinking. Duse's ability to produce a blush without the aid of makeup became, for many, emblematic of changing artistic attitudes. Thus, in 1895, when Duse acts Sudermann's *Magda*, the blush is spoken of in revealing terms. Shaw, for example, in his review of June 15, 1895, in which he compares the cosmetic acting of Bernhardt with the acting of Duse, is overwhelmed. When Magda confronts her former lover, she blushes because of what the meeting brings to mind. Shaw goes on to observe,

> She began to blush; and in another moment she was conscious of it, and the blush was slowly spreading and deepening until, after a few vain efforts to avert her face or to obstruct his view of it without seeming to do so, she gave up and hid the blush in her hands. After that feat of acting I did not need to be told why Duse does not paint an inch thick. I could detect no trick in it: it seemed to me a perfectly genuine effect of the dramatic imagination. (*Our Theatre* 162)

Shaw then goes on to qualify in relation to Duse's acting the theatrical trick as opposed to the ''genuine effect of the dramatic imagination.'' There are ways to produce a theatrical blush, but Magda's blush, Shaw says, cannot be explained away.

As Le Gallienne shows, a critic in New York in 1896 comments on the same phenomenon (137–38), but what is important here is the mystery associated with the natural blush as opposed to an understandable and artificial blush. The impact of the blush is based upon the fact that it appears to be natural, suggesting that Duse is, herself, moved by the action of the play. The soul acts and controls the body.

The audience, therefore, is moved as well by the sincerity of the action. The purely aesthetic and artificial acting of Bernhardt, on the other hand, tends to separate the viewer from the experience. Appropriately, Shaw goes on in his review to suggest that the experience has given him a renewed sense of faith in the theatrical arts. An almost spiritual validity which is absent from the more ordinary entertainments comes into play: "And for me, at least, there was a confirmation of my sometimes flagging faith that a dramatic critic is really the servant of a high art, and not a mere advertiser of entertainments of questionable respectability of motive" (*Our Theatre* 162). The religious overtones correspond with the sense that Duse is, as an actress, a mystic moved by greater forces.

Symons sees Duse as a resolution of artistic concerns. He often quotes her saying that the theatre as it is must be destroyed: "To save the theatre, the theatre must be destroyed, the actors and actresses must all die of the plague. They poison the air, they make art impossible. It is not drama that they play, but pieces for the theatre" (*Works* 9:217). The New Theatre, which, as we have seen, Gordon Craig felt he was ushering in, brings many of Symons's concerns into line, and Duse's acting is a primary motivating force: "At every moment of a play in which emotion becomes sincere, intelligent, or in which it is possible to transform an artificial thing into reality, she is profoundly true to the character she is representing, by being more and more profoundly herself" (*Works* 9:222). Duse's acting creates a vision of a new world in which the personal impersonality of Verlaine becomes real and inhabitable, so to speak. So Symons presents the sense of a world refreshed by a new validity: "And she creates out of life itself an art which no one before her had ever imagined: not realism, not a copy, but the thing itself, the evocation of thoughtful life, the creation of the world over again, as actual and beautiful a thing as if the world had never existed" (*Plays, Acting, and Music* 1909, 65).

3

The Art of Travel

In his preface to *Plays, Acting, and Music*, Symons alludes to the significance of travel writing and the spirit of place in his overall aesthetic: "And, as life too is a form of art, and the visible world the chief storehouse of beauty, I try to indulge my curiosity by the study of place and people" (preface). The dedication to *Cities* (1903), the first collection of his travel writings, further suggests not only why the writing of travel literature appeals to him, but also why such work should be considered an integral part of his general aesthetic principles: "As you know, and, I sometimes think, regret, I am one of those for whom the visible world exists, very actively; and, for me, cities are like people, with souls and temperaments of their own, and it has always been one of my chief pleasures to associate with the souls and temperaments congenial to me among cities" (v). He describes a poetic response to the visual aspects of the world, and that response finds its expression in his impressions of cities.

There is in Symons's statement an implicit qualification. The visible world exists, but it is the starting point, the essential surface with which he begins in order to discover deeper truths. This qualification or distinction is one which is evident throughout Symons's work. His development as a poet and critic of all the arts always involves a rather complex consideration of the relationship between the visible and invisible worlds. *The Symbolist Movement in Literature* (1899) represents the zenith of this discussion; however, the earlier work, such as the impressionistic poems in *Silhouettes* (1892) or his evaluation of Browning as a poet of situations in *An Introduction to the Study of Browning* (1886), shows an interest in the visible world that is not without a corresponding interest in the more mysterious aspects of reality. And at the core of this dialectic exists for Symons a desire to seek and find an essential truth. He had described *vraie vérité* in "The Decadent Movement in Literature"; the same concept applies to *Cities:* "It is part of my constant challenge to myself, in everything I write, to be content with nothing short of that *vraie vérité* which one imagines to exist somewhere on this side of ultimate attainment" (vi–vii).

The discussions of cities which make up this initial volume of travel writings are, therefore, more than various essays describing Symons's subjective sojourns.

And yet, subjectivity is inevitably an element of what he seeks, for it is only through the subjective response that the truth Symons desires can be attained, particularly among the great cities of Europe. It is at this point that one of the many echoes of Pater is heard. Quoting Arnold, Pater says, " 'To see the object as in itself it really is,' has been justly said to be the aim of all true criticism whatever; and in aesthetic criticism the first step towards seeing one's object as it really is, is to know one's own impression as it really is, to discriminate it, to realize it distinctly" (*Renaissance* viii). Symons defines his objective in his travel writing in *Cities* similarly:

> I have put myself as little as possible into these pages; I have tried to draw confidences out of the stones that I have trodden but a few weeks or a few months, out of the faces that I have seen in passing, out of the days of sunshine that have after all warmed a stranger. I have respected the sight of my eyes and the judgement of my sense, and I have tried to evoke my cities in these pages exactly as they appeared to me to be in themselves. (vi)

The restatement of Pater's theory of the aesthetic critic helps Symons develop his own purpose as an aesthetic traveller.

The nature of Symons's travel writings, then, involves an evaluation of confidences drawn painstakingly from stone, of insights into what Symons believed to be the souls of the cities he visited. It is evident, however, that any analysis of this aspect of his work has to take into account a number of related and equally essential issues, for Symons saw his travel books as more than the contribution to the mass of travel literature that was expected from any self-respecting nineteenth-century writer. His travel writings, although individual in some very important ways, reflect social and artistic concerns of the late nineteenth and early twentieth centuries. He is, to use V. S. Pritchett's distinction, a writer who travels (693), but Symons also carries the imprint of his age. The aspects of Symons's thought and work that best focus his travel writings in relation to this period are his interest in wanderers and vagabondia, the development of his aesthetic from impressionism through the inclusion of symbolist theories, and his work on Italy and Spain, the countries that most interested him as a traveller and travel writer.

Wanderers and Vagabondia

Symons begins *Spiritual Adventures* (1905) with the autobiographical fragment, "A Prelude to Life." It seems quite evident, however, that this piece is intended to evoke a number of themes which will be developed further in the stories that follow it in the volume and that the piece itself is organized dramatically to depict aspects of the narrator's temperament, a narrator who in the final analysis is Symons. It is, in other words, not only an exercise in autobiography; there is an added sense of dramatic integrity. From this point of view, "A Prelude to Life" is an earlier and shorter example of the same genre as *A Portrait of the Artist as a Young Man* (1916), setting up a contrast, as Joyce does much more extensively, between the artist and his rather narrow and inartistic environment. Life, or rather the artistic life, does not begin until each narrator has physically left behind his past life. The conclusion to "A Prelude to Life," the title of which suggests clearly the interesting ambiguity contained in the meaning of "life," offers some useful parallels which inform both works. The narrator has left his family home in the country in order to live in London. His approach to life now, as opposed to his early religious upbringing, involves a different sort of religion: "If there ever was a religion of the eyes, I have devoutly practised that religion. I noted every face that passed me on the pavement; I looked into the omnibuses, the cabs, always with the same eager hope of seeing some beautiful or interesting person, some gracious movement, a delicate expression, which would be gone if I did not catch it as it went" (*Works* 5:32). The conclusion describes the moment of escape through which the narrator hopes to facilitate a more sound and inspired artistic life. The connection to Joyce's novel is clear. As Stephen Dedalus puts it, with typical youthful exuberance, "Welcome, O life! I go to encounter for the millionth time the reality of experience and to forge in the smithy of my soul the uncreated conscience of my race" (257).

Within this context, "A Prelude to Life" can be seen as, to use Symons's phrase, a "personal document" which describes, on a very important level, his own artistic development in relation to his socio-economic background, a background which very much reflects its Victorian origins. His overt desire to escape the confines of his provincial life in order to travel and experience life more fully is very much a part of the general aesthetic we see developing. This ambition, however, does not seem to be totally positive. Symons feels that his past life, which has determined his present attitudes, is an odd mixture of good and bad: "If I have been a vagabond, and have never been able to root myself in any one place in the world, it is because I have no early memories of any one sky or soil. It has freed me from many prejudices in giving me its own unresting kind of freedom; but it has cut me off from whatever is stable, of long growth in the world" (*Works* 5:4). The same issue of freedom arises, and Symons certainly values the attraction of what might be called vagabondia, for it offers an escape from the commonplace, along with corresponding sense of instability. He feels "cut off from whatever is stable" in the world. As is the case throughout this autobiographical fragment, such personal characteristics can be seen and evaluated within a larger, social context. In this case, Symons's internal conflict very interestingly mirrors the difference in attitude historians such as Walter E. Houghton have identified with Matthew Arnold and Walter Pater. These two figures have come to represent the two basic conceptions of the human mind that emerged during the Victorian period. Symons's temperament, as it is described in the above passage, shows the influence of the conflict between the relativistic, as well as individualistic, spirit of Pater and the desire for stabilizing cultural force, "the authority of culture, with its inherent power of discovering truth" (17). This extension does not force the Symons passage to carry too much ideological weight. It is clear that "A Prelude to Life" is meant to reflect a number of issues important to the late Victorian world; and, additionally, the answer to this conflict for Symons is implicitly related to his development as an artist, as well as a writer of travel literature.

Symons's primary aim, as described in this autobiographical sketch, is to achieve an important sense of personal freedom. When, for example, he describes his early difficulties with reading, the memory of his first exposure to Cervantes's *Don Quixote*, a book, he says, from which he would not be separated, brings back the sense of freedom and escape he found within its pages. It opened his eyes to an imaginative world outside himself. Reading, with the addition of music, or, to carry the argument a step further, the arts in general, became for the young Symons a method of escape from the more pedestrian world: "Books and music, then, together with my solitary walks, were the only means of escape which I was able to find from the tedium of things as they were" (*Works* 5:18). And things as they were involved being surrounded by commonplace, middle-class people. The accompanying sense of enclosure was, perhaps, what Symons disliked most, along with the middle-class values he felt the enclosure was built upon.

This attitude is one of many he shares with W. B. Yeats. In "What is 'Popular Poetry'?" and "Poetry and Tradition" Yeats defines his interest in a literate aristocracy and an emotionally, as well as artistically, attuned peasantry. Symons, as we shall see, develops similar ideas, particularly in relation to his aristocracy of the men of letters and his interest in gypsies. For both writers, however, the middle class, dominated by commercialism and the rhetoric of journalism, controls the industrial world and has left it wanting in all that is artistically and socially sound. The middle class represents the true social decadence, not the artists and writers who are often associated with decadence during the late nineteenth century.

In line with this feeling of restriction associated with middle-class society, there is in "A Prelude to Life" a developed contrast between imprisonment and escape. During a visit to the convict settlement at Princetown, Symons describes his feelings about the prisoners. He sees escape plots in their faces. Later, after narrating the story of an actual escape, he declares his sympathy with the convicts' situation: "I sickened at the thought of the poor devils who would be captured and brought back between two muskets. Once I saw an escaped convict being led back to prison; his arms were tied with cords, he had a bloody scar on his forehead, his face was swollen with heat and helpless rage" (*Works* 5:9). Interestingly enough, it is also at Princetown that Symons is first introduced to *Don Quixote*.

The imagery associated with prisons and entrapment appears throughout Symons's writings and, in fact, becomes an obsession after his emotional breakdown in the late summer of 1908. In his essay, "Nantes," written in 1925 and published in *Wanderings* (1931), the rather rhetorical style gives a very clear sense of the way in which this theme dominated Symons's mind: "These infamous houses are so close in these narrow lanes that one all but touches them: some go inward to a point and vanish: and everywhere squalor, crime, filth, and slime. In one you look up a fearful stone corridor just like one in a prison" (218). Symons's rhetorical style, the accumulation of adjectives and nouns, becomes more obvious in his later work. It can be assumed that in this case part of the rhetoric is due to the fact that this sort of scene undoubtedly recalled in Symons's mind his own unfortunate imprisonment in Italy during his breakdown, as well as his institutionalization in England once he had been brought home. He describes these experiences in similarly horrifying tones, with the same type of intense subjectivity, in *Confessions: A Study in Pathology* (1930). But it is also apparent that these experiences were the terrible fulfillment of nightmares that were developing years before.

Symons's hatred of the middle-class world into which he was born, a hatred which is clearly expressed in the prison imagery of "A Prelude to Life," becomes an essential motivating force in his life. In this case, it is particularly strongly felt in his desire to travel beyond the bounds of his inherited world, to experience life more fully than tradition and convention allow. Additionally, this ambition is the expression of a want for what is pleasurable and beautiful. In this respect, it is interesting that men like Thomas Cook were beginning to offer travel as a form of diversion. But what began with Cook as a method of enlivening life became a very strong form of delusion for some, as Edmund Swinglehurst points out: "Foreign travel was the perfect setting for people who liked to deceive themselves about the true condition of their society: foreign countries, particularly the poorer ones, confirmed their belief that everything was all right at home, and the servility which they commanded from the poor who fought for their patronage was interpreted as a natural respect for superior people" (138).

Symons's travel writing is somewhat associated with this type of social delusion; his interest in travel certainly relates to a negative reaction to his environment. His motives are also artistic. Unlike most middle-class travellers who followed the lead of such magazines as *Queen*, which described fashionable places to visit, he travels with a sense of awareness that is absent in his middle-class counterparts. This awareness, however, does not negate the desire to escape the ugly, industrialized world. Thus, the excitement he associates with travel reflects more general attitudes of the period. When he describes in "A Prelude to Life" his first real journey outside the limited world he has become used to, the event takes on a combination of qualities: "I pushed my way through the crowds in those old and narrow streets, in an ecstasy of delight at all the movement, noise, colour, and confusion. I seemed suddenly to have become free, in contact with life" (*Works* 5:27). The feeling of excitement is associated with and contained in the sense of confusion and disruption this passage describes, all of which is in marked contrast to the moral and social stasis of his family life. Equally, the impulse to see this experience as a broadening one is strengthened near the end of this story when he meets a sailor, who is described as a sort of Odysseus figure: "It was the first time I had seemed to come so close to the remote parts of the world; and, as he went on his way, he turned back to urge me to go on some voyage which he seemed to remember with more pleasure than any other: to the West Indies, I think. I began to pour over maps, and to plan to what parts of the world I would go" (*Works* 5:28).

Symons's interest in travel, however, is not left unqualified in this essay. As we have seen, the contrast between his rather commonplace background and what he expects to find in the outside world determines much of the dramatic action of the piece and reflects some important late-nineteenth-century attitudes. But Symons's response to geography is unique. He travels through instinct and sight rather than by maps. He describes his temperament which is, ultimately as a positive characteristic, only able to deal with place in terms of actual experience. The rather abstract notion of name, as it is given in a book, or location on a map has no real meaning for him. This attitude, in fact, is further supported by Symons's "religion of the eyes." The last sentences in "A Prelude to Life" accent the same concept, tied in with Pater's belief in flux as the only adequate description of experience: "At every moment, I knew, some spectacle awaited them [his eyes]; I grasped at all these sights with the same futile energy as a dog that I once saw standing in an Irish stream, and snapping at the bubbles that ran continually past him on the water. Life ran past me continually, and I tried to make all its bubbles my own" (*Works* 5:32). The allusion to the "Conclusion" of *The Renaissance* is apparent, particularly in the stream image which Pater uses as a metaphor for our lives and experiences. And the passage from Pater continues with a more elaborate analysis, concentrating on the need for "constant and eager observation": "Every moment some form grows perfect in hand or face; some tone on the hills or the sea is choicer than the rest; some mood of passion or insight or intellectual excitement is irresistibly real and attractive for us,—for that moment only" (*Renaissance* 236–37).

Almost all that Symons deals with in "A Prelude to Life" is contained in this passage from Pater. In fact, this autobiographical sketch is, without direct attribution, an extended depiction of Pater's influence on Symons's early development as an artist and critic. But we cannot help noticing by the time we reach the conclusion of "A Prelude to Life" that there is a strong difference in attitude expressed in the two passages. Pater's "Conclusion," although recognizing the brevity of life and intense experience, does not leave the reader with a sense of futility and despair. The Symons passage seems dominated by this attitude. The difference, however, is easily explained and does not represent a break with Pater; Symons, rather, wants to qualify the pure impressionism implicit in Pater's view. We have to remember that the Symons who has written "A Prelude to Life" has also written *The Symbolist Movement in Literature* and that the symbolist theories involve more than mere impression. Symons describes an interest in a metaphysical and more permanent aspect of our experience, which the early theories of Pater would have to deny. In his travel writing, Symons wants to establish the sense of wonder and excitement he experienced in various locations, but he also wants to add an element of drama associated with what he often refers to as "the attraction of the center." He is seeking a truth or, as he puts it in the dedication, a soul, which involves more than surface impression.

"A Prelude to Life," then, presents the development of Symons's artistic personality in such a way as to show that his interest in the arts was bound to include an equal interest in travel and travel literature. Certainly the influence of Pater helped to determine this aspect of his character.

Symons often expressed his individuality through rebellion, and he found additional fuel for this impulse in the pages of *Cornhill Magazine*. Churchill Osborne, Symons's tutor who functioned as an intellectual guide throughout Symons's early life, sent him the complete set of the magazine around 1881 or 1882. The importance of this incident is commented on in "A Prelude to Life." He explains that he read all the bound volumes, which included many stories and articles by Robert Louis Stevenson. He first developed a taste for the gypsy element in literature through Stevenson's work. When he discovered George Borrow's *Lavengro* this taste became a passion. He says much the same thing about George Borrow's *Lavengro* in an essay on English and French novels published in *Dramatis Personae* (1833): "I was very young when I read his masterpiece *Lavengro* (1851) in its original three volumes, from which I got my first taste for a sort of gypsy element in literature. The reading of that book did many things for me" (74–75).

This autobiographical novel does seem to have appealed to Symons in a number of personally and artistically significant ways, in more ways, in fact, than has been fully appreciated. As a young man with artistic ambitions trapped in a middle-class world from which he felt quite alien, Symons found Borrow's account of his own early life oddly, and perhaps uncannily, familiar. Borrow describes himself as an outcast who identifies more with other social outcasts, particularly gypsies, than with his own family. Borrow's father, through a description of his son, focuses the conflict: "Why he has neither my hair nor my eyes; and then his countenance! why 'tis absolutely swarthy, God forgive me! I had almost said like that of a gypsy . . ." (I:185). The early sections of *Lavengro* are dominated by the sense of alienation the narrator feels, an alienation which is imagistically accented by his older brother, who is fair-skinned and more like the other members of the family. This dark and light motif also is associated with individual temperament. At one point, George, the narrator in the novel, identifies these qualities for us, using aspects of nature to develop the description: "So I stood on the Alpine elevation, and looked now on the gay distinct river, and now at the dark granite-encircled lake close behind me in the lone solitude, and I thought of my brother and myself. I am no moralizer; but the gay and rapid river and the dark and silent lake, were, of a verity, no bad emblems of us two" (I:12–13). The temperamental differences are elaborated so as to pit traditional, Christian values against the rebellious, pagan attitudes of George. As the result of this difference, identified with the darker side of nature, George becomes, as does Symons, something of a recluse. He becomes "a lover of nooks and retired corners" and develops "the habit of fleeing from society" (I:13).

The parallels between "A Prelude to Life" and *Lavengro* are strong. Symons was, as he says in a letter to James Dykes Campbell on January 2, 1888, "a fervent Borrowian.'' Borrow, and the interest in gypsy lore he generated, offered another form of escape, another possible view of the world. As Symons says, humanity began to exist for him, but in a very unique form, representing values radically opposed to his background:

> *Lavengro* took my thoughts into the open air and gave me my first conscious desire to wander. I learned a little Romany, and was always on the lookout for gipsies. I realized that there were other people in the world besides the conventional people I knew, who wore prim and shabby clothes, and went to church twice on Sundays, and worked a business and professions, and sat down to the meal of tea at five o'clock in the afternoon. (*Works* 5:21)

The desire to wander is part of the need for novelty in this stereotyped world Symons describes. As a young man, Symons had written to Osborne expressing his desire to see Italy, and *Lavengro* fed this desire. George's reactions in the novel to his brother's travels and his stories of strange regions helped to generate similar attitudes in Symons.

Gypsies, as Symons says, are emblematic of an alternative life-style and of the vagabond spirit Borrow describes. They are representative of a more internal Bohemian existence that is often associated with the artist-outcast of this period. From Yeats's point of view, for example, the artist is necessarily an outcast who will eventually usher in a new order. In his chapter on Prague in *Cities*, Symons discusses the character of Bohemia, particularly in relation to *The Labyrinth of the World* by John Amos Komensky. In this text, as Symons sees it, the wanderer is a critic of life and seeks a more ideal world. The book is, therefore, identified with other pilgrimages, such as *Pilgrim's Progress* and *Guilliver's Travels*. The conclusion sums up the ideal of travel: ''The pilgrim learns how he may live in the world without living as the world lives, realizing now 'that the world is not so heavy that it may not be endured, nor so valuable that its loss need be regretted' '' (146).

Wanderers personified for Symons, among other things, his own ideas of freedom and, by extension, his desire for artistic freedom. His relationship with Frank Willard, who, under the name of Josiah Flynt, published accounts of his wanderings around the world as a tramp, was in many respects based on Willard's history as a vagabond and Symons's admiration of this life-style. References to Willard crop up throughout Symons's work. In an essay in *Wanderings*, his last collection of travel writings, he reminisces about his trip to Berlin to visit the Willard family. Katherine Willard, Frank Willard's sister, was an early love of Symons, as he says in ''Berlin's Discomforts'' (1920), to whom he dedicated *Silhouettes* (1892); but at this point he is also quite interested in Frank Willard as a soul mate: ''Curiously, perhaps, one reason why we got on so well was that both were never quite at home under a roof or in the company of ordinary people'' (135). In his longer evaluation of Willard in *London: A Book of Aspects* (1909), Symons's observations also tend to describe his own fascination with wandering and travel. He relates the desire to travel to many foreign lands with that half-unconscious instinct which makes a man a vagabond. In Willard and, by extension, in Symons the ultimate nature of this instinct involves additional, Paterian ideals: "He has no mission, only a great thirst; and this thirst for the humanity of every nation and for the roads of every country drives him onward as resistlessly as a drunkard's thirst for drink, or the idealist's thirst for an ideal. And it seems to me that few men have realised, as this man has realised, that 'not the fruit of experience, but experience itself, is the end'" (*Cities and Sea-Coasts* 193–94).

Although Symons never became as extreme a vagabond as Willard, he felt in his own travels a real affinity with this lifestyle. He often enjoyed a direct association with Willard's vagabond adventures. Travelling with such vagabonds, as Symons says in *Charles Baudelaire: A Study* (1920), is to roam with "the moral and immoral people, who are alone worth knowing" (11). In such poems as "The Wanderers," first published in *The Savoy* and collected in *Amoris Victima* (1897), he uses the same imagery he used to describe Willard, as well as himself in "A Prelude to Life":

> Wanderers, you have the sunrise and the stars;
> And we, beneath our comfortable roofs,
> Lamplight, and daily fire upon the hearth,
> And four walls of a prison, and sure food.
> But God has given you freedom, wanderers! (35)

The issue here is again freedom from the conventional world, from the habitual which Pater had also seen as a hindrance to a more complete life.

Symons's identification with wanderers and wandering is perhaps most strongly and idiosyncratically felt in a late essay, "Unspiritual Adventures in Paris" (1931). This essay was written after his breakdown and shows a very unfortunately disturbed and obsessed mind. He says at one point that the spirit of Baudelaire, among others, possesses his own spirit: "Now, for certain occult reasons, known to them as much as to myself, certain great writers and great artists have given me part of their souls" (*Wanderings* 86). The general tone and critical procedure of *Charles Baudelaire: A Study* is based upon this very personal sense of identity, which is seen by Symons as a form of possession. His essay tries to retrace the steps of Baudelaire's vagabond existence, visiting the various locations of his residence. This form of research, tracing footsteps, becomes for Symons a way of invoking all those who are eternal wanderers. He includes himself, Balzac, Baudelaire, and Augustus John, as well as Blake, in this group, quoting his own poem, "The Wanderers," to help describe and define this category of people. He goes on to say that wandering is "the only relief for those who have become overweary of their own existences; it magnetizes our very vertebrae" (*Wanderings* 87–88).

What is evident here is that to Symons these eternal wanderers are true pilgrims; they seek a truth or aspect of experience that outstrips our normal experiences. Richard Middleton, perhaps known best as a wanderer, said much the same thing, particularly in terms of personal identity: "We shall never discover arcadia or escape the anguish of existence but in a fresh environment we may succeed in exploring some untold byway of our own natures" (qtd. in Savage 551).

The passion for discovery that "Unspiritual Adventures in Paris" describes and that "A Prelude to Life" is partially based upon is certainly due in part to Symons's fascination with *Lavengro*. B. A. Redfern's observations about Borrow's work also relate to Symons: "And it is worth noting that he is able to pass on this sense of curiosity and wonder to his readers who enjoy their excursions with him into the fields and dingles of Romance, and feel a lively interest in the strange beings and happenings which he introduces to them" (57). Redfern's comment on Borrow gives us some insight into Symons and into Symons's interest in Borrow's work.

But the aspect of Borrow's writing that Symons notices the most is his interest in gypsies and gypsy lore, as has already been suggested. Symons was, in fact, a member of the Gypsy Lore Society most of his life and published various articles, reviews, and notes in their publication, *The Journal of the Gypsy Lore Society.* The first of these, entitled "In Praise of Gypsies," appeared in 1908 and was followed by "Thomas Browne on the Gypsies" in 1911 and "Notes on the Romani Rai" in 1928, to name only two others. For Symons, the gypsy was the quintessential wanderer and outcast, as well as the embodiment of a number of important values. In many ways, this interest in gypsies as social outcasts mirrors Yeats's interest in other forms of outcasts as emblematic of the artist. The article Symons wrote for *The Journal of the Gypsy Lore Society* in 1908 was prompted by an aspect of this association. The Movable Dwellings Act of 1908 was being supported by such organizations as the New Forest Good Samaritan Charity, whose annual report at this time states that "it is to the public advantage that the Gipsy life, only another name for Nomadic thievish tramps, should be made impossible" (qtd. in Symons, "In Praise of Gypsies" 294). Symons's reaction to this sort of public opinion centers on a belief in the value of gypsy tribes which he considers greater than the middle-class world is able to understand or even recognize:

> They are the symbol of our aspirations, and we do not know it; they stand for the will for freedom, for friendship with nature, for the open air, for change and the sight of many lands; for all in us that is a protest against progress. Progress is a heavy wheel, turned backward upon us. The Gypsy represents nature before civilization. He is the wanderer whom all of us who are poets, or love the wind, are summed up in. He does what we dream. He is the last romance left in the world. His is the only free race, and the tyranny of law and progress would suppress his liberty. That is the curse of all civilization, it is a tyranny, it is a force of repression. To try to repress the Gypsies is to fight against instinct, to try to cut out of humanity its rarest impulse. (296)

This passage incorporates much that has been dealt with in relation to Symons's interest in vagabonds. Frank Willard's life as a traveller, which was to Symons's mind a model existence, and Symons's desire to escape the confines of his family home become united in his fascination with gypsies. The argument raised here focuses on those aspects of society which he found most distressing and distasteful. The same type of inversion of attitude—that is, progress seen as decadence—is described as well. The merchant middle class which has taken over the world is seen as a destructive force. Later in this essay, Symons qualifies this attitude further, relating it to the more common association of decadence and degeneracy with the writers and artists at the turn of the century:

> There has been great talk of late of degeneracy, decadence, and what are supposed to be perversities: such as religion, art, genius, individuality. But it is the millionaire, the merchant, the money-maker, the sweater, who are the degenerates of civilization, and as the power comes into their hands all noble and beautiful things are being crushed out one after another, by some mechanical device for multiplying inferiority.
> Civilization, as it was thousands of years ago, in China, in India, was an art of living, beside whose lofty beauty we are like street urchins scrambling in a gutter. (298)

A very strong echo of Yeats comes in here, although Yeats expresses it most clearly in poems written many years after this essay. Symons identifies gypsies with the impulse of past civilizations. Unlike the more conventional citizens of the modern, industrialized world, they have escaped contamination.

In his discussion of Sarojini Naidu, the Indian poet for whose first volume he wrote an introduction, he develops this idea further. Gypsies are the "Eternal Wanderers, and they are our only link with the East, with Magic, and with Mystery" (*Mes Souvenirs* 38). These are, of course, qualities which are present in the best art as well, and, interestingly enough, the mystery of the gypsy language is part of what attracts Symons. Because of its historical associations, it seems expressive of original secrets. It is, he feels, "an aboriginal language—perhaps the most ancient of all" (39).

Symons's interest in the Romany language began, as he tells us in "A Prelude to Life," with the reading of *Lavengro*; and the suggestion that it is, perhaps, the most ancient language of all, possessing original secrets of existence, is an important part of Borrow's novel. "Lavengro," means "word master" in Romany. In the novel, George learns the language from Petulengro, the gypsy king, who is "a dark, mysterious personage," and the language itself is full of mystery; there was the "strangeness and singularity of its tones; then there was something mysterious and uncommon associated with its use" (II:267). All of these characteristics come into play because of the vast historical and mythological associations gypsies embody: "We are an old people, and not what folks in general imagine, broken gorgios; and, if we are not Egyptians, we are at any rate Rommany Chals!" (I:227). George's interest in language in general, and Romany in particular, centers on a desire to establish basic similarities, to find those secrets and innate aspects of language that existed before Babel.

The most characteristic description of Gypsies, as Symons sees them, comes in his essay, "Notes Taken in Constantinople and Sophia" (1902). In Constantinople Symons watches a gypsy girl who seems the reincarnation of ancient life. She is "like a Sphinx that had come to life" (*Wanderings* 141). In line with his thinking about gypsies, he also states that her eyes reflected an Eastern darkness. After describing a meeting between her and a street vendor, from whom she tried to steal a package of cigarette paper, he recounts a moment in which he and the gypsy seem to have developed a spiritual contact in a mere glance:

> Her eyes rested on me, and passed over me; but, just before I went on, she looked across, with a look of one equally outside things, and smiled brilliantly at me, with eyes and teeth and mouth, in a manner of perfectly disinterested friendliness. I never saw anyone so fiercely and violently alive, or with such electricity in her eyes. As I went back through the Grande Rue de Pera, elbowing that motley crowd, I seemed to be passing through a menagerie of jackals and hyenas, after coming from the presence of a wandering princess whom I had met by the way. (142)

The modern world pales when compared to this ordinary gypsy girl. He sees in her what he saw in gypsies throughout his life: the sense of freedom he sought in life and art, the impulse of a mysterious and symbolic aspect of reality, and his own ambition to identify with both.

Impressionism and *Vraie Vérité*

Gypsies embodied for Symons a number of important concepts, both artistic and social. "A Prelude to Life" shows that there was a very personal, as well as symbolic, aspect to his appreciation. But what is also interesting in this autobiographical sketch is that, as well as showing that Symons's temperament was particularly well suited to the writing of travel literature, it also suggests that he developed and changed his prose techniques in order to deal with his artistic and metaphysical interests. In other words, if we see Symons as evolving into a symbolist from his earlier work as a Paterian impressionist, this process is significantly elaborated in his travel writings.

Symons's first travels abroad, in the company of Havelock Ellis in September 1889, were, understandably, to France. He was, at this time, beginning to develop an interest in French literature and culture. In 1886 he published an article on Frédéric Mistral, the leader of a movement in France to bring back or invigorate Provençal language and literature, and in 1889 he wrote an article on Villiers de L'Isle-Adam for Oscar Wilde, then editor of *Woman's World*. This first trip, however, was arranged primarily to see the Exhibition Celebrating the Centenary of the Revolution, and Symons did not do much more than that. The two men travelled again to Paris in the spring of 1890, during which time Symons met various French writers including Verlaine, who was to have a profound effect on his literary theories.

The influence of things French, however, was focused, more or less, through Pater. In 1891 Symons published "A Visit to Roumanille" in *Black and White*. The essay describes his visit with the French poet during the time he and Ellis were travelling south to Spain. Although included in *Wanderings* (1931), it is primarily literary in orientation. The opening sentences, however, focus on the value of travel, which adds adventure to life: "And all these add to one's life a sense of adventures, for adventures are to be found wherever one follows them; and a life without adventures is really no life: a negation, a refusal" (48). This passage describes an attitude very reminiscent of Pater, accenting, as it does, a life based upon new sensations. The relevant idea in *The Renaissance* is the failure of formed habits which turns our experience of the world into stereotypes.

Pater's influence has been discussed somewhat in the opening chapter in relation to "A Prelude to Life," but it is important at this point to discern further the implications of this influence in relation to a number of other writers who influenced Symons as well. The character of his impressionistic travel writing is best understood in relation to Pater's work, but writers like John Addington Symonds were also involved in Symons's artistic development. J. A. Symonds, in fact, wrote to Symons during the first stages of their acquaintance about the similarity of their names. J. A. Symonds thought they might be related.

Symons wrote to Michael Field about the sort of poems he was then able to publish, most of which, he said, were in the "impressionistic manner" (letter, September 7, 1888). Later, in 1893, he wrote about J. A. Symonds's essay, "In the Key of Blue": "One of the most interesting things he has done" (letter, January 11, 1893). J. A. Symonds had, in fact, discussed this essay with Symons in their correspondence, suggesting that it was "something in the line of impressionism" (*Letters* III:690). J. A. Symonds then sent the proofs to Symons, saying in a letter dated September 27, 1892, "I wonder what you will think of it as a form for presenting one's impressions of nature?" (III:753). Symons reviewed the book, *In the Key of Blue and Other Prose Essays*, for *The Athenaeum*, May 13, 1893, and he is somewhat more critical, but his sympathy with this form of writing is still strong: "The first section, which gives its name to the book, is a somewhat curious experiment in literary impressionism. It is a colour-study, in mingled prose and verse, an attempt to paint in words the actual tints and tones of a single colour" (598). Symons's objections to the essay, which he describes in this review, are not due to a disagreement with the method. He would like, in fact, to see the method refined. He is not sure, however, whether J. A. Symonds's command of verse is up to the task. What Symons admires in J. A. Symonds's work, though, what he is writing to Michael Field about, is its quality of impressionism which reflects personality. In his earlier review of *Our Life in the Swiss Highlands* (which J. A. Symonds wrote in collaboration with his daughter, Margaret Symonds) for *St. James's Gazette*, Symons states that the most impressive aspects of this volume deal with and relate to personal impression. He says, for example, that the essay, "A Page of My Life," which must have influenced Symons's "A Prelude to Life," is successful because it is so personal. Symons concludes that "in the act of writing down these impressions, intense recollection turns into a fascinating kind of literature, a personal form of it, which Mr. Symonds attains thus, and thus only" (6). Symons's critical attitude is, it seems, based upon an interest in personal impression, intense recollection, suggesting a slight reworking of Wordsworth's famous phrase, and he found these qualities in aspects of J. A. Symonds's work.

Although *In the Key of Blue* is a particularly nineties book and seems especially well suited to Symons's interest, its antecedents can be discovered in J. A. Symonds's earlier work. "Lombard Vignettes" in *Sketches and Studies in Italy* (1879) has similar qualities. He mingles terms from various arts, which is characteristic of the nineties color study, in order to create a sense of harmony of form and impression. In fact, it should be noted that the change in form from travel narrative to travel sketch suggests a change in artistic ambition. An impressionistic view, framed as if it were a painting, is preferred to the rather strict and pedantic travel narrative.

J. A. Symonds's influence on Symons, then, is consistent with and prior to Pater's. Symons had been interested in the older scholar's work for some time when in December 1885 he sent a copy of *Titus Andronicus*, for which Symons had written an introduction. He says in "A Study of John Addington Symonds" that when he was sixteen he "read some of the prose of Symonds before I came on the rare first edition of Pater's *Studies in the History of the Renaissance*" (MS). He had probably read much of the work J. A. Symonds published in *Cornhill Magazine*. Approximately a year after he first wrote to J. A. Symonds, in December 1886, he began to correspond with Pater. He had sent Pater a copy of his first full-length critical study, *An Introduction to the Study of Browning*, which was published in that year. They did not meet, however, until August 7, 1888.

Pater's influence was prepared for, then, by Symons's reading of J. A. Symonds. But the effect of Pater's work on Symons can best be described and evaluated by isolating the central concepts of flux and the essential relativity of all ideas, for it is Symons's belief in these ideas which leads to the literary impressionism he practices at this time. As we have seen in "A Prelude to Life," Symons identified himself with the conflict implicit in Arnold's and Pater's writings. Pater's view is the more radical, centering as it does on relativity and flux when all those around him are desperately trying to fortify their world with absolutes and a belief in convention. In fact, the prevailing Victorian belief in progress, the belief that Western, Christian culture was continuously bettering itself, is completely undermined by Pater's view. Johann Herder had suggested earlier that the belief in progress was, indeed, a misconception, that there was no constant, uniform standard, no absolute.

Pater's attitude towards relativity becomes a positive characteristic of the modern world. His essay on Coleridge in *Appreciation* (1889) expresses this idea best: "Modern thought is distinguished from ancient by its cultivation of the 'relative' spirit in place of the 'absolute.' Ancient philosophy sought to arrest every object in an eternal outline, to fix thought in a necessary formula, and the varieties of life in a classification by 'kinds,' or *genera*. To the modern spirit nothing is, or can be rightly known, except relatively and under conditions" (66). Coleridge, to Pater's mind, is a man who has wasted his life seeking absolute truth in a relative age; whereas Winckelmann is an example of a man who has not sought absolute truth and who is involved in the direct contemplation of art. It is at this point that Pater's notion of flux enters the argument. Our ordinary experience can only be defined in terms of continuous flux. Life, for Pater, is equated to a stream, and the same sort of stream image is used by Symons at the conclusion of "A Prelude to Life." We must, therefore, turn to the life of the senses in order to appreciate the best moments as they pass.

The literary impressionism this theory was bound to produce explains the sort of color studies J. A. Symonds was writing, as well as a number of Symons's early poems. The latter, in fact, tend to be impressionistic travelogues rather than poems. The first section of *Silhouettes* (1889), which describes his visit to Dieppe on his way home from Paris in 1890, is entitled "At Dieppe" and clearly reflects the ambition to present the scene as impressionistically as possible:

> The sea lies quieted beneath
>   The after-sunset flush
> That leaves upon the heaped grey clouds
>   The grape's faint purple blush.
> Pale, from a little space in heaven
>   Of delicate ivory
> The sickle-moon and one gold star
>   Look down upon the sea.
>   (*Works* 1:98)

This poem, "After Sunset," is the first in "At Dieppe," and it establishes a mood, evokes the late afternoon hush and repose. Unlike Yeats's moods, however, Symons wants to create the sense of impermanence associated with this time of day. This impressionism is momentary, not a Yeatsian moment of eternity. Symons's poem is a color study and intends nothing more. In his next volume of poetry, *London Nights* (1895), he prints two poems under the title, "Colour Studies." The first, "At Dieppe," is dedicated to the impressionistic painter, Walter Sickert, and is meant to be a verbal equivalent of his paintings of this area of France. In addition, the autumnal quality, the sense of decay, is strongly accented. Autumn, along with early evening, is a time of great poetry, as Yeats suggests in *Celtic Twilight*, but it is equally a time in which the transitory qualities of life are felt most strongly.

The theory of impressionism that informs this poem is very much evident in Symons's prose as well; he is, above all else at this point, concerned with faces, makeup, the surface expression of mood. The second section of *Silhouettes*, appropriately enough, is entitled "Masks and Faces." An early discussion of this interest in the impressionistic technique occurs in a review article Symons wrote on Richard Jefferies's work. The article was first published in *Hour-Glass* in October 1887, and later reprinted in *Studies in Two Literatures* (1897). In it he points out that Jefferies's early work, such as *The Game-Keeper at Home* (1878) and *Wildlife in a Southern County* (1879), is limited because his only strengths are "quickness of eye and faithfulness of hand" (*Works* 8:29). After quoting a passage from

The Game-Keeper at Home, Symons goes on to analyze the general characteristics of the passage, using a terminology and critical perspective that define his own concerns as well: "Here the interest is in the thing itself, there is no attempt at painting a picture or making an impression, but simply at describing a curious circumstance which has been observed" (*Works* 8:30–31). In Jefferies's later work, however, Symons ascertains a change in artistic intention and method, a change which is most strongly felt in *The Open Air* (1885). Again, after quoting a passage from the work, he describes how it is different: "Here the thing in itself is of no interest; it is but a company of drunken men and women outside a village pothouse; but see how cunningly it is taken, how the touches of colour, making a picture of this piece of vulgar reality, are noticed and brought out, just as a painter would bring them out on his canvas. The straight forward observer has become an impressionist, he values Nature now for her suggestions" (*Works* 8:31). Symons's interest in impressionism determines his interest in Jefferies's work. A writer should not deal with reality in terms of details; rather, he must look for form, composition and, most particularly, the suggestive quality reality has to offer. The quality in language that is poetic is associated with the discovery of "suggestion" in nature. Realism eliminates this quality with detail. Théophile Gautier, interestingly enough, is too exact in his travel books: "What Gautier saw he saw with unparalleled exactitude: he allows himself no poetic license or room for fine phrases; has his eye always on the object, and really uses the words which best describe it, whatever they may be. So his books of travel are guide-books, in addition to being other things; and not by any means 'states of soul' or states of nerves" (*Prose and Verse* 45). In other words, the more or less objective depiction of place fails to capture what is most important.

Although Pater's concept of experience lies at the theoretical heart of Symons's work, we begin to see that there are other artistic and intellectual influences which Symons uses to fortify these ideas. In his essay, "Edmond and Jules de Goncourt," he describes his interest in these writers, as well as other artists. Their art is based upon their ability to present "an exaggerated sense of the truth of things" (*Figures* 348). He then goes on to discuss them in relation to other writers and artists: "What the Goncourts paint is the subtler poetry of reality, its unusual aspect, and they evoke it, fleetingly, like Whistler; they do not render it in hard outline, like Flaubert, like Manet." The essay also states that "the Goncourts only tell you the things that Gautier leaves out; they find new, fantastic points of view, discover secrets in things, curiosities of beauty, often acute, distressing, in the aspects of quite ordinary places" (348–49). The Goncourts and Whistler, like Pater, elaborate delicate, artistic impressions for the reader or viewer to contemplate. Symons, in fact, incorporates this passage in *A Study of Walter Pater* (1932), showing that he felt there were close theoretical and methodological ties between these writers and artists.

The figure missing from this list, however, is Paul Verlaine. In *Colour Studies in Paris* (1918) Symons collects in a section on Verlaine a number of earlier articles and reviews, and many of his comments on the poet's work focus on the same qualities, particularly the twilight atmosphere: "His verse is as lyrical as Shelley's, as fluid, as magical—though the magic is a new one. It is a twilight art, full of reticence, of perfumed shadows, of hushed melodies. It suggests, it gives impressions, with a subtle avoidance of any too definite or precise effect of line or colour" (171-72).

The painterly techniques and the impressionistic language of the artists and writers Symons admired very readily apply to his travel writings. As we have seen, travel became for Symons the source of new sensations. The suggestive quality of Verlaine's verse and the secrets of beauty the Goncourts sought were aspects of reality Symons also tried to define and recreate in his travel sketches. Such minor figures as Hubert Crackenthorpe, among others, had produced similar works, particularly *Sentimental Studies* (1895) and *Vignettes* (1896). What they sought was the artistic moment, or what William Gilpin had defined earlier, albeit much more formally, as the picturesque. Symons is also looking for and trying to recreate in prose the moment of magical glow. This amounts, certainly, to living life as art. In a sense, he looks for in a landscape or cityscape what, as we have seen, he also finds in ballet, the paradox of art in life. The moment when life crystallizes into art, the Paterian moment, is "magical":

> The most magical glimpse I ever caught of a ballet was from the road in front, from the other side of the road, one night when two doors were suddenly thrown open as I was passing. In the moment's interval before the doors closed again, I saw, in that odd, unexpected way, over the heads of the audience, far off in a sort of blue mist, the whole stage, its brilliant crowd drawn up in the last pose, just as the curtain was beginning to go down. It stamped itself in my brain, an impression caught just at the perfect moment, by some rare felicity of chance. (203-4)

This moment, the perfect pose, appropriately at the completion of the ballet, is a metaphor for what Symons seeks in more ordinary experiences.

He is, as is Henry James in his travel writing, a passionate pilgrim seeking aesthetic pleasure. Also like James he self-consciously works to construct a picturesque scene. It was for this reason that James liked to arrive at his destination at sunset, when something like Rossetti's "magical robe" came into play. In Symons's early work we see this quality in his interest in silhouettes, which was the title of his second volume of poems. At dusk, detail diminishes, form increases and suggestion, as well as mystery, dominates the scene. It becomes an accomplished artistic whole well suited to a mind dominated by literary impressionism. This quality is central to his appreciation of Budapest, which he visited in 1902 in order to fill out *Cities*: "At sunset every point of the abrupt hill opposite is detailed in sharp silhouette against a glowing sky, out of which the colour is about to fade; the whole uninteresting outline of the palace, seen under this illumination, becomes beautiful" (190-91). One feels that this is, perhaps, a verbal sketch for a Whistler painting. Belgrade offers a similar situation: "After the sun has set the river grows colder and paler, and the short grass of the plain turns to exactly the colour and texture of the Infanta's green velvet dress in Velasquez's picture at Vienna" (199).

The scene acquires a harmony of composition; what was a literal dreariness takes on artistic charm.

The aesthetic procedure Symons elaborates here is quite in keeping with the ideals of aestheticism that developed in the late nineteenth century. He deals with the transformation of the literal, and he often effects this transformation by borrowing painterly techniques. Again, we are reminded of Henry James, whom Symons had met in Italy in 1894 and whose work he published in *The Savoy*. James's *Portraits of Places* was published in England in 1883. The title of the volume suggests an interest in carrying over of techniques from one art form to another. James often looks at a landscape in terms of a painting; Winchelsea, for example, which he describes in *English Hours*, recalls a Turner or a Claude (299). For Symons, the environment, at times, works in harmony with the observer: "The English mist is always at work like a subtle painter, and London is a vast canvas prepared for the mist to work on" (*Cities and Sea-Coasts* 102). But the same issue of transformation is paramount; this is not Lamb's London, which can be celebrated unequivocally, even if it does appear to Symons, to use Lamb's words, as a "multitudinous moving picture" (76).

In other sections of his travel writing Symons alludes to the paintings through which he sees an area; the areas become important partially because of these literary and artistic associations. "Bergamo and Lorenzo Lotto," in *Cities of Italy* (1907), is a case in point: "All around Bergamo one sees the landscape backgrounds of early Italian pictures: on one side the mountains, and, stretching out to the mountains or to the sky, wide flat plains, set with short trees like bushes, and with square patches of cultivated ground, a green level space ending on the sky in a mist" (247). His essay on Montmartre in *Colour Studies in Paris* describes a similar process; this time, however, the painter who determines the view is Manet: "The place and moment where the Quartier Latin becomes—what shall I say?— its best self, are upon those fine Sunday afternoons when the band plays in the Luxembourg Gardens. Does everyone know Manet's picture of the scene: the long frock coats, the long hair, the very tall hats, the voluminous skirts of the ladies, and the enchantment of those green trees over and between and around it all?" (*Colour Studies* 27).

Symons continued, throughout his travel writing, to see his environment in terms of familiar paintings as well as in terms of impressionistic composition in general. Conversely, a city like Sofia was criticized because there seemed to be a "mingling of elements that do not unite" (*Cities* 205). His essay, "Impressionistic Writing" in *Dramatis Personae* says much the same thing but from a more theoretical point of view: "Impressionistic writing requires the union of several qualities; and to possess all these qualities except one, no matter which, is to fail in impressionistic writing. The first thing is to see, and with an eye which sees all, and as if one's only business were to see; and then to write, from a selecting memory, and as if one's only business were to write" (343). The selecting memory seeks recreation over truth to detail. The relation of beauty to truth, of course, was raised with the advent of realism. The belief that a harmonized world is solely dependent upon the observer is as pure an impressionistic view as we get in Symons, and it is, according to this passage, the harmony that is the source of the revelation. Later in the essay he elaborates further, using Whistler and Verlaine as examples: "A fine composition may, in the most subtle and delicate sense, be slight: a picture of Whistler, for example, a poem of Verlaine. To be slight, as Whistler, as Verlaine, is slight, is to have refined away, by a process of ardent, often of arduous, craftsmanship, all but what is most essential in outward form, in intellectual substance" (346). This statement is partially in answer to the complaint that paintings by Whistler, or the impressionists in general, do not manifest true craftsmanship, primarily because they do not show the quality of finish the Victorians had come to associate with good art, an issue which will be dealt with more fully in the next chapter. He argues that the rather vague and atmospheric language of Verlaine and the formal, shadowy paintings of Whistler exemplify an unusually refined art.

By the turn of the century the influence of impressionistic techniques on travel writing in general was strongly felt. E. V. Lucas, for example, published a series of travel books, entitled "Impressions of Travel," which saw many editions. The cover piece to *A Wanderer in Florence* (1912) gives a very accurate description of its contents and methodology: "This is the fourth of a series of impressionistic travel books by Mr. Lucas, the other three of which—*A Wanderer in Holland*, *A Wanderer in London*, and *A Wanderer in Paris*—have all run into many editions. In this work the author follows his accustomed line, blending latter-day impressions with historical lore, and recording minutely the sensations of pleasure produced by beauties of art, architecture and natural scenery" (cover piece). The terminology is directly from Pater, showing that his influence has continued significantly. Certainly such twentieth century travel writers as Norman Douglas owe a great deal to Pater's theoretical base. The best of the nineteenth- and twentieth-century travel writers, however, sought more than mere impression. The work was designed to create a taste, an instructional aspect one would not expect to find in works seemingly aimed at giving pleasure only but which is certainly present in the travel writings of D. H. Lawrence and Norman Douglas. Much of the travel writing also centers on a personal quest for more permanent values. This aspect of the work is somewhat related to its instructional characteristics. The revelation Symons begins to describe in "Impressionistic Writing," as well as the truth that can only be discovered through beauty, can be seen as an allusion to this more permanent realm. These characteristics, although implicit in Symons's earlier work, become particularly apparent after his trip through Ireland with Yeats.

In 1892 Symons visited Ernest Rhys in Wales, a visit which began to renew his interest in his Celtic identity; but it was not until 1896, during his travels with Yeats and Edward Martyn, that this identity began to show itself in his work. These travels accomplished more of a reinitiation, actually, for his reading of *Lavengro* during his childhood, with its rather elaborate linguistic associations of the mysteries of various Celtic languages and Romany, had already instilled in Symons a fascination with these worlds. As a result, however, of his travels with Yeats, he wrote and published in *The Savoy* "A Literary Causerie: From a Castle in Ireland" (Edward Martyn's Tulira Castle), "In Sligo: Rosses Point and Glencar," and "The Isles of Aran." He makes the following observation in "The Isles of Aran," an observation which is striking in relation to his earlier writing:

> I have never realized less the slipping of sand through the hour-glass; I have never seemed to see with so remote an impartiality, as in the presence of brief and yet eternal things, the troubling and insignificant accidents of life. I have never believed less in the reality of the visible world, in the importance of all we are most serious about. One seems to wash off the dust of cities, the dust of beliefs, the dust of incredulities. (*Cities and Sea-Coasts* 313–14)

One almost feels that this is the moment at which Symons changes the name of his projected book from *The Decadent Movement in Literature* to *The Symbolist Movement in Literature*. The now-famous essay, "The Decadent Movement in Literature" was published in November 1893 in *Harper's Monthly*, before this trip to Ireland. Now Pater's concept of drift, in which momentary intense sensations are sought, is coupled with "eternal things." The sense of despair implicit in the final passage of "A Prelude to Life" is overcome. This passage also recalls Baudelaire's "Correspondences," for the aspects of this world "mingle more absolutely." He is describing what amounts to a revelation, the symbolic moment of correspondence. In *The Symbolist Movement in Literature* he refers to the authority of Thomas Carlyle for his definition: "In the Symbol proper, what we call a Symbol, there is ever, more or less distinctly and directly, some embodiment and revelation of the Infinite; the Infinite is made to blend itself with the Finite, to stand visible, and as it were, attainable there" (qtd. 2).

The development of Symons's theory of the "symbolist moment" is largely due to the combined influences of Browning, Pater, and the French symbolists, with Yeats as a focusing device. But it is also worthwhile to note Symons's discussion of the relationship between impressionism and symbolism. As he says in "The Decadent Movement in Literature," in trying to define impressionism and symbolism as the two main branches of what he now calls the Decadent Movement, there are some interesting similarities: "Now Impressionist and Symbolist have more in common than either supposes; both are really working on the same hypothesis, applied in different directions. What both seek is not general truth merely, but *la vérité vraie*, the very essence of truth—the truth of appearances to the senses, of the visible world to the eyes that see it; and the truth of spiritual things to the spiritual vision" (*Dramatis Personae* 98–99). At this point, he suggests, perhaps rather vaguely, that each seeks "the very essence of truth," but it is not until the introduction to *The Symbolist Movement in Literature* that he finds, to again use Baudelaire's appropriate word, a further correspondence. It is only through the visible that the invisible can be attained. He finds that, truly, his earlier interest in impressionism accommodates symbolism.

Much of Symons's best travel writing centers on this same issue of correspondence. In *Cities*, as we have seen, he identifies *vraie vérité* with the soul. The aesthetic moment becomes, perhaps, more than the momentary impression; it is the recognition of more essential and more permanent aspects of reality. This concept is similar to Joyce's epiphany, and both of these notions clearly developed from Pater. Browning also tries to isolate the significant moment within a dramatic context. "A Gingerbread Fair at Vincennes," published in *The Savoy*, shows Symons developing similar artistic aims. The essay is based upon an outing with Ellis and Remy de Gourmont in 1892 but is constructed so as to show the scene in terms of drama. The opening paragraphs describe the fair before "the hour of disguises has begun" (*Colour Studies* 6), in other words, before the play has begun. The third section of the essay, perhaps better described as the third act, brings the drama to its climax: "But it is at night, towards nine o'clock, that the fair is at its best. The painted faces, the crude colours, assume their right aspect, become harmonious, under the artificial light" (*Colour Studies* 13–14). Although this essay is, as the title of the collection suggests, a color study, it is also a very self-consciously created drama which elaborates a significant moment.

The quality of experience which Symons seeks, particularly as seen in his travel writing, is due in part to the influence of some other writers as well: Heinrich Heine and Vernon Lee (Violet Paget). Although Symons mentions in "A Prelude to Life" that he dislikes the German language, he had written to Osborne as early as June 15, 1883 that he was involved in translating Heine's poetry, but he never really mastered the language. He also felt that Heine's travel writings were truly extraordinary. Symons's interest in Heine at first seems unusual, for the irony and humor that is the hallmark of much of Heine's work would have been somewhat alien to Symons's temperament. The aspects of Heine, however, that appealed to Symons (particularly in *Reisebilder*, his collections of travel writings) are related to the evocation of the soul.

One's first reaction to Heine's travel writings is that they are very colloquial and anecdotal, almost slight, as well as being traditional in their narrative structure. But this anecdotal quality is considerably transformed by Heine. His use of what seem to be minor incidents becomes a form of synecdoche and symbol. He describes, for instance, an experience in Trent Cathedral; he sees a woman in a confessional, but her face is concealed: "Yet there came to view a hand, which at once held me fast. I could not help looking at it; its blue veins and the aristocratic gleam of its white fingers were so strangely familiar to me, and all the power of dreams in my soul was stirred into life to shape a face to match this hand" (III: 54). From the woman's hand he wishes to construct a face to match. In his travels he does much the same thing, finding an object or person that will define, symbolically and almost magically, the area. In the following passage, he lights on the figure of a woman selling fruit at an open market as emblematic of much more than her mere physical presence would suggest: "I gazed on this woman with the same rapt attention with which an antiquary would pore over a newly discovered torso—

yes, I could detect far more on this living human ruin. I could see on her traces of all the civilization of Italy—the Etruscan, the Roman, the Gothic, the Lombard, down to our own powdered modern age . . .'' (III:56). The individual detail represents Italy; the history that has passed stands in the midst of a more modern marketplace. Often for Heine, such symbols are experienced "as in a dream, and one of those dreams, too, wherein we strive to recall something we have dreamed long ago" (III:51). There is, in this phrase, the suggestion of archetypal symbols, but mostly he seems interested in discovering the secret of a place which is best contained in symbol. Symons defines this same sort of experience in his essay, "Montserrat": "When I have seen a face, a landscape, an aspect of sky, pass for a moment into a sort of crisis, in which it attained the perfect expression of itself, I have always turned away rapidly, closing my eyelids on the picture, which I dread to see fade or blur before me" (*Cities and Sea-Coasts* 126).

Vernon Lee offers a similar perspective, and her work was vitally important to Symons during his formative years. On October 4, 1886, he wrote to Dykes Campbell saying that the introduction he had written to *Venus and Adonis* (published in 1885) was modelled on the style of Vernon Lee, whose *Euphorion* he admired. Additionally, he was reading Lee's work on Italy in conjunction with his Browning studies. Several of the notes he published in the *Browning Society: Monthly Abstract of Proceedings* (1884–85), such as "Galuppi—Vernon Lee" and "Vernon Lee on 'The Ring and the Book'," reflect his interest in and knowledge of her work. Many of her essays were published in *Cornhill Magazine*, copies of which Symons had received from Osborne. Finally, the connection between Pater and Lee suggests that her influence coincides well with Pater's. Lee met Pater in 1881, during her visit to England, and she corresponded with him throughout his life. Pater's influence on her writing was strong as well; so when Symons writes to Osborne in March, 1885, that he is interested in Pater's style, it is evident that the influences of those two writers are working well together.

Lee's travel articles, most of which were published in the *Westminster Gazette* before she collected them in individual volumes, gained her more recognition than she could understand, particularly since she considered her other work in literature and aesthetics to be more substantial. Her travel writing, however, has continued to interest a number of writers. Aldous Huxley, for example, wrote to her after reading *The Golden Keys* (1925), which was, it turned out, the last collection of travel essays to be published before her death in 1935: "How much I like, too, your generalizations about the Genius Loci!" (248). As Huxley rightly observes, it is Lee's theory of *genius loci* that is the most important aspect of her travel books. Certainly Lawrence Durrell's more recent theory of *deus loci* owes something to Lee's earlier generalizations, and, as we shall see, Symons's theory of *vraie vérité* is, no doubt, partially due to Lee's influence.

Lee's first travel book, *Limbo* (1897), is more formative than the volumes which follow, but it does contain many interesting initial discussions of her theory of *genius loci*, although it is not until her second volume of travel essays, *Genius*

Loci (1899), that she actually uses that phrase. In the essay, "In Praise of Old Houses," for example, she develops what amounts to an early formulation of her theory: "I feel, I say, walking day after day through these streets, that I am in contact with a whole living, breathing thing, full of habits of life, of suppressed words; a sort of odd, mysterious, mythical, but very real creature" (31). In "The Lie of the Land" in the same volume she deals with what she feels is the impossible artistic ambition of recreating the qualities she experiences. Both the ambition and phraseology recall Symons's work: "I want to talk about the something which makes the real, individual landscape—the landscape one actually sees with the eyes of the body and the eyes of the spirit—*the landscape you cannot describe*" (45). The "something" she wants to depict is, as the title of the essay suggests, the lie of the land, and, as Symons also formulates, the vision or revelation is based upon a combination of eye and spirit. The impressionistic method, as she says later in the essay, "represent[s] rather a necessary phase in the art, than a definite achievement," for "where there is a faithful, reverent eye, a subtle hand, a soul cannot be far around the corner" (57).

By the time *Genius Loci* is published, her ideals, as well as the theory that informs them, are clearly defined: "The Genius Loci, like all worthy divinities, is of the substance of our heart and mind, a spiritual reality" (5). And later in this essay, like Heine and Symons, she notes that often the individual becomes the symbol; some aspect of the environment speaks for the whole. The soul still remains a mystery, but some qualities of it can be gleaned from these features.

J. A. Symonds was undoubtedly an influence in the development of these ideas as well. Many of his travel articles, which were published in the 1880s in *Cornhill Magazine,* evolve a theory of *genius loci*. In "Spring Wanderings," for example, he makes the following statement: "There is something arbitrary in the memories we make of places casually visited, dependent as they are upon our mood at the moment, or on an accidental interweaving of the impressions which the *genius loci* blends for us" (678). In "May in Umbria," which was published several months later, he develops this idea further: "It is sometimes the traveller's good fortune in some remote place to meet with an inhabitant who incarnates and interprets for him the *genius loci* as he has conceived it" (450).

The connection with Symons is plain. His search for the soul of Rome, for example, leads him to pagan Rome rather than the city of the Popes. But above all, he sees Rome through the Campagna: "To realize the greatness of Rome, it is not enough to have seen the Colosseum, St. Peter's churches, palaces, ruins, squares, fountains, and gardens; you may have seen all these, and yet not have seen the most beautiful possession of Rome: the Campagna" (*Cities* 25). It is in this landscape that he has a sense of "the soul's ecstasy before eternal things" (29). And, as he says later in the essay, the Campagna is composed of the aspects one expects in *genius loci*: "All the changes of the earth and of the world have passed over it, ruining it with elaborate cruelty; and they have only added subtlety to its natural beauty, and memories to that beauty of association which is a part of the spirit of places'' (31). What both Lee and Symons seek, as does Heine, is what Ezra Pound refers to as ''luminous detail,'' events, moments, landscapes, that crystalize, that burn with a ''hard, gemlike flame.'' The association with Pater, too, is further clearly developed in *The Enchanted Woods* (1905): ''As we continue to live, and see more of our own and other folks' lives behind, or along-side of us, there arises a dim comprehension of some mysterious law by which the good things of life, all the happiness—nay, the very power of being happy—are not life's aim but life's furtherance, and their true possession depends on willing and uncalculating response to life's multifold and changing beckonings and behests'' (8).

Not only does this passage recall Pater, but it is reminiscent of Symons's statement about the nature of travel in his early essay, ''A Visit to Roumanille.'' In addition, one can go back to Symons's review article, ''Three Contemporary Poets,'' in the January 1886, issue of the *London Quarterly Review*, to see that the development of his aesthetic, the significant or symbolic moment, was quite consistent with his earlier thinking. Thus, he says the following of Browning's *Ferishtah's Fancies*: ''It is as if one caught a wave at its poise, and held it for a moment, motionless with all its suspended thrill and fury of movement. In an eloquent pause and silence, when life lived to the fullest culminates in one crisis of joy, pain, passion, or disgust, Browning seizes and poses his opportunity'' (243). The moment achieves symbolic status.

Italy and Spain

Symons's obvious and strong attachment to France, due primarily to his extensive and intense interest in French literature and culture, remained with him throughout his life. *The Symbolist Movement in Literature*, which elaborates the most important aspects of his aesthetic, is a tribute to the country in which the movement originated. His love of France, in fact, is expressed throughout his travel writings. *Colour Studies in Paris*, a collection of essays he had published in various periodicals years earlier, depicts the artistic flavor of the city in which he felt art and life mingled more completely and ideally than in any other modern city. For Symons, one could suppose, Paris was the Florence of a modern Renaissance based upon the Symbolist theories he describes in his book. In *Wanderings*, he collects many of his earliest travel essays on France to form the first section, ''Wanderings in France,'' and, additionally, he gathers a number of later essays, all of which were written after his breakdown, to form the third section, ''Further Wanderings in France.'' If he had not had his breakdown, or if he had survived it more substantially, he might have developed a more clearly focused travel book on France.

In terms of his early interests in travel, however, he looked elsewhere in Europe for stimulation, particularly to Italy and Spain. As he says in *Cities of Italy*, which he published to supersede his earlier volume, *Cities*, he hoped at this point to organize two major books of travel essays: ''Here I have brought together, into something more like unity, all that I have to say about Italy, and I hope later to do the same with my scattered writings, in 'Cities' and elsewhere, on Spain'' (vii). Symons, however, had his breakdown before he was able to complete his book on Spain. We are left with the first section of *Cities and Sea-Coasts and Islands* (1918), which is entitled "Spain," as the only collection he put together on that country. But it is clear that these two countries were important to Symons, and his writings on them warrant further evaluation.

In the spring of 1894 Symons made his first of many trips to Italy. He spent most of the two months in Venice, just as Gautier had during his first visit to Italy. It was in Venice, in fact, that Symons first met Henry James. This initial trip to Italy for Symons was actually the fulfillment of a long-standing ambition. He had written to Osborne of his rather intense desire to see Italy, a desire which was, no doubt, fueled by the writers who interested him at this time. At thirteen he had read most of Byron. He says in "Notes on My Poems," an article written when he was destroying his "juvenile verses," that at thirteen he had written "thirty-nine stanzas of Canto I of 'Don Ismaeli' done after 'Don Juan' and laid on 'the iron-bounded coast of Cornwall' " (112). In "A Prelude to Life," he comments: "I turned to Byron, at twelve or thirteen, as to a kind of forbidden fruit, which must be delicious because it is forbidden" (*Works* 5:10). Byron, as well as representing a form of rebellion, must also have instilled a sense of wonder in Symons about the great countries of the world. *Child Harold's Pilgrimage* became the quintessential romantic travelogue and established for the generations that followed that in places like Greece and Italy, "Where'er we tread 'tis haunted, holy ground" (176). Symons was also at this time reading Browning. In 1879, when he completed "Volume II" of his "juvenile verses," there was already a trace of Browning in his poetry (112), and Browning was one of the great heroes to nineteenth century travellers. The country of his greatest celebration is Italy. Symons's interest in Browning alone would have led him there.

Symons's ambition to see Italy, of course, is in keeping with the more general Victorian attitudes about that country. *Lavengro*, that book Symons found so personally appealing, is emblematic of the prevailing mood. George describes Italy and the wonderful artists it produced. Now he wished "to see Italy, or rather Rome, the great city, for I am told that in a certain room there is contained a miracle of art" (I:233). The specific work of art is "The Transfiguration" by Raphael, but for most of this late Victorian world, all of Italy was, to use Durrell's phrase about Greece, "miracle ground."

During the eighteenth century, The Grand Tour, as established in such texts as Thomas Nugent's *The Grand Tour* (1749), as well as focusing on the sort of instruction one was to obtain as a grand tourist, had codified Italy as the most central place to visit. In this case, however, the interest was due to a completely different temperament. As Richard Jenkyns observes, the eighteenth century "valued classical correctness next to godliness" (1), and the interest in Italy during this period stemmed in part from its connection with "classical correctness" in literature, art, and architecture. Nugent's text is emblematic of this aspect of the period and showed the seriousness with which the young English gentleman was supposed to regard his travels abroad. The travel book, as a genre, was defined in line with this thinking, concentrating, as it did, on a narrative of details in terms of topography and relying on as much objectivity as could be maintained. The scientific mind, which was the result of a general growth of rational, scientific interest in the world, viewed even the personal travelogue as something of a science. Writers were, therefore, encouraged to avoid the egotism inherent in the first-person narrative.

With the advent of the nineteenth century, attitudes changed significantly, as did the genre of travel writing. Encouraged by the late-eighteenth-century publication of such books as Laurence Sterne's *A Sentimental Journey Through France and Italy*, the sentimental traveller took over where the splenetic traveller, like Tobias Smollett, left off. Sterne's parody of The Grand Tour is the beginning of a reorientation of perception and consciousness which comes to fruition with the romantic movement. In terms of the travel writing of this period, the reorientation allowed for a more poetic and imaginative response to one's environment. As F. A. Kirkpatrick observes, the sort of scientific accuracy embedded in earlier travel accounts is no longer required. Borrow's *Bible in Spain* is a case in point: "But, in reading Borrow's *Bible in Spain*, one of the finest travel-books ever written, no one pauses to ask whether every page depicts actual occurrences exactly as they happened. For Borrow, catching the very spirit of the picturesque romance, gives a truer picture of Spain than any accurate description could offer. He views and depicts the country in the light of his own sympathetic genius" (241). This sympathetic genius, of course, is what Byron cultivates as well; he is concerned with man in relation to his surroundings.

Symons inherited this tradition and seems to see it very much in contrast to the eighteenth century. As we have seen, part of what he intends in *The Romantic Movement in English Poetry* (1909) is the establishment of a tradition with which he feels artistically identified. The eighteenth century represents a break with that tradition. Much of the introduction to the book elaborates this concept of tradition, and the eighteenth century is always associated with qualities of society which are antithetical to the poetic spirit of the Romantics. The point of this argument, however, is used to develop an analogue. Just as Pater, in *Marius the Epicurean*, uses the later stages of the Roman Empire to evaluate aspects of Victorian England, so Symons uses the antipoetic characteristics of the eighteenth century to evaluate similar attitudes in the late Victorian world. This tactic is particularly striking in relation to the scientific interests which dominated both ages. The great Romantics, Wordsworth and Coleridge, Shelley, Keats, and Byron, are poets we should admire, but their place in a technological and industrial world is difficult to determine. Again, Richard Jenkyns's observations about the scientific temperament of the Victorian age focuses on this dilemma: "Firstly, there was a feeling that the new era was in intellectual terms a scientific age; that scientific thought; hard, remorseless and factual, was draining the magic and fantasy out of the world" (25). This view is one that Yeats certainly maintained, and Symons felt quite comfortable with it as well. The industrial world, which seemed to grow uglier and uglier, was the deadening expression of the scientific mind.

Italy, conversely, surfaced as the place where poetry, magic, and fantasy still thrived. It was, in fact, three times more poetic for Victorian writers than anywhere else in the world. The writers of the romantic period had celebrated its magical landscape, as had the great writers and artists of the Renaissance, and, finally, it is the land associated with the great writers of antiquity. The artistic and poetic associations of any single area were almost endless. Additionally, since Italy was relatively unindustrialized, it offered a refreshing contrast to the cold and mechanically abstract North. It was, in many respects, the area in which the nineteenth-century admiration for the primitive impulse could focus its attention. In our own century, this idea has been popularized by Norman Douglas and D. H. Lawrence. But the ideological contrast really originated in the nineteenth century, and Symons's essay, "Notes Taken in Switzerland" (1903) shows its influence. Switzerland, with its northern disposition, has no mystery: "The Lake of Geneva, with its exquisite clearness of colour, has neither mystery nor luxuriance; even at Lucerne the beauty is contrived on the romantic pattern, and has no allurement; the Lake of Zurich is like a reservoir; and one imagines it at work for some useful purpose." When he crosses the boarder into Italy, however, something new is added: " 'At last I am in Italy!' No, there is no doubt, the Italian lakes have a quality of unconsciousness which is wholly lacking in the lakes of Switzerland" (*Wanderings* 132–33).

This passage comparing Switzerland and Italy predates all of Lawrence's work, but both writers come to similar conclusions. The imaginative and sublime quality of the Alps, which we associate with Wordsworth and Shelley or, for that matter, with Leslie Stephen and The Alpine Club, is left out of account. Like Lawrence, Symons tends to see the Swiss temperament, and by extension the industrial North, as self-conscious and restrictive. There is a lack of the essential spontaneity associated with the unconscious impulse of the South. Shelley, when he visited Italy, noted a similar contrast, although he did except the Alps from it:

> Our journey was somewhat painful from the cold & in no other manner interesting until we passed the Alps: of course I except the Alps themselves, but no sooner had we arrived at Italy than the loveliness of the earth & the serenity of the sky made the greatest difference in my sensations—I depend on these things for life for in the smoke of cities & the tumult of humankind & the chilling fogs & the rain of our own country I can hardly be said to live. (II:3–4)

This letter to Thomas Love Peacock uses the same type of contrast, physical and metaphysical, as does Lawrence in *Women in Love*. For many people during this time Italy was the place of life; the industrial, mechanical North, the place of death in life.

J. A. Symonds is an example of one of the writers of this period who sought physical and spiritual sanctuary elsewhere. He eventually settled in Davos, Switzerland, but his attitudes to the Italian landscape are representative as well. An important article, "Amalfi, Paestum, Capri," which Symons undoubtedly read in *Cornhill Magazine*, refers to the poetic and impulsive nature of the Italian environment, which no artist seems able to capture: "What is wanted, and what no modern artist can successfully recapture from the wasteful past, is the mythopoeic sense—the apprehension of primeval powers akin to man, growing into shape and substance on the borderline between the world and the keen human sympathies it stirs in us" (*Sketches and Studies in Italy* 11). The Italian landscape generates the mythopoeic sense. Gabriele d'Annunzio, whom Symons had met during his 1896 trip to Italy after *The Savoy* had failed, embodies the qualities of the South Symons found most artistically appealing. In his introduction to G. Harding's translation of *Il piacere* (*The Child of Pleasure*) in 1898, his analysis of the work involves the contrast between the North and the South:

> D'Annunzio comes to remind us, very definitely, as only an Italian can, of the reality and the beauty of sensation, of primary sensations; the sensations of pain and pleasure as these come to us from our actual physical conditions; the sensation of beauty as it comes to us from the sight of our eyes and the tasting of our several senses; the sensation of love, coming to us from the root in Boccaccio, through the stem of Petrarch, to the very flower of Dante. (vi)

Symons identifies d'Annunzio with other Italian writers in order to show his connection with what J. A. Symonds called the primeval powers. He deals with, as Symons says later in this introduction, the "spirit which can be known only through the body" (vi), an edict Lawrence was to popularize years later and which certainly relates to Symons's religion of the eyes.

Italy was, it seems, the ideal environment for the practice of the Paterian aesthetic Symons had developed, but in conjunction with the contrast of North and South, which saw Italy as impulsive, there developed an historical contrast as well. The past and the present are compared in terms of the quality of civilization. The more disaffected from their society the writers of the late nineteenth century became, the more they tended to idealize the past. Italy, in relation to this tendency, is a country which exists as a palimpsest, one civilization on another only partially rubbed out. Certainly, the wonderful associations that Vernon Lee evokes are due to this historical perspective. She, in fact, refers to this activity, as the "historical habit," which involves our supplementing our present life with a life in the past, a life which is larger and richer than our own, "multiplying our emotions by those of the dead" (*Limbo* 29). J. A. Symonds, again in his article, "Amalfi, Paestum, Capri," makes a similar observation. Various civilizations, including Greek, Latin, Moorish, and medieval, have flourished on the same soil: "In Italy, far more than in any other part of Europe, the life of the present is imposed upon the strata of successive past lives" (*Sketches and Studies in Italy* 12). Henry James comments upon the same phenomenon in *Portraits of Places*, but he is—if not equally then partially—interested in "the vulgarity of the Italian genius of to-day." He clearly allies himself, however, with the tradition of which J. A. Symonds and Lee, as well as Symons, are a part: "After thinking of Italy as historical and artistic it will do him no great harm to think of her, for a while, as modern, an idea supposed (as a general thing correctly) to be fatally at variance with the Byronic, the Ruskinian, the artistic, poetic, aesthetic manner of considering this fascinating peninsula" (44–45).

Symons's interest in Italy followed this "historic habit" and is particularly apparent in his admiration of the Renaissance in Italy and England. He had written to J. A. Symonds for ideas or themes for his poetry from the Italian Renaissance. Browning's use of the Renaissance as material for poetry probably encouraged Symons in this interest. Certainly his more general interest in J. A. Symonds's work was related to the latter's Renaissance studies. In his letter of July 12, 1888 to Michael Field he says as much to her, suggesting that she could benefit from a study of the period as well: "I have often wished you would take up a Renaissance subject—surely no period is so full of fine suggestions as that." He goes on to mention J. A. Symonds's *Italian Byways* as good source material. It seems clear, in fact, that Symons sought in the modern world an artistic revival that would mirror the Renaissance. As has been suggested already, *The Symbolist Movement in Literature* can be seen as a book which intends to revive the world dominated by "a materialistic tradition." As such, it tries to usher in a modern Renaissance, a new era of artistic hope. In fact, the connections, both in form and theme, between Symons's book and Pater's *The Renaissance* are striking, suggesting that Symons wanted to do for the present and future what Pater had done by using the past. Pater's form of criticism is, in a sense, an appreciation. After the "Preface," which offers some general characteristics, *The Renaissance* contains a series of related essays which are actually appreciations of individual, representative figures. The "Conclusion," of course, brings the argument full circle, relating it again to the modern world. Although Symons says very little about the organization of *The Symbolist Movement in Literature*, the influence of Pater's work is telling. Symons seems to be following the same pattern. Additionally, his admiration for the Elizabethan period, as described in his introduction to *Venus and Adonis*, for example, echoes not the symbolist aesthetic but the more general sense of artistic vigor, "that sudden Samson-like uprising of the slumbering intellect" (iv), that he felt was a part of the symbolist movement.

Cities of Italy is also, somewhat loosely, organized around the interest in the Renaissance in contrast to the modern world. In his essay on Sienna, he observes the effect of the modern world on these ancient cities: "The modern spirit has spoiled Rome, and is daily destroying there. It is more slowly, but not less certainly, destroying Venice, with a literal, calculated destruction. Florence has let in the English, who board there, and a new spirit, not destructive, reverent of past things but superficial with new civilization, has mingled the Renaissance with the commonplace of the modern world" (210). "Florence: An Interpretation" functions as central to the organization of the book, for he sees it as the artistic center of the Renaissance: "Florence is a corridor, through which the beauty and finery of the world have passed. That new Spring which Botticelli painted, and which was the Renaissance, flowered into the Florentine lilies with more of its ardour, and a more 'hard and determined outline,' than in any other Italian soil'' (133). The essay continues in this vein, organized around the artistic development of Florence. Life and art, as in modern Paris for Symons, mingle perfectly in this ''city of all the arts'' (136). It is important to see this city in terms of all the arts, as does Symons in this essay; for not only does life mingle perfectly with art, but the arts themselves seem to correspond magically as well.

Symons found support for these ideas in the work of one of his friends, Edward Hutton. Rather than go to university once he had finished school, Hutton chose Italy as the source of his further education. He had read heavily in Ruskin, Pater, and Vernon Lee, which set his mind on Italy. When in 1902 he met Symons, his ideas about Italy were more fully rounded and they corresponded well with Symons's. The sense of Italy as a holy, haunted place is established in *Studies in the Lives of the Saints* (1902), and there is a sense throughout his travel writing that, indeed, saints have walked the same ground. He also develops a very striking contrast between the modern world, often exemplified by the modern tourist, and the ideal past. The Renaissance in Italy, therefore, is an age we can hardly study too much. The disease of the modern world is the decay of sympathy for this time and the simultaneous decay of the great Italian cities. In *Italy and the Italian* (1902), he describes the decay of Venice: ''Perhaps Venice may stand for the tragedy of our modern world. She is dying so slowly under the glittering indifferent stars. Through her streets rush the penny streamers, like horrible bacilli in the veins of one dying of a dreadful fever. They care nothing for her beauty, and are perhaps unconscious that they are destroying her, being occupied with their own thoughts, their own little life'' (274).

For Symons, the cities of Italy are emblematic of the same loss of beauty, while they are the places where beauty is most strongly felt. Symons sees each city as expressing certain moods and attitudes, all of which are related to the historical habit we have identified. This unique interest in cities was probably partially the result of J. A. Symonds's influence. His essay, ''Monte Oliveto,'' which appeared in the May 1882 issue of *Cornhill Magazine*, describes how difficult it is to finally ascertain the essential character of cities:

> It is hardly possible to define the specific character of each Italian city, assigning its proper share to natural circumstances, to the temper of the population, and to the monuments of art in which these elements of nature and of human qualities are blended. The fusion is too delicate and subtle for complete analysis; and the total effect in each particular case may be compared to that impressed on us by a strong personality, making itself felt in the minutest details. Climate, situation, ethnological conditions, the political vicissitudes of past ages, the bias of the people to certain industries and occupations, the emergence of distinguished men at critical epochs, have all contributed their quota to the composition of an individuality which abides long after the locality has lost its ancient vigour. (*Italian Byways* 22)

J. A. Symonds has a particular interest in the general character of place and people. At one point in *Our Life in the Swiss Highlands* he mentions his reading, with considerable interest, Emile Hennequin's *La critique scientifique*, and although he does not admire the too limiting scientific approach, he is intrigued by *ethnopsychologie*, that is, national literature taken as a sign of national character. In "The Love of the Alps," which he reprinted in *Sketches and Studies in Italy and Greece*, J. A. Symonds explains the appeal the Alps had to the nineteenth century very much along these lines and, interestingly enough, suggests that the interest is part of a new Renaissance: "It may seem absurd to class them altogether; yet there is no doubt that the French Revolution, the criticism of the Bible, Pantheistic forms of religious feeling, landscape-painting, Alpine travelling, and the poetry of Nature, are all signs of the same movement—of a new Renaissance. Limitations of every sort have been shaken off during the last century; all forms have been destroyed, all questions asked" (296).

Symons follows J. A. Symonds's lead and tries to determine, mostly through poetic intuition, the *vraie vérité* of the cities he visits. Implicit in his evaluation of the great historic cities of Italy is a criticism of the northern cities of his own time. Like Ruskin who looked to the medieval world for the ideal city, Symons draws a picture of Renaissance beauty in opposition to the modern industrial city.

Within this context, Symons's rather dominant interest in dead cities, associated with decadence, surfaces significantly. Throughout his travel writings he continually deals with or alludes to cities that have retreated from the world and that appear to be emblems of decay. *Spiritual Adventures*, for example, includes a story entitled "An Autumn City," which is about a traveller, Daniel Roserra, who "tended his soul as one might tend some rare plant; careful above most things of the earth it was to take root in" (*Works* 5:119). The character has a number of things in common with Symons, particularly those aspects of Symons's personality which were suggested in "A Prelude to Life." Both are innately interested in travel and what amounts to the spirit of place. Roserra, like Symons, "thought much of the influence of places, of the image a place makes for itself in the consciousness, of all that it might do in the formation of a beautiful or uncomely disposition" (*Works* 5:119). This statement is very close to the aesthetic procedure Symons outlines in *Cities* and repeats in *Cities of Italy*.

The soul of the city in this story, as the title suggests, is autumnal, and it is this quality, exactly this quality, that Roserra appreciates. Arles, where the story takes place, is essentially a dead city:

> When the soul of Autumn made itself a body, it made Arles. An autumn city, hinting of every gentle, resigned, reflective way of fading out of life, of effacing oneself in a world to which one no longer attaches any value; always remembering itself, always looking into a mournfully veiled mirror which reflects something at least of what it was, Arles sits in the midst of its rocky plains, by the side of its river, among the tombs. (*Works* 5:123)

What Roserra seeks in this city and what Livia, his wife, can neither appreciate nor understand, is this element of autumn, of twilight. The escape or retreat into this shadowy world is emblematic of the isolation of the artist and of the more permanent, immaterial world. In contrast, Livia, who thrives on the external world, "wants something definite to do, somewhere definite to go" (*Works* 5:129). Thus, the conclusion of the story draws out the differences in their natures in terms of a contrast of cities; the more commercial city of Marseilles is set in opposition to the timeless, withdrawn world of Arles. Roserra's reaction to Marseilles sets up the contrast: "A nausea, a suffocating nausea, rose up within him as he felt the heat and glare of this vulgar, exuberant paradise of snobs and tourists" (*Works* 5:131). Livia, however, is in her element.

Much of this story is drawn from the travel writing Symons published on Arles, three essays in all, which are reprinted in *Wanderings*. Symons's description of Bologna, however, equals the mood of his writings on Arles. His reaction to the artifacts in the Museo Civico is a case in point: "But gradually, as I moved from room to room in that silence, amongst all those spoils of Etruscan and Italic sepulchres, the weight of so much, so ancient, and so forgotten death began to weigh upon me" (*Cities of Italy* 241–42). And later, looking at coins and medals, he says, "I could see only that they were the portraits of dead men and women, and that the pride of life which had perpetuated them was after all only another glory which had gone into dust, ridiculously despoiled by death" (242). Part of the atmosphere of this scene is undoubtedly drawn from Heine, who, in the last chapter of his travel book on Italy, describes a series of portraits of Genoese women in the Palace Durazzo in much the same way: "Nothing in the world inspires the soul with melancholy as the sight of portraits of fair dames who have been dead for centuries. Sadness steals over the soul when we reflect that of all the originals of those pictures, of all the beauties who were so lovely. . ." (122–23). Much of the mood is due to the characteristics of the traditional *ubi sunt* theme which both Heine and Symons evoke. Heine even alludes to François Villon's "Ballade des dames du temps jadis." But an additional quality, not associated with this traditional theme, surfaces. The sense of death and decay implicit in all life is tied in with a sense of world decadence. Civilization is moving further and further away from an understanding and appreciation of the beauties and art of these dead cities. The contrast in "An Autumn City" focuses on this concept, as does Yeats in *A Vision*, albeit with a much more extensive perspective. It is in this way, in fact, that the nineteenth-century interest in ancient cities, Vernon Lee's "historic habit," is related to the late-nineteenth-century discussion of decadence.

Spain, on the other hand, offers another alternative to the modern world and becomes the ultimate contrast to the industrial, middle-class environment Symons disliked so intensely: " 'Stung by the splendour of a sudden thought,' there came to me, night after night, in Fountain Court, in the year 1891, the obsession of seeing what I could see, during a limited space of time, in Spain: that one country which I was afterwards to adore beyond all others" (*Wanderings* 48). He and Ellis had made their first trip there as a result of this impulse, and the country had a profound effect on both of them. Indeed, the impact was so great that they proposed collaborating on a book on the country. Although the book was never written, Ellis did write his own book, *The Soul of Spain* (1908) and Symons, after he had recuperated somewhat from his breakdown, collected a number of articles he had written earlier to form "Spain" in *Cities and Sea-Coasts and Islands*.

Aspects of Spain's appeal appear to be deeper versions of similar qualities in Italy, but on the most immediate level, the country offered novelty no longer available elsewhere in Europe. Italy had by then become overrun with tourists, as well as overdescribed in works written about it. James's comment about Venice in *Portraits of Places* is a case in point: "Venice had been painted and described many thousands of times, and of all the cities of the world it is the easiest to visit without going there. . . . There is nothing more to be said about it" (1). For many of the writers of this period, Spain became an alternative. As Ellis says in *The Soul of Spain*, "Spain, indeed, has not yet attained the depressing exuberance of renovated Italy" (2).

The alternative it offers is clearly identified with the temperament and character of the people and the geography. In his article, "The Poetry of Santa Teresa and San Juan de la Cruz" (1899), Symons describes what amounts to an essentially poetic temperament: "The Spanish temperament, as I have been able to see for myself during the three months I have already been in Spain, is essentially a poetical temperament. It is brooding, passionate, sensitive, at once voluptuous and solemn. Here is at least the material for poetry" (65). And, in his essay, "Moorish Secrets in Spain" (1899), he identifies the temperament of Spain with its Moorish history; the secrets of the life force apparent in Spain comes from, in part, the Moors who once inhabited the country. This quality is particularly apparent in the Malaguena, which is a music almost without origin: "It is as Eastern as the music of tom-toms and gongs, and, like Eastern music, it is music before rhythm, music which comes down to us untouched by the invention of the modern scale, from an antiquity out of which plain-chant is a first step towards modern harmony" (102). The music of Spain as Symons interprets it is the expression of initial creative forces, the same impulses that Nietzsche describes in *The Birth of Tragedy*. Dancing, which comes from the same source, is perfected in Spain by the gypsies: "As I have watched a Gitana dancing in Seville, I have thought of the sacred dances which in most religions have given a perfectly solemn and collected symbolism to the creative forces of the world. . . . It is another secret of the Moors, and must remain as mysterious to us as those other secrets, until we have come a little closer than we have yet come to the immaterial wisdom of the East" (104–5).

Ellis, whom Symons joined for part of his 1898–99 trip through Spain, describes Spain in similar terms. The two men undoubtedly collaborated on their perceptions, if not on an actual book. Ellis viewed the Spaniard as "the child of a European father by an Abyssinian mother" and as serving as an important "connecting link between Europe and the African continent it was once attached to and

still so nearly adjoins'' (29). Symons described the violence in ''A Bull Fight at
Valencia'' (1898), but for both men ''Spain represents, above all, the supreme
manifestation of a certain primitive and eternal attitude of the human spirit'' (vii–
viii). The world of Spain ''reminds'' Symons and Ellis of the past, recalls more
essential impulses: ''It would be easy to enumerate many details of life in Spain
which remind us of a past we have long left behind'' (14).

For Symons particularly, Spain became the country most closely allied with
the same qualities he saw in the gypsies. Spanish art focused these characteristics
especially well, for they express a primitiveness that the nineteenth century admired, and, as a result, they are associated with the more modern schools of painting which oppose the high finish of traditional Victorian art. Symons, in fact, sees
El Greco as discovering the world anew: ''Theotocopuli seems to have discovered
art over again for himself, and in a way which will suggest their varying ways to
some of the most typical modern painters. And, indeed, I think he did discover his
art over again from the beginning, setting himself to the problem of the representation of life and vision, of the real world and the spiritual world, as if no one had
ever painted before'' (50). There was in England at this time, as in times past, a
revival of interest in Spanish art. In 1895 the New Gallery Exhibition of Spanish
Art was held, and in 1901 the Guildhall Exhibition of Spanish Pictures was also
held. Symons's description is emblematic of this increased general interest.

Perhaps Ellis gives the best summation of the interest in Spain. His book is certainly more scientific than Symons would have allowed if they had collaborated,
but his appreciation of the Spanish temperament is, as we have seen, consistent with
Symons's. In his description of the physical grace of the Spanish people, the contrast of civilizations which brings into perspective the late nineteenth century's appreciation of Spain is strikingly drawn:

> The adequate adjustment of nervous force to muscular movement is, in the best sense, an animal
> quality; it is the quality which gives animals, living in nature, their perfect grace. In Northern
> France, in England, in America, the influences of civilizations lead to an excess of irritable ner-
> vous energy, which is always overflowing, meaninglessly and therefore ungracefully and awk-
> wardly, into all the muscular channels of the body. In this excess of restless nervous energy the
> qualities of our modern civilized temperament largely lie, and it is this probably, more than any-
> thing else, which removes us so far from the Spaniard. (81)

4

Art and Artists

In 1891 Symons published in *Black and White* a descriptive review of the Royal Minuet Party. The title, "Watteau in Piccadilly," emphasizes the variety of artistic experiences it incorporates in the review. He finds that he is involved in a world of mixed sensations, of synaesthesia: "And passing through a doorway I found myself suddenly transported into a delicious country, which I seemed to recognize, as though I had once lived in it. 'Watteau!' I cried, as I sank upon a seat, for I found that I had strayed out of the November weather into the afternoon sunshine of one of the *Fêtes Galantes*" (757).

At one point we are involved in the characteristics of a world dominated by music; at another point we are very much a part of a world described as if it were a painting. It might be said, in fact, that the variety of sensations is the topic of the piece. Appropriately, then, the final sentence alludes to Pater as an important theoretical force: "One seemed to see a Watteau in movement under the Watteaus of white and gold walls, as one sees them at Sans Souci—the only place in the world where the 'Prince of Court Painters' is still at home" (757). Symons suggested that the figures dancing as part of the Royal Minuet Party recall the figures in a Watteau painting, that his impression of the entire experience involves the generation of one art form as the reflection of another.

Symons is interested in what can be gained critically by speaking of one art form in terms of another. In order adequately to describe eighteenth-century dance, it seems appropriate to rely on the visual sophistication of a Watteau painting. The critic has to adopt this critical methodology in order to adequately deal with various forms of artistic expression. As Symons suggests in "An Art Critic and Criticism": "Every art has not only its own language, but its own world of existence. The musician hears the world, the painter sees the world, and neither can ever put precisely into words what he has heard or seen. It is the business of the critic to divine this, and to find some approximate means of transposing it into the terms of another language" (2). The critic who has to transpose the language of painting or the language of music often finds that the language associated with one art helps him describe another. This same type of overlapping of artistic terms was used by Pater and Swinburne, and Baudelaire's ideal of correspondence certainly figures significantly in the tradition. Symons derives much of his own thinking from all of these figures.

The fact that these sorts of critical issues are so quickly generated by a review such as ''Watteau in Piccadilly'' shows not only the importance of synaesthesia in Symons's works, but also the importance the visual arts played in the development of his overall aesthetic. In his earlier work, such as *An Introduction to the Study of Browning*, many of the same artistic concerns come into play. Browning's quality as an artist, according to Symons, is partially based on the fact that he incorporates ideas from various arts: ''But the latent qualities of painter and musician have developed themselves in his poetry, and much of his finest and very much of his most original verse is that which speaks the language of painter and musician as it had never before been spoken'' (22). Browning's inspired use of the visual arts, both as a source for technical ideals and as a source for subjects for his poetry, helped to motivate Symons's interest in this art form.

Reading through Symons's art criticism, then, it becomes apparent that, like Browning, he found in the visual arts grounds for his technique as a poet and writer, and that he also found that within the context of the visual arts the difficulties of developing an overall aesthetic could readily be debated. The nature and value of art, as Symons understood these issues, receive considerable attention. We can best deal with these aspects of Symons's criticism of the visual arts by dealing with two major areas, his overall theory of visual experience and his discussion of several individual artists.

Symons's Theory of Visual Arts

Symons says in a letter to Edmund Gosse that his book, *Aubrey Beardsley*, was his first major piece of art criticism: ''I am so glad you like my Beardsley. It is my first serious attempt at art criticism, and I am hoping to do more in that line, as soon as I feel quite confident of myself'' (letter, May 9, 1898). He had, however, up to this point written a number of articles in art criticism, including ''A French Blake: Odilon Redon,'' which appeared in the *Art Review* in July 1890, and ''Mr. Holman Hunt's New Picture,'' which appeared in *The Academy* on September 6, 1890. His early poems also show a strong influence from the visual arts. Rather than show homage to the old masters as Browning does, Symons's poems tend to derive from more avant garde sources. ''The Temptation of Saint Anthony,'' for example, which was completed in 1887, develops the theme of the temptress and is generated by the designs of Félicien Rops. ''The Wood-Nymph'' is somewhat more traditional in its appeal and finds its source in a painting by Edward Burne-Jones. Other poems, which he published later in life but which were written in the nineties, such as ''Aubrey Beardsley'' and ''Faint Love,'' based on a fan by Charles Conder, have an equally strong visual orientation.

Also during the nineties, especially with the publication of *Silhouettes* in 1892, the influence of Whistler and impressionism becomes particularly apparent in Symons's poetry and prose. His travel writings, as we have seen, are impressionistic sketches of the great cities of Europe. His poems, too, rely heavily on impressionistic techniques. Robert L. Peters, in "Whistler and the English Poets of the 1890's" develops this point. Symons, among others, was "eager to assert a new and vital era in English poetry" and drew "upon the techniques and subject matter of other media" (251). Symons's interest in Whistler as a source for literary technique is consistent with his earlier appreciation of Browning, for as he says in relation to Browning's "Old Pictures in Florence," "the principles which Mr. Browning imputes to the early painters may be applied to poetry as well as art" (*Browning* 100).

Symons's fascination with Whistler, however, and with Walter Sickert, who during this time was a dedicated follower of Whistler's, is based upon technique which avoids discursive content. As Peters says, the poems written along the lines of impressionist paintings "demand of the reader a certain purity of attention, and ability to perceive form and pattern rather than message or sentiment" (257). As Symons's statement on Browning suggests, the appeal of expression and technique must be coupled with the deeper values of the soul. He does, however, wish to avoid the more superficial moralities which had at this time impinged on artistic expression. Symons often tries to solve this artistic problem, as in his review, "The New English Art Club": "Truth in art is the means to an end, and the end is beauty; an end which can be reached only by way of truth" (519).

It is obvious, then, that Symons is very much involved with the theories of the visual arts that surfaced throughout the late nineteenth century. His own literary, as well as overall aesthetic, ideas are influenced by the various artistic trends. It was not, however, until early in the twentieth century, particularly with the publication of *Studies in Seven Arts* (1906), that he began to write fully about his ideas and show more exactly the influences that determined them. A rather long essay, "The Painting of the Nineteenth Century," part of which originally appeared as an extended review of D. S. MacColl's *Nineteenth Century Art* but which was expanded for publication in *Studies in Seven Arts*, evaluates the art critics Symons finds most significant in terms of his sense of tradition. John Ruskin, as we would in some respects expect, stands at the head of the list, for he certainly established for the generations that followed the terminology and the general criteria of art theory. Additionally, his belief in the value of beauty was important to the more extreme aesthetic theories that emerged during the late nineteenth century. Symons, it seems, sees Ruskin within this framework: "The influence of Ruskin has undoubtedly been a good influence; beauty was to him, literally, what a Frenchman has called it, a religion; and he preached the religion of beauty at a period almost as much absorbed in the pedantries of science and the ignominies of material success as the present period" (*Works* 9:20). Ruskin, indeed, saw his role as critic along very similar lines. Society seemed no longer able to understand or appreciate the value of artistic beauty, which for Ruskin was finally "witness to the omnipotence of God" (*Modern Painters* I:22). The failing in society was reflected by the popular press, and he felt, as he says in the second volume of *Modern Painters*, the need "to summon the moral energies of the nation to a forgotten duty, to display the use, force, and function of a great body of neglected sympathies and desires" (28). In his preface to the first edition he says much the same thing in relation to English artistic taste: public taste seems to have plunged deeper into degradation, and the press promotes all that is false and affected in art. The critic, then, has "to declare and demonstrate, wherever they exist, the essence and the authority of the Beautiful and the True" (*Modern Painters* I:4).

Ruskin's ambition, his desire to demonstrate the ultimate value in art of the Beautiful and the True, is, in terms of the content of his message, contained in the combination of those terms. Beauty functions in relation to truth. This attitude is contrary to Symons's usual view, where truth is a means to an end. In "The New English Art Club" he self-consciously echoes Ruskin in order to accent what he considers to be the more accurate view: "Have even the best, have the best especially, of the painters of the New English Art Club remembered that, if truth does not result in beauty, it is, in painting, so much paint spilt fruitlessly on canvas?" (519). Symons goes on to argue the point further in this study, *Dante Gabriel Rossetti*, part of which gives a thumbnail sketch of the history of English painting. Here Symons alludes to Ruskin's sincere devotion to nature as a primary artistic standard. This concern seems to lead to an interest in minute detail in painting, and it is this aspect of Ruskin on which Symons focuses. Ruskin, however, actually describes an overall concern with a combination of detail and design which will express the ultimate truth about nature and, therefore, God. Detail is not sought for its own sake. That would be the lowest form of art. The artist uses detail "for the sake of the inestimable beauty which exists in the slightest and least of God's works, and treated in a manly, broad, and impressive manner" (*Modern Painters* I:32). Symons, if we could exclude the religious overtones, would agree with this point of view. It is also within this theoretical context that Ruskin is able to appreciate Turner's later impressionistic style and the Pre-Raphaelites, as he points out in "Of the Use of Pictures" in volume three of *Modern Painters*.

For Symons, however, Ruskin is too insistent, too concerned with detail and artistic finish: "He demanded strict drawing as a foundation, and only after all its modulations and precision the wonders of light" (*Rossetti* 41). The Pre-Raphaelites emerged as artistic models, but Symons finally sees Rossetti as branching off from this group or tradition and as somewhat more appropriately allying himself with those who do not manifest strict drawing. Like Blake, who takes the perspective that the imagination is more perfect and more organized than anything seen by the mortal eye, Rossetti relied on internal vision and suggestion rather than traditional artistic finish. Symons was at this point also fascinated by light and shade, by the qualities of silhouette. In relation to the tradition of visual arts established and defined by Ruskin, Whistler appears as a refreshing innovator. Symons stresses this point in "On the Purchase of a Whistler for London":

> The painting of Whistler came at a time when the public was beginning to accustom itself to the minute religion of the eyes which the Pre-Raphaelite pictures had brought in; and the public, though it may have many loves contemporaneously, can have but one creed at a time. Ruskin by much preaching had brought the public to its knees; it was not convinced that it liked Pre-Raphaelite pictures, but it was certain that its duty to its higher self condemned it to accept them as what it ought to like. (*Studies in Modern Painters* 44)

Symons obviously sympathizes with Ruskin's essential aim, that is, to educate the public in the qualities and importance of artistic beauty, but he feels that the evangelical aspects of his work are disruptive to the ideal of true artistic expression. Pater's influence, therefore, functions, as does Whistler's, as a corrective; he reevaluates artistic ideals which are in some ways based upon Ruskin's religion of beauty but which evolve their own intrinsic doctrines.

Pater, then, brings to art criticism a different perspective, one Symons finds more appealing. He "corrected many of the generous and hasty errors of Ruskin, and helped to bring back criticism to a wiser and more tolerant attitude towards the arts" (*Works* 9:20–21). "The School of Giorgione" is undoubtedly the central text for Symons. As "Watteau in Piccadilly" shows, Symons found the notion that "each art may be observed to pass into the condition of some other art" (an idea which Pater derives from the German term, *Anders-streben*) critically and artistically useful (*Renaissance* 133–34). Additionally, the belief that "all art constantly aspires towards the condition of music" functions as grounds for dealing with Ruskin's moral perspective, which had led to literary and anecdotal interpretations of paintings (*Renaissance* 135). Pater tries to establish a purely artistic and, in many respects, ideal standard of art; and it is a standard which by definition directly confronts Ruskin's influence.

J. A. Symonds, in fact, defines more generally the nature of this confrontation in "Is Music the Type or Measure of All Art?" in *Essays Speculative and Suggestive* (1890). As J. A. Symonds describes the situation, two standards of art have evolved. Poetry had been established as the standard which accented the discursive qualities (that is, the mental qualities of art); but music as a standard, according to J. A. Symonds, accents the nondiscursive and sensuous qualities of artistic experience: "Thus is it manifest that critics who refer to the standard of poetry, and critics who refer to the standard of music, differ in this mainly that they hold divergent theories regarding the function of art in general" (191–92). J. A. Symonds's comment is very astute, for Pater's entire discussion is self-consciously aimed at establishing the new anti-Ruskinian standard. For Pater art always strives "to be independent of the mere intelligence, to become a matter of pure perception, to get rid of its responsibilities to its subject or material." Ultimately, "form and matter, in their union or identity, present one single effect to the 'imaginative reason,' that complex faculty for which every thought and feeling is twin-born with its sensible analogue or symbol" (*Renaissance* 138). Pater strikes a blow for artistic form in this passage, although ostensibly he professes the union of form and matter as the ideal. It might be more accurate to observe that he accents the transforming powers of artistic form. The subject or material of a work of art are altered or transformed so as no longer to have any discursive validity. His concept of "imaginative reason" rather than mere intellect is also part of his ambitions to remove art from a purely moral realm.

Pater represents a very important and needed addition to the tradition of Ruskin by integrating antiliterary standards in the visual arts. Symons, therefore, begins to admire those painters who do not tend to paint for the sake of the subject. In a review for *Outlook* in 1905, "From Stevens to Sargent," for example, he describes Stevens's art within this context: "And Stevens, like Millais in the 'Mrs. Bischoffshein,' is content to paint aspect, not subject; to realize that painting need not attach itself to a story" (574). He also felt that the paintings at the Royal Academy for that year failed because they were too clearly limited by the requirements of storytelling ("The Royal Academy" 645). And throughout Symons's art criticism, J. K. Huysmans is referred to pejoratively because he tends to turn paintings into literature. The point Symons makes involves the incongruity between Huysmans's ability to identify and fight for the most important contemporary artists and his inability to deal adequately with them as artists. In "An Art-Critic and Criticism" he describes the problem more fully: "You will realize that Huysmans is not concerned with pictures as pictures, only with pictures as symbols, and that he is prepared to lay aside the critical faculty altogether, in his aim at completing in words some inadequate attempt of a painter to express himself through the medium of paint" (2). Symons objects to Huysmans's apparent association with the literary standard of the visual arts, which is historically identified with Ruskin and the Pre-Raphaelite movement.

Even though he very much appreciates some aspects of the various Pre-Raphaelite artists, particularly Rossetti, Symons still finds fault with some of their artistic procedures. As has already been suggested, Rossetti, in his less detailed later work, diverged from Pre-Raphaelite objectives. Holman Hunt, on the other hand, is more characteristic of the movement. As Symons states, "Hunt's attitude towards art may be inferred from the quality of his pictures; their strenuous search after minute truthfulness, their didactic spirit, their religious earnestness" (Review of Hunt's *Pre-Raphaelitism* 872). This statement represents Symons's more seasoned attitude toward the movement, one obviously influenced by the more ideal, musical standard introduced by Pater. In "The Pre-Raphaelites at Whitechapel" he defines clearly his attitude toward the movement: "Remember, it was the period of George Eliot, the period when Comte was a prophet; there was something of the scientific spirit in these painters, with their deliberate fidelity to what seemed to them fact" (450).

The literary or anecdotal quality of English art which Symons rightly associates with Ruskin and Pre-Raphaelitism receives its fullest and most sympathetic discussion in his essay, "The Art of Watts." He points out, for example, that Watts's paintings involve more than mere artistic expression: "More than most painters, most at least of those painters who have the genuine pictorial sense, Watts's quality of vision is conditioned by a moral quality of mind" (*Works* 9:52). The pictorial or representational quality of his work leads naturally to literary and moral overtones. The issue of pictorial limitation, therefore, becomes significant: "I do not always feel that in every one of his allegories he is quite sure of the limits of pictorial expression, that he surrenders himself quite fully to the thing seen, without undue confidence in the meaning behind it. But the mind which sees visible things as the symbols or messengers of moral ideas has conceived a whole world upon canvas in which there is not a mean or trivial corner" (*Works* 9:52–53). This statement involves an interesting qualification. The moral principle, which is clearly allied to the pictorial qualities of Watts's paintings, refers directly to Ruskin who, as we have seen, sees the natural world as if it were the Bible. Beauty has ultimately moral connotations: "Ideas of beauty, then be it remembered, are the subjects of moral, but not of intellectual perception" (*Modern Painters* I:111). Symons, it seems, tries to show that Watts's paintings, in spite of their allegorical overtones, have aesthetically much to offer. The distinction between allegory and symbolism, in fact, determines the overall artistic qualities of the paintings. In the tradition of Pater, he wants to show that there is no conflict between form and meaning. The symbol, therefore, means more than allegory, and the picture becomes more than a painted poem. Watts is seen as following in the tradition of Blake and Rossetti; through his control of the pictorial qualities of his paintings, he "remains a painter, instead of failing to be a poet" (*Works* 9:61). In some ways, in fact, he is superior to Rossetti; he embodies more completely the Paterian ideal:

> Rossetti had never so great a command over his material as Watts, but his pictures are good or bad just in proportion as he admitted or refused to admit the limits of pictorial expression, and the degree to which idea or sensation can be symbolized in form, of which the idea or sensation is only a passing guest. As his intention over-powered him, as he became the slave and no longer the master of his dreams, his pictures became no longer symbols, but idols. (*Works* 9:60)

Watts, at his best, does not fail in this way. His content is not separate from the artistic form. In fact, it is transformed by the artistry, as Pater had suggested it should be, and, therefore, what would have been pedantic and allegorical achieves the status of symbolism. Artistically, then, symbolism aspires to the union of artistic form and material content. Symons's evolution from his early aestheticism to symbolism undoubtedly had much to do with this notion that symbolism is, artistically, a combination of aesthetic ideals and aspects of the ultimate concept to which all art refers.

In line with his opposition to the literary content of paintings, Symons often follows Pater's lead by identifying the visual arts with music. Monticelli, for example, interests Symons because he seems to unite a number of the characteristic tendencies of modern art, particularly because of his association with music. As Symons says, the synaesthetic effects are striking: "I confess that he interests me more than many better painters. He tries to do a thing wholly on his own, and is led into one of those confusing and interesting attempts to make one form of art do the work of another form of art as well as its own, which are so characteristic of our century, and which appeal, with so much illegitimate charm, to most specu-lative minds" (*Works* 9:37). "Watteau in Piccadilly" shows an equal interest in the illegitimate charm of the mixed sensations of various arts. Ultimately, what Symons values most in Monticelli's work is the synaesthetic quality of his color, the harmony of color. By accenting color above line the paintings tend to transcend visual representation; they approach the condition of music. An evaluation of his work seems to require musical terminology, for "all his painting tends towards the effect of music, with almost the same endeavour to escape from the bondage of matter" (*Works* 9:38).

Symons tends to approve of the ideal which relates to the teachings of Pater, but he maintains certain reservations. He, like Pater, recognizes that each art has "its own specific order of impressions, and an untranslatable charm" (*Renaissance* 133), but that there is also an intriguing overlap of effect. Interestingly, Symons refers to Monticelli's "illegitimate charm" as due to his use of music as a standard for his use of color. What Symons objects to, however, is the desire to suspend the methods of one art form in order to utilize the methods of another. Correspondence becomes superimposition. Additionally, Monticelli's overreliance on the musical analogy is based on a misinterpretation: "On true principles of analogy, music cor-responds to a picture in which there is first of all very careful drawing. But that is not the way in which it is seen by theorists like Monticelli, whom we must take as he is: a painter who would make pictures sing, not according to the rules of music, but according to a seductive misinterpretation of them" (*Works* 9:39).

Symons's reservations, however, over Monticelli's methodology do not hinder an appreciation of his ambitions. Music as an artistic standard maintains its interest and validity. Elsewhere in his art criticism he continues to object simultaneously to the use of the musical correspondence while retaining some sense of faith in it. In his review, "Fantin-Latour and Whistler," for example, he approves of and ob-jects to Fantin-Latour's paintings on grounds similar to those in his discussion of Monticelli. Fantin-Latour's lithographs, which are mostly dedicated to music, at-tempt to depict musical visually. Symons approves of this objective in concept, but "one cannot abandon oneself to what it says with these shapes, upward motions and scattered lights, as one can to the vast and exquisite ebb and flow of the tidal music" (*Studies in Modern Painters* 32). Again, Symons appreciates the ambitious designs which try to approach the state of music, but he holds back slightly because finally the visual elements of painting have to be digested as well. Painting is a material art form after all. On the other hand, it should avoid a too material orien-tation as well. There is, however, a median ground, as Symons's quotation from

Leonardo implies: "A good painter has two chief objects to paint: man and the intentions of his soul. The former is easy, the latter hard, for it must be expressed by gesture and movements of the limbs" (*Cities of Italy* 147).

Symons's belief in music as a standard for all art obviously tends to force him in the direction of pure aestheticism, which is an aspect of his character and aesthetic that emerges often. "Watteau in Piccadilly," with its allusion to Pater, is an example in 1891. "A Prince of Court Painters" in *Color Studies in Paris*, Symons's more analytical essay on Watteau which derives its title from Pater's imaginary portrait, shows that aestheticism is very much a part of his twentieth-century makeup as well. The appeal that Watteau has for Symons is located in Watteau's use of musical instruments in his paintings as an analogue for his artistic ideals. He, more than any other artist, seems to state pictorially that music is his standard of artistic excellence: "Watteau was a great lover of music, and he has placed instruments of music even in hands that do not know how to hold bow and handle. Like music, his painting is a sad gaiety, and I rarely look at his pictures without receiving almost a musical sensation" (209). The quality of Watteau's figures also approximates musical sensations. His women, "themselves like a delicate music," also invoke "some of the mystery of music" (209–10). The design and the decorative qualities bring the paintings into the realm of music. In some respects, these works appeal on a nonreferential level.

In relation to the history of painting the musical quality becomes important to Symons. His discussion of Botticelli in "The Painting of the Nineteenth Century" shows a profound orientation toward the musical standard. The painter organizes his figures in a rhythm which unites the painting in a fine music. Whistler is a significant force in this tradition, one with whom Symons sympathizes and to whom he appeals often for support. The relation between the two figures is especially important because Whistler functions for Symons as both a critic and a painter. Thus, in "The Painting of the Nineteenth Century," where he identifies those critics who are important to him, Whistler follows Pater, and his value as a critic of the arts is made very apparent. Symons adds, in another essay, "Whistler," "I wish I could remember half the things he said to me, at any one of those few long talks which I had with him in his quiet, serious moments" (*Works* 9:69). Much that Symons derives from Whistler's writing has already been covered well in general in relation to the late nineteenth century by Graham Hough in *The Last Romantics* and by William Gaunt in *The Aesthetic Adventure*. Hough elaborates a view which relates well to Symons's: "Whistler is, among other things, such a mountebank that it is easy to underrate the importance of what he was doing. In fact he is turning the whole aesthetic tradition derived from Ruskin into a different channel" (176).

The connection between Whistler's various comments on artistic theory and Symons's ideas is striking, particularly in relation to several of Symons's artistic principles with which we have already dealt. In relation to the moral aspects of a work of art, especially as they come to the forefront of the Pre-Raphaelite paintings, Whistler argues strongly against literary orientation and moral overtones. The problem is that people have acquired the habit of looking "not *at* a picture, but *through* it, at some human fact, that shall, or shall not, from a social point of view, better their mental or moral state" (9). Whistler reiterates Ruskinian ideals which have filtered down through society and have become ingrained in the attitudes of the public, and his reiteration is a form of criticism. He adds to this a slap at the art critic who propagates this ideal of literary morality in the place of artistic interest:

> For him a picture is more or less a hieroglyph or symbol of story. Apart from a few technical terms, for the display of which he finds an occasion, the work is considered absolutely from a literary point of view; indeed, from what other can he consider it? And in his essays he deals with it as with a novel—a history—or an anecdote. He fails entirely and most naturally to see its excellence, or demerits—artistic—and so degrades Art, by supposing it a method of bringing about a literary climax. (17)

It is on these grounds particularly that Whistler attacks Ruskin, as is shown in Whistler's publication, *Whistler v. Ruskin. Art and Art Critics* (1878). Painting, according to this pamphlet, does better without art critics at all. Ruskin, in fact, should "resign his present professorship, to fill the Chair of Ethics at the University" (17).

It is apparent that Symons's discussion of Watts is, to a large extent, based on the attitudes voiced by Whistler. As Symons says, the fact that Watts's paintings seem to lend themselves to literary interpretation, that his intention is to convey literary rather than pictorial content, "is the severest condemnation which could be passed upon the work of a painter" (*Works* 9:56). In many respects, it is the severest condemnation because it is Whistler's severest condemnation.

Other significant aspects of Whistler's writings surface throughout Symons's writing on art. In "New English Art Club," for example, he comments on a painting by William Rothenstein which produced a sense of reality so complete that the quality of paint was lost: "And in thus going so far towards making a picture cease to be a picture, and become, in another than that literal and disturbing sense, a mirror, does not the painter take really a step backward, towards that external reality which, because it is nature, is certainly not art; from which art is perhaps our one means of escape?" (519). Symons draws on two seemingly contradictory concepts from Whistler. When Whistler wrote the introduction to his exhibition catalogue, "*Notes*"—"*Harmonies*"—"*Nocturnes*" (1884), he established that "the work of the master reeks not of the sweat of the brow,—suggests no effort,—and is finished from its beginning" (1). By emphasizing the fact that the artist's effort is not to be considered, he was attacking a Ruskinian principle. For Ruskin the difficulty of a project was directly related to its beauty and power: "We shall find, in the course of our investigation, that beauty and difficulty go together; and that they are only mean and paltry difficulties which it is wrong or contemptible to wrestle with" (*Modern Painters* I:97). This issue was also a part of the overall conflict over artistic finish, which many believed manifested effort and therefore quality. Burne-Jones, for example, testified during the famous libel trial in Ruskin's behalf: "In my opinion complete finish ought to be the object of all artists. A picture ought not to fall short of what has been for ages considered complete finish" (qtd. in Whistler, *The Gentle Art* 14).

Symons sides with Whistler in this debate, as he shows in his discussion of Rothenstein's painting. Combined with this allegiance is the belief that art should appear to be artificial. As Symons states, it should not be presented as if it were a mirror held up to nature. Whistler's ambition to do away with false artistic finish requires, finally, that a painting look like a painting rather than like nature. It is for this reason, again during the trial, that Whistler claims that he did not intend for *Nocturne in Blue and Silver* to be a correct painting: "It is only a moonlight scene and the pier in the center of the picture may not be like the piers at Battersea Bridge as you know them in broad daylight" (*The Gentle Art* 8). The distinction between nighttime effects and one's vision during broad daylight is artistically important. Whistler uses references to night to show the artistic effect of outline and silhouette. The daylight world is dominated by hard lines and reality as we see it in the mirror. The effect of a moonlit scene is also artistically self-conscious. As Symons says, Whistler "wishes you to know that you are looking at a picture, a work of art, and not at yourself or your neighbour in a mirror" (*Works* 9:83).

Whistler's use of musical terminology, which Symons found so appealing, was something of an accident. *The Woman in White* in 1861 generated commentary from Paul Mantz which included the phrase "symphony in white" (Spalding 29). He was probably motivated by the appropriateness of the phrase, as well as by the fact that writers like Gautier had given their poems titles like *Symphonie en Blanc Majeur*. Additionally, the critical response to *The Woman in White*, as Francis Spalding has observed, was determined for the most part by literary allusions: "Critics were naturally eager to seize upon the central meaning of Whistler's canvas and references were made to Wilkie Collins's popular novel, *The Woman in White*, though Whistler refuted this possible source" (29). The musical terminology, then, surfaced as a way of accenting the nonliterary qualities of the painting, especially since, as Whistler says, "the vast majority of English folk cannot and will not consider a picture as a picture, apart from any story which it may be supposed to tell" (*The Gentle Art* 86). When Pater published "The School of Giorgione" in the *Fortnightly Review* in 1887 he espoused more completely the artistic standard of music that Whistler's paintings embodied. In 1878, Whistler stated a similar view in an interview for *The World*: "Art should be independent of all clap-trap—should stand alone, and appeal to the artistic sense of eye or ear, without confounding this with emotions entirely foreign to it, as devotion, pity, love, patriotism, and the like. All these have no kind of concern with it; and that is why I insist on calling my works 'arrangements' and 'harmonies'" (*The Gentle Art* 48).

Symons, following in the path of Pater, obviously responds to this attitude. Symons's discussion of Whistler's paintings, as will be shown more fully in the next section of this chapter, often relies on the musical analogy, which contains the artistic standard he finds most appropriate. Symons, in fact, recognizes the historical importance of this tendency. Gautier had generated some of the conceptual base, "and to the painter of Sarasate, music could hardly have failed to represent the type of all that his [Whistler's] own art was aiming at, in its not always fully understood or recognized way" (*Works* 9:75). As Symons realized, he came to the rescue of an artistic tradition which had been misled: "Great critics like Ruskin and great artists like Watts have done infinite harm by taking the side of the sentimentalists, by attaching moral values to lines and colours, by allowing themselves to confirm the public in some of its worst confusions of mind" (*Works* 9:77).

As Symons tries to show in "The Painting of the Nineteenth Century," Whistler was not entirely alone in his battle against public misapprehension. George Moore, for example, is a critic who Symons feels is sympathetic and whose importance has been unfortunately neglected. Moore, whom Symons had met in Paris in 1890, shared and undoubtedly influenced many of Symons's views. Symons's Fountain Court location was not far from Moore's rooms in King's Bench Walk, Inner Temple, and, as his dedication to Moore in *Studies in Two Literatures* shows, they often discussed various artistic issues, particularly in relation to French and English literature and art. Moore, as well, looked to France for a renewal of English culture, and he derives from France many of the same artistic ideals as Symons. *Modern Painting*, as Symons suggests, presents something of an overall aesthetic, based upon various articles Moore had written for *The Speaker*. In "The Failure of the Nineteenth Century," for instance, which originally appeared in *The Speaker* in 1891, he develops the thesis that the nineteenth century brought a new intention into the visual arts, a primary interest in the subject. Prior to the nineteenth century, he asserts, beauty was the essential requirement. Neither in the more purely imaginative traditions (such as in Italian painting) nor in the more realistic traditions (such as in Dutch art) did subject dominate other considerations. Moore is, of course, altering art history for his own purposes; but, in relation to his own time, his point is well taken. Symons follows in the same tradition. When an interest in subject predominates, art declines: "And ever since the subject has taken first place in the art of France, England and Germany, and in like measure as the subject made itself felt, so did art decline" (*Modern Painting* 52).

Moore, like Symons and Yeats, turns the idea of decadence on its head. The artistic progress toward the moralizing associated with Ruskin, which required from painting exactness of detail and truth of effect, led to a decay in artistic quality. On the other hand, the art which, by the public and by Ruskin, is considered decadent, the art of Degas and of Whistler, to name two, is seen as reestablishing the proper tradition of beauty of which the nineteenth century seemed to have lost sight. Moore, characteristically, argues against the "vice of subject for subject's sake" (*Modern Painting* 53). In "Monet, Sisley, Pissarro, and the Decadence," he makes his point even more forcefully:

Great art dreams, imagines, sees, feels, expresses—reasons never. It is only in times of woeful decadence, like the present, that the bleating of the schools begins to be heard; and although, to the ignorant, one method may seem less ridiculous than another, all methods—I mean all methods that are not part and parcel of the pictorial intuition—are equally puerile and ridiculous. The separation of the method of expression from the idea to be expressed is a sure sign of decadence. (*Modern Painting* 96)

Moore everywhere in his writing about art argues against standardized modes of seeing. Symons, as we shall see, also finds this a significant failure in the artist's creation and in the public's appreciation of artistic creation. Moore goes so far as to state that all great artists must be self-educated so as to avoid a stereotyped vision of the world.

Whistler, of course, figures importantly in Moore's aesthetic and functions as a common theoretical source for both Symons and him. The first section of *Modern Painting*, "Whistler," is derived from three reviews which Moore had written for *The Speaker*: "Society of Portrait Painters" (July 22, 1891), "Mr. Whistler: The Man and His Art" (March 26, 1892), and "Mr. Whistler's Portraits" (April 2 and 9, 1892). To the second edition of *Modern Painting* he added "The Whistler Album," which originally appeared in *The Speaker* on December 16, 1893. As with Symons, he feels that Whistler's influence functions as a corrective, that he offers a more sound tradition which "helped to purge art of the vice of the subject and the belief that the mission of the artist is to copy nature" (24). Whistler offers a new way of seeing which breaks down the mental framework established by the schools and, particularly, the Academy. Moore, for the most part, associates this aspect of Whistler's work with the Japanese influence: "We Westerners had thought it sufficient to copy Nature, but the Japanese knew it was better to observe Nature. The whole art of Japan is selection, and Japan taught Mr. Whistler, or impressed upon Mr. Whistler, the imperative necessity of selection" (12).

Moore develops these perceptions in relation to the quality of Japanese art more fully in "Some Japanese Prints." He combines, as do Whistler and Symons, pictorial art with musical terminology. The Japanese artist "thought of harmony, not of accuracy of line, and of harmony, not of truth of colour" (261). Later in this essay, he even more forcefully makes connections between the Japanese prints of Utamaro, Whistler's paintings, and the musical standard of art: "Ladies under tree, by Utamaro! That grey-green design alternated with pale yellow corresponds more nearly to a sonata by Mozart than to anything else; both are fine decorations, musical and pictorial decorations, expressing nothing more definite than that sense of beauty which haunts the world" (262).

The ideally decorative quality of music defines the perfected qualities of these prints; they express nothing. For Symons, Charles Conder—who owed much to Whistler and the Japanese prints of Utamaro—follows in this tradition. Symons, indeed, appreciates Conder's depiction of the beauty of the music-hall ballet, a form of ideal spectacle which combines with the musical standard. Symons often preferred letting music absolutely determine, even to the point of it becoming a purely imaginative experience, the gestures of the dance. In this way, the physical reality of the dancer is transformed. Symons describes Conder within this same framework. Using the same correspondence between decoration and musical qualities, he defines Condor's art in relation to Watteau. We feel that "Watteau in Piccadilly" is being resurrected: "Since Watteau no painter has had a subtler sense of the beauty and decoration of clothes, or has made rarer harmonies out of the modern opportunities of fancy dress" (*Studies in Modern Painters* 16). He goes on to elaborate: "I said that the rarest art is in creation of a new world. Conder has created a new world, with its sky, earth and people. His world is a park, with water and moonlight, in which a perpetual *fête galante* is in progress; or it is Triana, with the masquers passing in a car; or a silken ballet" (16).

In "The Lesson of Millais," which originally appeared in *The Savoy*, Symons states that Millais died at the age of thirty-five, for from that time on he was what Symons considered to be a popular painter. He abandoned a career which might have made him a great painter in order to become the richest and the most popular. At the heart of Symons's objection is an antagonism toward the reduction of art to any popular standard and, equally, an intense opposition to the influence of the marketplace. Symons believed, as did Moore, in the ultimately aristocratic quality of art: "Art, let it be remembered, must always be an Aristocracy; it has been so, from the days when Michelangelo dictated terms to Popes to the days when Rossetti cloistered his canvasses in contempt of the multitude and its prying unwisdom" (*Studies in Modern Painters* 4). Millais fails because he dedicated himself to pleasing the multitude.

Moore undoubtedly picked up from Whistler some of his aversion to the amateur and the dilettante, particularly in relation to the history of industrial society. The disaffection of the artist accompanied the emerging impact of commercialism. Whistler describes his version of the progress from the beautiful to the manufactured:

> Then sprang into existence the tawdry, the common, the gew-gaw. The taste of the tradesman supplanted the science of the artist, and what was born of the million went back to them, and charmed them, for it was after their own heart; and the great and the small, the statesman and the slave, took to themselves the abomination that was tendered, and preferred it—and have lived with it ever since! And the artist's occupation was gone, and the manufacturer and the huckster took his place. (*Ten O'Clock* 10)

The Biblical quality of Whistler's rhetoric and syntax is used to describe the genesis of an art that is no longer associated with a true artistic tradition. The Royal Academy, in turn, became emblematic of all that was bad and commercial about nineteenth-century art. In "Our Academicians," Moore objects to the Academy on two inextricably related grounds. First of all, its purpose seems to be defined in relation to its commercial success. He regards it, then, as a commercial enterprise, a shop like any other shop. It exists to sell art and will value the paintings that sell well. It cannot, therefore, establish an independent standard of art. Whistler made the same point earlier in "The Commercial Travellers of Art," which appeared in *Truth* in 1886. He criticizes popular artists because they "are the commercial travellers of art, whose works are their wares, and whose exchange is the Academy" (*The Gentle Art* 137). But, and this is Moore's second point, to the public the Academy is the institution which sets artistic standards. As a result, in Moore's view, a false standard of art is created in the public mind.

Symons confirms this view. In "Art and the Royal Academy," published in 1903 in *The Weekly Critical Review*, he states that in order to locate true artistic standards, we have to look elsewhere. The Royal Academy is, as Moore had said, a shop. He also compares the Academy to a popular magazine. The editor, who has to select his articles based upon their popular appeal, becomes the equivalent of the selection committee. In each case the quality is reduced because of the commercial restrictions that have been imposed.

Implicit in Symons's criticism of the current state of public opinion and the official standard of art as established by the Royal Academy is a lament over the fact that a more ideal society which would allow for and even cultivate true artistry does not exist. Although Whistler argues against the prevailing notion that "the Greeks were, as a people, worshippers of the beautiful, and that in the fifteenth century Art was ingrained in the multitude" (*Ten O'Clock* 10), he still describes the Greek world as one in which the quality of artistic design permeated all levels in society. As we have seen, Renaissance Italy, as it could still be experienced by travelling through the great cities and art galleries of that country, for many late-nineteenth-century writers functioned as an artistic and social ideal. Symons shows his allegiance to this tendency in much of his travel writing. Pater had established the same pattern in his imaginary portrait, "Denys L'Auxerrois," to which Symons often refers as Pater's most important. The premise for the piece is the reincarnation of the poetic spirit: "What follows is a quaint legend, with detail enough, of such a return of a golden or poetically-gilded age (a denizen of old Greece itself actually finding his way back again among men) as it happened in an ancient town of medieval France" (*Imaginary Portraits* 47). J. A. Symonds expresses a similar state of mind, particularly in relation to Renaissance Italy, in his various writings, such as *The Life of Benvenuto Cellini* (1888), *The Life of Michelangelo Buonarroti* (1893), and in the seven-volume *Renaissance in Italy* (1875–76).

Moore, in "Long Ago in Italy," offers an even more dramatic presentation of the same idea. He establishes a sense of the society and art of Italy in contrast to London by opposing the contents of the New Gallery with its exterior environment: "We shall enter an enchanted land, a land of angels and aureoles; of crimson and gold, and pure raiment; of beautiful youths crowned with flowers; of fabulous blue landscape and delicate architecture. . . . Know ye the land where Botticelli and Filippo Lippi dreamed immortal dreams? Know ye the land, Italy in the fifteenth century?'' (*Modern Painting* 283). The association with current artistic issues is implicit. Italy in the fifteenth century is, in fact, appealed to as an artistic standard. Moore, then, allows this discussion to reflect more recent controversies: "Of truth of effect and local colour they knew nothing, and cared nothing. Beauty for beauty's sake was the first article of their faith" (283). He had used the discussion of "truth of effect and local colour" in his essay, "The Failure of the Nineteenth Century," as we have already seen. He also in this passage alludes to art for art's sake, as well as the related issue of the public's inability to perceive beauty. Thus, part of the point he is making in this essay hinges on the fact that during the fifteenth century in Italy art seemed for the entire society. This attitude, although historically completely inaccurate, is very much in line with the writings of Pater and J. A. Symonds.

Undoubtedly, however, the most important figure in this tradition is William Morris. Symons wrote a number of articles on Morris, including "Morris as Poet," which appeared in *The Saturday Review* on October 10, 1896, and "William Morris's Prose," which appeared in *The Saturday Review* on December 11, 1897; but in "The Painting of the Nineteenth Century," he tends to dismiss Morris rather quickly as a figure who was really continuing the work which Ruskin began. Of course, Moore's and Symons's notion that art is finally an aristocratic force would not settle well with Morris's theories. But, paradoxically, they seem to share his desire to see an art that emanates from society as a whole. As Morris points out in "Art and the People," the condition of the fine arts is determined by two opposing camps, the same camps Symons and Moore identify. On the one hand there is "the higher intellectual art, the work of poets, painters and the like, a very small remnant struggling amidst a thicket of pretence and imposture." On the other hand, a pretence of ornament remains "which is nothing but a commercial imposture, or at best but a foolish survival of half-remembered habit" (391–92). Morris's ultimate ambition was to create a popular art that was not bound by these extremes, nor tied to any class structure. He wanted to facilitate an art that sprang from the life of the people. Renaissance Italy and the Greek world, as many late-nineteenth-century critics saw them, were ideal societies in which this sort of art was possible.

Symons, in "The Decay of Craftsmanship in England," stresses the same ideal aspect of Greek society: "If you pass from a Greek statue to the contents of a Greek woman's toilet-table, or indeed to the pots and pans of her kitchen, you will be conscious of no such sudden change as in passing from a modern host's private picture-gallery into the bedroom where you are to sleep" (*Works* 9:125). The spirit of craftsmanship, the appreciation of beauty as it is embodied in the perfected form of a Greek statue, permeates the entire society. Symons sees this quality not only in Greek civilization, but also in the history of British civilization. Old silver, dating from the time of Charles I to George III, is equally dynamic because its line gives a sense of perfection. The sense of beauty exists within the civilization of this time as a soul does within the human body. In turn, he asks whether "the sense of beauty, the sense of proportion, has gone completely out of the modern English mind'' (*Works* 9:122).

The appendix Symons added to *Studies in Seven Arts* in 1906, which deals with the lack of craftsmanship in England, corresponded with his writing another article on the arts and crafts movement, ''The Failure of the Arts and Crafts,'' which appeared in *The Outlook* on January 20, 1906. The final sentences of the appendix are also the final sentences of this article. Earlier in it, however, he describes the nature of the movement, describing it in opposition to machine production: ''The Movement may generally be characterized as a search for increased beauty, refinement and sincerity in design and workmanship in the accessories of human life, united by an architectonic ideal, and as affording scope in what may be considered the useful arts for the artistic expression of individual taste and in contradistinction and protest against purely commercial, mechanical and machine production'' (90). The influence of the machine is, for Symons, extensive and dangerous, for a sense of machine production seems to dominate individual perception as well. The dominance of commercialism, as we have seen in his discussion of the Royal Academy, is in many ways an extension of the machine mentality. Ruskin had made much the same point, especially in ''The Moral Landscape'' in volume three of *Modern Painters* and in ''The Nature of Gothic'' in *The Stones of Venice*. In the latter, in fact, Ruskin contrasts man as a tool and man as human: ''Let him but begin to imagine, to think, to try to do anything worth doing; and the engine-turned precision is lost at once'' (II:192). And in ''The Moral Landscape'' he states that ''the great mechanical impulses of the age, of which most of us are so proud, are a mere passing fever, half-speculative, half childish'' (III:380). Symons, as well, objects to the psychology that is created by the machine, which is also the basis for the unnatural character of craftsmanship: ''Modern craftsmanship is the craftsmanship of the machine, those deadly pistons and hammers have got into our very brains, and a serious artist, who gives himself the time to think out a piece of work, and do it with his own hands, can no longer either think or do anything that is not mechanical'' (*Works* 9:128).

Symons's reaction to the antiartistic and mechanical present finds even more complete expression in his appreciation of D. S. MacColl as an art critic. As he says in ''An Art-Critic and Criticism,'' ''We have in England, at the present day, one art-critic, and one art-critic only, who is at once a good critic, and a good painter, and a good writer'' (1). In ''The Painting of the Nineteenth Century'' he adds, ''Mr. D. S. MacColl's book on *Nineteenth Century Art* is the most important book on painting which has been published since Ruskin's *Modern Painters*'' (*Works* 9:19). Symons's exposure to MacColl's art criticism was not, however, limited to this text. As MacColl states in *Confessions of a Keeper*, he was the art critic for *The Spectator* from 1890 to 1896, and then for *The Saturday Review* through into the twentieth century. But *Nineteenth Century Art* does bring together much of his thinking about art. In a number of ways, Symons solidifies a number of his own artistic ideals in relation to his appreciative review of MacColl's book.

As already observed, "The Painting of the Nineteenth Century," which has its origin in Symons's review of MacColl's book for the *Fortnightly Review*, rapidly expanded into a complete statement of artistic beliefs.

The central concept of Symons's art aesthetic is derived in part from MacColl's statement defining the nature of nineteenth-century art. Symons quotes the following passage in order to begin his own argument: "What exactly was the special and final addition made to the instrument of painting in the nineteenth century? It may be expressed by saying that painting accepted at last the full contents of vision as material, all that is given in the coloured camera-reflection of the real world" (2). MacColl goes on, in light of this notion, to make a case for impressionism as the dominant artistic mode in the nineteenth century, and he defines impressionism in relation to its natural rather than decorative logic of effect. At first, what he describes seems to be a particular form of naturalism. The acceptance of the world as if man's vision equalled a camera's is not, however, what he has in mind. The disinterested view, which would be associated with science, represents no artistic ideal. J. A. Symonds in his essay, "The Model," says the artist "must at one and the same time obey and control the model, departing at no point from its teaching, but utilizing its character and individuality for the further purpose of expression" (211). MacColl offers a similar view, suggesting that the mind, indeed, selects significant values from the visual world and that this action is related to the central artistic issues of the period: "This action of the eye and mind, of knowledge, interest, and attention, this choice of the most significant lines and values, and sacrifice of others, this picture-making we are engaged in as long as our eyes are open, has raised when transferred to painting, all the questions of 'finish,' 'faithfulness of detail,' and so forth, that are part of the impressionistic debate" (11). MacColl tries to show that artistic finish as embodied by the Pre-Raphaelites, the pictorial detail of which, as shown earlier, becomes part of the moral import of their paintings, is too unnatural. With the impressionists of the nineteenth century a true relation is developed between the artist and the visual world which he paints. Symons, in reference to MacColl's writing, defines the same ideal. The visual world is not accepted without some human intervention: "Is it not rather that modern painters have tried to do with the aid of nature what the old painters did without it? to find the pattern and rhythm of their pictures in nature itself, rather than in their brains and on their own palettes?" (*Works* 9:23).

The type of impressionism that both MacColl and Symons are describing is distinct from much French impressionism, although it obviously owes a considerable amount to French impressionist painters. Symons, however, always translates French influence into an English context; he tries to establish an English equivalent. It is for this reason that his first major article of art criticism is titled "A French Blake: Odilon Redon." He wants to alter French artistic ideals so that they can suit the English tradition. For the impressionist tradition, he relies on the work of Whistler, who was suspicious of French impressionism, and Walter Sickert, who defined English impressionism. Symons was friendly with the latter from around

1895 onwards. Sickert, years later, reviewed *From Toulouse-Lautrec to Rodin* (1929) for *The Fortnightly Review* in 1929. Additionally, Symons printed a number of Sickert's drawings in *The Savoy*.

By the time the two men had met, Sickert had written his introduction to the catalogue of the *London Impressionists' Exhibition*. The exhibition was held in December 1889, and the introduction Sickert wrote, drawing heavily on Whistler, established the nature of impressionism for the British artistic scene:

> Essentially and firstly it is not realism. It has no wish to record anything merely because it exists. It is not occupied in a struggle to make intensely real and solid the sordid or superficial detail of the subjects it selects. It accepts, as the aim of the picture, what Edgar Allan Poe asserts to be the sole legitimate province of the poem, beauty. In its search through visible nature for the elements of this same beauty, it does not admit the narrow interpretation of the word 'Nature' which would stop short outside the four-mile radius. (qtd. in MacColl, *Steer* 176)

This statement contains a number of elements which also make up Symons's theory of visual art. Impressionism forms an essential part of this theory in its opposition to inartistic realism. Finish and detail, as we have seen, do not create the correspondence between observer and observed, nor do they give a true sense of the reality. But, it has to be realized, the French impressionists (such as Monet), who aim at creating the effect of light are also excluded from Sickert's form of impressionism. He makes this point clearly several years later in "French Pictures at Knoedler's Gallery," which appeared in *The Burlington Magazine* in 1923: "The theory that it is the main business of an artist to paint a half dozen views of one object in different lights cannot be seriously maintained. It would be nearer the truth to say that the artist existed to disentangle from nature the illumination that brings out most clearly the character of each scene" (39).

Sickert often relies on analogies with the verbal arts in order to describe the methodology of the visual arts. In arguing against realism in "Modern Realism in Painting," he uses literary language as an example of what painting strives to create:

> Few would be found to defend the proposition that a stenographic report of events and words as they occurred would constitute the highest literary treatment of a given scene in life. A page of description is distinguished as literature from reporting when the resources of language are employed with cunning and mastery to convey, not a catalogue of facts, but the result of the observation of these facts on an individual temperament. (qtd. in Theuriet 140–41)

Symons makes this same point about impressionistic writing in his essay on Richard Jeffries's prose; and, as we have seen, this sense of verbal artistry—as well as the accompanying perception—was particularly relevant in relation to Symons's travel writing. He sought in his travel articles to create *la vraie vérité* of place. The form of impression that Sickert described and practiced seeks to accomplish the same illumination of the scene. The artistic beauty is directly related to *vraie vérité* that is evoked.

Symons, in turn, elaborates on these aspects of impressionism in relation to Whistler and MacColl. In his essay on Whistler, for example, he actually suggests the merger of symbolism and impressionism: "It has taken new names, and calls itself now 'Symbolism,' now 'Impressionism'; but it has a single thing to say, under many forms: that art must never be a statement, always an evocation" (*Works* 9:85). Symons sees impressionism as part of the sounder artistic tradition, as an opposition to the scientific and imitative mind. MacColl, in "Painting and Imitation," makes the same point, using dance as the analogue: "*For drawing is at bottom, like all the arts, a kind of gesture, a method of dancing upon paper.* The dance may be mimetic; but it is the *verve* of the performance, not the closeness of the imitation, that impresses, and tame additions of truth will encumber and not convince. The dance must control the pantomime" (*Confessions* 89). In line with this concept of drawing, Symons argues for a form of impressionism that is distinct from the work of Monet. Thus, in terms of what MacColl defines as the nature of nineteenth-century painting, Symons tries to make the definition even more explicit:

> There is the devout sincerity of the eye to things seen; there is the mind's acceptance of the principle of life in visible things. From the conjunction of this thought and sight we get the special character of modern painting. Impressionism, in a broad sense the pictorial art of the century, is, in its essential aim, limited to an immediate noting of light, movement, expression; to the exquisite record of an instant. Is it, in Browning's phrase, "the instant made eternity"? (*Works* 9:25)

It is apparent, particularly when we consider the above quotation in relation to the other aspects of Symons's writing on the visual arts, that he vacillates between a rather pure interest in art, an interest which manifested itself in his writing on Watteau, Conder, and Whistler, and an equal interest in life. He recognizes that pure aestheticism, allied with music as an artistic standard, is ultimately crippling. It is for this reason, in fact, that impressionism as Sickert and MacColl have defined it was so important.

Symons was not alone in his struggle with the relationship between art and life. R. A. M. Stevenson, whose book, *Velasquez*, was quite influential when it was published in 1895, and who was the art critic for the *Pall Mall Gazette*, deals with the same issues. The musical standard is qualified by the visual—and, therefore, less pure—characteristics of the visual arts. But artistic expression still dominates: "Our faith in any art reposes, however, upon the belief that its material, even if unavoidably adulterated with foreign significations, is nevertheless as capable as the sounds of music of expressing character in virtue of artistic arrangement. Otherwise, no medium of expression but the symphony should deserve the name of art" (33). The musical standard is maintained, even if the material of art innately signifies more than itself. This issue becomes crucial in relation to Velasquez in whose art life, or the reality of the visual impression, has to be retained as well: "Plainly, then, there are two interests to be reconciled in a picture, the facts and the impressions of nature on one hand, and, on the other, the beauties and exigencies of the framed pictorial world. A *modus vivendi* must be established between the imitative and the decorative, and the compact between these two may be called the convention of the art of painting'' (34).

For Symons Velasquez is a painter who, in relation to the tradition of Spanish painting, discovered the world. His evaluation of this painter embodies many important artistic issues. *Venus and Cupid*, for example, is emblematic of an ideal relationship between the flesh and the spirit, truth and beauty. Symons's belief that truth in art is the means to an end is reiterated in ''Portrait Painters and a Velasquez'' in *Studies in Modern Painters*: ''How precisely Keats had defined what is ultimate in art when he said 'Beauty is Truth, Truth Beauty.' In this picture there is no mere marriage or happy union of truth and beauty, but a transubstantiation. The woman who lies there on the canvas is the divine animal; the flesh, which is merely flesh, and untouched by the desecration of the ideal, is as innocent and as mysterious as life'' (78). Symons describes the artistic ideal which, as Stevenson had shown, adds life to art. At this point, he argues that the artist must, in fact, return to the visible world. Thus, he objects to those painters who seem to have rejected reality for a more insubstantial vision. Although he admires the aesthetic qualities of Monticelli, Rossetti, and Watts, each fails because ''the visible world has seemed too narrow for them'' (*Works* 9:32). In many ways, in fact, Symons appreciated the qualities of Spanish art because there is an overpowering serious sense of reality.

In another context, ''On a Rembrandt in Milan'' contrasts what he considers to be the rather sterile beauty of Italian painting with the sense of life found in Rembrandt. The dominant concern with beauty above every other concern excludes an important sense of life: ''But after an hour in the Brera I begin to feel a certain monotony and a certain lifelessness in these beautiful persons, who seemed to have existed in the world only that they might be painted; in these scenes that had never happened except in a painter's studio; in all that was artificial from the beginning in these pictures painted for ornament'' (*Cities of Italy* 263). Symons defines this form of art as ''an enchanting box of toys,'' a derogatory expression he often uses. The same notion is developed in ''Water Colours and Toys'' in *The Outlook* for February 18, 1905. In contrast to this quality in art, Rembrandt accepts the facts of nature more frankly. Symons elaborates from this characteristic a set of specific artistic criteria: ''Life must be a motive for decoration, and beauty must be added, like a garment, to whatever natural charm life may seem to suggest by its existence'' (*Cities of Italy* 266).

Related to this renewed interest in nature and its peculiarities is the perpetuation by Symons of some aspects of romanticism which he derives from Baudelaire, as well as from Pater. The quality of life which manifests itself in painting tends to be disruptive to the decorative line. This characteristic is part of its value; it instills an important sense of strangeness. Baudelaire, in ''The Universal Exhibition of 1855,'' makes this observation: ''Beauty always has an element of strangeness. I do not mean a deliberate cold form of strangeness, for in that case it would be a monstrous thing that had jumped the rails of life. But I do mean that it always contains a certain degree of strangeness, of simple, unintended, unconscious strangeness, and that this form of strangeness is what gives it the right to be called beauty" (119). The quality of strangeness is connected to the essential individuality of the work of art. A universality of line and form would exclude any sense of individual peculiarity which is part of the life art reflects. Pater picks up this idea from Baudelaire (who derived it from Poe), as his essay on romanticism shows: "It is the addition of strangeness to beauty, that constitutes the romantic character in art; and the desire of beauty being a fixed element in every artistic organization, it is the addition of curiosity to this desire of beauty, that constitutes the romantic temper." And later in the essay he elaborates further:

> With a passionate care for beauty, the romantic spirit refuses to have it, unless the condition of strangeness be first fulfilled. Its desire is for a beauty born of unlikely elements, by a profound alchemy, by a difficult initiation by the charm which wrings it even out of terrible things; and a trace of distortion, of the grotesque, may perhaps linger, as an additional element of expression, about its ultimate grace. (*Appreciations* 246–47)

Symons, in his essay on Whistler, alludes to Baudelaire's use of the term to define the quality of Whistler's art: "And, like Poe, it was a combination of beauty and strangeness which Whistler sought: 'l'étrangeté, qui est comme le condiment indispensable de toute beauté'" (*Works* 9:80). Elsewhere, such as in *Cities of Italy*, the same artistic ideal is referred to, "that there can be no perfect beauty without some strangeness in the proportion" (*Cities of Italy* 148).

Strangeness in beauty is related to the sense of life art manages to retain. Baudelaire makes this point clearly. Symons, particularly in his essay, "Raphael," offers a similar perspective. Raphael is the perfect example of the artist who is dominated by the pure sense of line. In line with Baudelaire and Pater, Symons objects to this sort of art and artist because all that is individual is kept out of his art. Somewhat rhetorically, Symons asks whether it is reasonable to complain about Raphael, "that his women have no strangeness in their beauty; that they do not brood over mysteries, like Monna Lisa?" (125). He is, of course, speaking of both the *Mona Lisa* and Pater's description of its strangeness and mystery. Finally, the question is answered; Raphael's correct drawings exclude life and, therefore, mystery.

The belief that strangeness is an essential characteristic of beauty also defines Symons's interest in exaggeration and caricature as an essential aspect of artistic technique. Blake, who will be dealt with more fully in the next section of this chapter, represents a typical example. The question at issue in his work involves the distinction between correct drawing and expression:

> The mistake of those who have praised such a painter as Blake for his conceptions, and condemned him for his technique, lies in a confusion between what is artistically right, that is, truthful to

beauty, and what is academically correct, that is, faithful to rule. God's arm, in the drawing at the beginning of *Europe*, is out of all human proportion in a figure done after the ordinary type of humanity; but the arm is technically superb, because it expresses the instant energy of omnipotence, not to the mind, but to the mind through the eye, unhesitatingly. Poor technique would have been to have drawn a faultlessly modelled arm, and to have left mind and eye uninterested and unconvinced. (*Works* 9:59–60)

The same issues which determined Symons's reaction to Raphael apply positively to Blake, and we sense that Baudelaire and Pater are the progenitors. Exaggeration gives a sense of life, a sense of surprise, which contributes to the overall beauty and expression of the painting. MacColl, in speaking about those artists he calls the Titans, that is, Goya, Blake, Delacroix, and so on, makes the same point. They do not rely on correct drawing but rather on caricature and exaggeration, on an essential sense of strangeness. They are "ready to sacrifice the still-life form to the effect of movement, or the expression of feeling, elongating, amplifying, distorting" (41). It is for this reason, among others, that Symons appreciated such figures as Goya, whom Baudelaire also admired for those "deformations of animality." Constintin Guys, Honoré Daumier, and Jean Louis Forain also figure importantly in Symons's writing about art. Daumier, for example, is valuable to Symons in part because he influenced a number of painters in the same way as Delacroix; in Daumier "there is an immense vitality in all his figures, abject or caricatured, deformed or transformed, wonderful, heroic, sordid, tragic, bestial" (*From Toulouse-Lautrec* 133).

The ability to express life in art so that what is produced gives a unique feeling of the correspondence between the two is, to Symons, finally related to one's ability to see. Standard modes of perception are to be avoided. Art is, thus, the embodiment of new insight and creates in the viewer, through its strangeness and surprise, new insights. Symons, in fact, often speaks of various artists as having rediscovered the world, for they have broken down an established sense of reality. El Greco set "himself the problem of the representation of life and vision, of the real world and the spiritual world, as if no one had ever painted before" (*Cities and Sea-Coasts* 50). In his short story, "Death of Peter Waydelin," Symons bases much of the plot on the conflict of modes of perception. Finally, seeing that is dominated by certain aesthetics is what one artistically needs to avoid; El Greco *needs* to paint as if no one had ever painted before. It is, as well, in the nature of seeing that true beauty is experienced and defined. As Peter Waydelin says, people do not see beauty in his work: "How should they, when we do our best to train them up within the prison walls of a Raphael aesthetics, when we send them to the Apollo Belvedere, instead of to the marbles of Aegina?" (*Works* 5:102). The story revolves around Peter's struggle to evolve in his painting, to rediscover a vision of the world, and, as we would expect, the sense of beauty he creates is not appreciated or understood by the public.

Within a more theoretical context, Symons deals with this same issue in "The Art of Seeing," which he published in *The Weekly Critical Review*. Here he makes explicit the connection between modes of seeing and the ability to depict a true sense of life. Historically, the art of seeing has determined much of art history: "Each age and each school has its own way of seeing, and the painter who really sees for himself has always been as rare as the poet who feels for himself or the philosopher who thinks for himself" (13). This is the point Symons made in relation to El Greco. He tends to admire those artists who represent the most apparent and radical break with conventional modes of pictorial expression, for he feels that they show life coming back into art. The great artist, within this framework, sees life directly, not through other painters' eyes: "To the great artist there is nothing but life; he must see nothing which is not alive with an organic life of its own, and he must see only through a temperament incessantly alive" (14). For all the reservation he has about Monticelli's work, Symons admires him because of his personal vision. This ability in Monticelli leads to a more general statement about modes of seeing and individuality. The artist does not depict things as the are: "Things as they really are! that paradox for fools. For everyone, probably, for the artist certainly, things are as one sees them; and if most people seem to see things in very much the same way, that is only another proof of the small amount of individuality in the average man, his deplorable faculty of imitation, his inability not only to think but to see for himself" (*Works* 9:40). The quality of vision, however, is often tied to an interest in the primitive, to untrained modes of seeing.

Finally, these aspects of Symons's visual aesthetic, his interest in the impressionistic technique because it strives to combine the aesthetic with the real and his belief that no beauty exists that does not include an element of strangeness, relate to his fascination with aspects of the modern world as the proper material for modern art. In "Modernity in Verse," for example, Symons uses this set of criteria to define the value of a number of artists:

> To be modern in poetry, to represent really oneself and one's surroundings, the world as it is to-day, to be modern and yet poetical, is, perhaps, the most difficult, as it is certainly the most interesting, of all artistic achievements. In music the modern soul seems to have found expression in Wagner; in painting it may be said to have taken form and colour in Manet, Degas, and Whistler; in sculpture, has it not revealed itself in Rodin? (*Works* 8:46)

These are, of course, the artists who matter most to Symons, and we will deal more extensively with Degas, Whistler, and Rodin in the next section of this chapter. At this point, it is useful to note first of all that Sickert, drawing on the teachings of Whistler, had established this same interest in the modern and, particularly, urban world in his introduction to the catalogue of the *London Impressionists' Exhibition* in 1889 referred to earlier. Symons, as well, is interested in the efforts of artists to depict the magic and the poetry which they daily see around them. Degas, of course, is an important source for this belief, particularly in relation to his ability to combine classical design with an inartistic subject matter. In a passage in "The Art of Watts," in fact, Symons identifies this quality in Degas. He has argued against those painters who have turned away from the world. Degas approaches the problem from a different point of view: "But to another, just now more accept-able, school of painters, the modern world is a thing to struggle with, to conquer in fair fight, to compel to one's purpose, no matter at what cost" (*Works* 9:63). At this point, however, Symons is using Degas and Moreau as two extremes. Velasquez is probably a better example. As Symons says, "Velasquez accepts life, making it distinguished by his way of seeing it, not so much choosing from among its moments as compelling a moment to give up the secret of a lifetime" (*Works* 9:64). In other words, he looked at life steadily, and Pater's description of roman-ticism, which seeks to make the difficult into the beautiful, serves as the theoreti-cal base. Velasquez brought the world artistically into his paintings, and, undoubtedly, the appreciation of aspects of the modern world as they were depicted in art led also to Symons's fondness for Guys, Forain, and Daumier. As he says in his essay on Guys, agreeing with Baudelaire who had written *Le Peintre de Vie Moderne* (1863),

> What Guys seeks with most passion is modernity; for on the Boulevard one sees every form of modernity in what is transitory, fugitive, eternally immobile. He seizes the dramatic moments, and as he draws them, exaggerates them. His imagination is so vivid that he can create furiously original drawings as he studies the dim lights behind the stages of music-halls, and the glaring lights along the Boulevard Saint-Martin. (*From Toulouse-Lautrec* 124)

Some Individual Artists

When Symons came in 1929 to publish *From Toulouse-Lautrec to Rodin* he was trying, it seems, to define the artistic tradition with which he had the most sym-pathy. *Studies on Modern Painters* (1925), which is mostly made up of reviews he published in *The Outlook* during 1905, tries on a less extensive scale to establish a similar sense of tradition within the nineteenth century. He reprints some por-tions of his essay, "The Painting of the Nineteenth Century," which had been printed in *Studies in Seven Arts*, as an introduction to the essays that follow it. Un-fortunately, these texts were put together after Symons's breakdown in 1908, and they clearly show that he has lost much of his critical power. Many of the essays included in *From Toulouse-Lautrec to Rodin* are mostly interesting from a patho-logical rather than critical point of view. They present the personality of the author in relation to his understanding of the disturbed personality of the artist. Personality actually becomes the basis of any critical judgments that are made.

The sense of tradition that Symons tries to establish, however, is very impor-tant to his overall aesthetic, but at times the interests he projects in his later work, the artists with whom he seems to identify, do not correspond with what seem to be the dominant concerns of his earlier art criticism. In *Parisian Nights* (1926), for example, he lists some of the artists whom he considers the most important. In order, they are, Degas, Toulouse-Lautrec, Beardsley, and Félicien Rops. But in *From Toulouse-Lautrec to Rodin* we get a sense that Lautrec and Rodin are the most significant figures for Symons, with the other artists scattered in between. Based upon the sheer volume of words Symons wrote about him, Whistler becomes extremely important as well. There is, along with a major essay on Rodin, an extensive study of Whistler published in *Studies in Seven Arts*. In *Studies on Modern Painters*, four chapters are devoted to Whistler. Blake also needs to be added to any list of artists that were important to Symons. A considerable portion of his study, *William Blake* (1907), is devoted to Blake as a visual artist. Symons often uses Blake as an English standard for evaluating and incorporating the artistic ideals of other artists.

Sorting carefully through all that Symons wrote about artists and art, it is possible, first of all, to identify the artists who figure most significantly in his life, who seem most influential; and, secondly, it is possible to establish a sense of the artistic tradition that is implicit in his choice of artists. Degas has to be placed at the head of the list, for it is through Symons's appreciation of this artist that the importance of Velasquez, Whistler, and Toulouse-Lautrec are established. Blake, as already mentioned, offers an English standard and relates to Symons's interest in drawing and expression. Then Symons's perspective on Beardsley, as well as on Augustus John, follows from his analysis of these earlier artists. Finally, Rodin rounds out his interests. Symons alludes to his significance in an undated letter to Austin Dobson: "I don't know if you agree with me in thinking Rodin a man of real genius, one of the greatest men of our time." Symons's discussions of Rodin's sculpture and drawing represent in many ways the fruition of various aspects of his earlier interests. The title *From Toulouse-Lautrec to Rodin* suggests that Symons saw Rodin as the artistic fulfillment of many of his ideals.

Symons's major essay on Degas, "On the Genius of Degas," was published in *Vanity Fair* in 1918 and reprinted in *From Toulouse-Lautrec to Rodin*. The essay is somewhat disappointing, primarily because it does not manifest much critical insight. But, as we have seen, references to Degas tend to surface at various times in Symons's writings. It is possible, then, to discern both the importance and the nature of Degas's influence through an evaluation of the essay and the various references to Degas elsewhere in Symons's work. In *Studies in Two Literatures*, for example, in the essay on James Thompson, Symons discusses what he calls the great problem: How does the artist be real, true to life, and yet poetic, true to art? This question forms a central part of Symons's aesthetic and is particularly relevant to the visual arts, as already seen. Degas functions as a particularly important figure in this debate, no doubt because he, almost more than any other artist of this period, dealt with the pictorial ramifications of this issue. Keith Roberts, in his study, *Degas*, elaborates on this aspect of Degas's work: "Always at the back of Degas's mind was a precise combination of lines and colours, and arrangements of form, that would combine the firmness and inevitability of classical design, the basis of Greek and Roman art and the painting of Raphael and Leonardo, Titian and Poussin, with an impression of life that was immediate and spontaneous" (8). Symons, in the 1890s, when he wrote his essay about Thomson, identified with

Degas's concerns: "For the real modernity we must turn to Degas; we find it in the new employment of a masterly and really classic art in the interpretation of just such actual things: the very race-horses, if you will, but how differently seen, and with what careful and expressive subtlety rendered" (*Works* 8:37). In this case, Degas's paintings, which combine an artistic interest with classical design and an individual interest in modern life, become for Symons the paradigm of art.

In his essay, "Jules Laforgue," in *The Symbolist Movement in Literature*, Symons again refers to Degas in order to discuss some relevant qualities of beauty in art. Laforgue, of course, relates well to Degas because of the use of colloquialism and slang in his poetry; he offers a verbal equivalent to Degas's subject matter. Traditional aspects of the poetic language have been eliminated, just as Degas dispensed with recognizable beauty in his figures. In "Gustave Moreau" in *Studies in Seven Arts* we get a fuller explanation of the same question of beauty: "And in Degas the beauty is a part of truth, a beauty which our eyes are too jaded to distinguish in the things about us. Degas finds in real things, seen at the right moment, all the flames and jewels of Moreau" (*Works* 9:50). Here, unlike his sentiment in the passage quoted from his essay on Watts, Symons values the beauty Degas manages to abstract from the real world. The particular quality of his paintings is thus derived from the fact that he draws on two planes simultaneously.

Symons undoubtedly evolved aspects of his appreciation of Degas through his friendships with George Moore and Walter Sickert. Moore published "Degas: The Painter of Modern Life" in 1890 in the November issue of *Magazine of Art*, and he reprinted it as "Degas" in *Impressions and Opinions* in 1891. Symons reviewed the book for *The Academy*, March 21, 1891. Moore's essay is especially important because it quotes statements that Degas made to him. Ian Dunlop in his study, *Degas*, refers to the quality of Degas's nudes, and he has to rely on Moore's article: "as he explained to George Moore, 'I show them deprived of their airs and affectations reduced to the level of animals cleaning themselves,' and pointing to one of his bathers, he remarked that the woman was like 'a cat licking herself'" (190). Symons refers to the same quality in Degas, especially in his essay, "The Art of Watts." The point here, however, as we have seen, is that Degas seems limited to the imposition of technique on material. His nudes are evidence of this aspect of his art. The same might be said for many of his paintings of ballet dancers, for he catches them often at odd moments when they are at their least beautiful. But he takes these odd, contemporary moments and adds a sense of composition and line. Jean Ingres, the great classical painter, was influential on his work, as Moore points out: "Degas was a pupil of Ingres, and any mention of this always pleases him, for he looks upon Ingres as the finest star in the firmament of French art" (*Impressions and Opinions* 310).

From Symons's point of view, the interest in the ballet and in the classical lines of Ingres combine in an overall interest in the beauties of artificiality, as well as in the qualities of sensuous experience. The worlds of ballet and cafe offered Degas a number of points of interest in relation to artificiality. He contrasts, first of all, the notion of the dancer as emblematic of a form of ideal beauty with the physical realities of ballet performance. Linda P. Muehling comments on this quality in his work in relation to *Little Dancer at Fourteen Years*: "Degas, of course, recognized the central irony of the dance, that the illusion of effortlessness is attained only by effort, and he may have seen in the awkward adolescent the personification of the long process of training that forms a dancer" (7). The contrast between illusion and reality in Degas's paintings of the ballet is further accented, as it is in Daumier, by setting in opposition the world of the stage—in which the lighting creates a glaring sense of artificiality—with the darker, more naturalistic world of the audience. In this way, the paintings function as a running commentary on the relation between art and life, the artificial and the real.

Symons responds clearly to these aspects of Degas's work. As we have seen in his music-hall criticism, he tends, in fact, to use the footlights as emblematic of the barrier between life and art, just as Degas does in his paintings. It is from this point of view as well that Symons identifies the influence of Ingres and classical drawing on the one hand, and Delacroix and the expressiveness of line on the other. In the last section of "On the Genius of Degas" Symons comments extensively on "the sensation of what such imaginations can create," which for Symons is "the finite in the infinite" (*From Toulouse-Lautrec* 119). In his essay on Watteau, "The Prince of Court Painters," Symons again refers to Degas in terms of his ability to combine artistic interests:

> For a similar gravity in the treatment of "light" subjects, and for a similar skill in giving them beauty and distinction, we must come down to Degas. For Degas the ballet and the cafe replaced the Italian comedy of masks and the afternoon conversations in a park. But in Degas there is the same instantaneous notation of movement and the same choice and strange richness of colour; with a quite comparable fondness for seizing what is true in artificial life, and what is sad and serious in humanity at play. (*Colour Studies* 208)

The artificial world is not left aloof in its atmosphere. As Theodore Reff has observed, Degas actually brings together the qualities of Ingres, Delacroix, and Daumier. The "Neoclassical ideal of harmonious form and incisive drawing" is combined with "a Romantic ideal of poetic conception and vibrant colouring" and with "a Realist ideal of trenchant observation and unconventional design" (86). These are, clearly, the artistic ideals Symons derives from Degas, whom he had met through George Moore and Walter Sickert.

Sickert quotes Degas as saying, "Beauty is mystery," a notion which appealed to Symons as well. As he points out in *The Symbolist Movement in Literature*, mystery is now evoked so that beautiful and magical things may be created: "Description is banished that beautiful things may be evoked, magically; the regular beat of verse is broken in order that words may fly, upon subtler wings. Mystery is no longer feared, as the great mystery in whose midst we are islanded was feared by those to whom that unknown sea was only a great void" (5). In much the same way, Degas was interested in the transformation of matter, and so he painted from memory rather than from nature. In this respect, he is distinct as a French impressionist, more allied with Sickert who wanted to paint for illumination rather than to depict illumination. Degas made this point himself: "It is all very well to copy what you see, but it is much better to draw only what you still see in your memory. This is a transformation in which imagination collaborates with memory. Then you only produce what has struck you, that is to say the essential, and so your memories and your fantasy are freed from the tyranny which nature holds over them" (qtd. in Roberts 12).

In his ultimate belief in the imaginative transformation of the world, Degas is like Blake, and Symons tends to identify with this aspect of both artists. In his study, *William Blake*, Symons quotes Blake's *Descriptive Catalogue* (1809) in order to show his dedication to the necessary, imaginative power of painting: "Shall painting be confined to the sordid drudgery of facsimile representations of merely mortal and perishing substances, and not be, as poetry and music are, elevated into its own proper sphere of invention and visionary conception? No, it shall not be so! Painting, as well as poetry and music, exists and exults in immortal thoughts" (*Works* 4:132). As we saw in the first section of this chapter, Symons also admired Blake for the expressiveness of his art. Symons admires Blake's belief that scholastic drawing, with its tyranny of representation, must be curtailed. Blake was "constantly on his guard against the deceits of nature, the temptation of a 'facsimile representation of merely mortal and perishing substances' " (*Works* 4:82). The imaginative and expressive, the conceptual, thus, are the aspects of Blake's work that Symons values most.

In "On a Sale of Blakes," however, which Symons wrote for *The Weekly Critical Review* in 1903, he describes some reservations with the purely conceptual approach, reservations which are in keeping with his renewed interest in the physical world: "But Blake's imagination is in rebellion, not only against the limits of reality, but against the only means by which he can make vision visible to others. And then he allows himself to be mastered by that against which he rebels: that power of the hand by which art begins where vision leaves off" (2). As Symons says, the fundamental conception is never lacking in Blake's work, but he is, at times, mastered by his own vision. But it is in conception, in the ability to create "all those magnificent suggestions" that value resides (2). In "A French Blake: Odilon Redon" Symons describes the quality of suggestion in both artists: "The drawing of Redon, like that of Blake, is only too often faulty; his men and women are only awkward spectres, his human faces lack the very elements of beauty. But he, like Blake, and like Blake only, has given the sense of the beyond, has seen across and through the visible" (207). Redon himself states that he wished to place "the logic of the visible in the service of the invisible" (qtd. in Werner xii).

Aubrey Beardsley represents for Symons the artist who, through the process of drawing, proves to the world that it has failed the artist. The rebellious spirit of

Blake is perpetuated in a satire that manifests beauty's degradation: "Beardsley is the satirist of an age without convictions, and he can but paint hell as Baudelaire did, without pointing for contrast to any contemporary paradise" (*Beardsley* 46). In keeping with the late-nineteenth-century sense that progress and perfectability of man was an illusion, he draws the world as something slightly grotesque. But by doing this he suggests the belief in beauty as well: "It is because he loves beauty that beauty's degradation obsesses him; it is because he is supremely conscious of virtue that vice has power to lay hold upon him" (41). The satiric quality is, as well, related to the quality of line in his drawings. Exaggeration and caricature, as we have seen, appealed to Symons because of their expressiveness. He admires this characteristic in Blake's work. Beardsley raises the same issue and elicits the same defence from Symons. Beardsley "could make a line do what he wanted it to do, express the conception of form which it was his intention to express" (42).

The quality of line and form which alters the conventions of representations ties in interestingly with Beardsley's satiric quality. Symons seems to see the world, as did Baudelaire, in relation to its corruption, its imperfections. Beardsley's vision corresponds well to this vision of reality. By viewing the world in this way, additional pressure is put on the artist to transform it. Ruskin had said that the artist need only reflect and interpret the ideals of God as they manifest themselves in the natural world. In a world dominated by sin and corruption, the artist is forced to transform rather than reflect. Symons makes this point in relation to Beardsley's *The Scarlet Pastorale*: "Need we go further to show how much more than Gautier's meaning lies in the old paradox of 'Mademoiselle de Maupin,' that 'perfection of line is virtue'? That line which rounds the deformity of the cloven-footed sin, the line itself, is at once the revelation and the condemnation of vice, for it is part of the artistic logic which is morality" (40). Appropriately, it is not the morality which alters the world but the artistic logic, which in its perfection of sin becomes a form of morality: "sin transfigured by beauty" (37).

To a large extent Beardsley's art has to be seen as a form of aestheticism, as primarily decorative. Symons appreciates the quality of his drawings in relation to that extreme of which Charles Conder was also emblematic. The influence of Japan and of Whistler can also be discerned:

> From almost the very first he accepted convention; he set himself to see things as pattern. Taking freely all that the Japanese could give him, that release from the bondage of what we call real things, which comes to one man from an intense spirituality, to another from a consciousness of material form so intense that it becomes abstract, he made the world over again in his head, as if it existed only when it was thus re-made, and not even then, until it had been set down in black line on a white surface, in white line on black surface. (43)

Years later, when Symons wrote about Conder, he dealt with the same sense that "one drifts into a rarer world than is lived in by lesser artists: a region of an almost morbid beauty where his fascinating creatures live exquisite lives" (*Studies in Modern Painters* 13).

The fact that Symons chose Beardsley as the topic for his first full-length study suggests the affinity he felt for this sort of artistic world. Degas, too, finally opts for an intense sense of artificiality in his work. ''Art is falsehood,'' he remarked once in his studio (Dunlop 133). The dominance of black and white in Beardsley's drawings accents this purity of artistic ideal. Objects and lines become beautiful rather than useful, accenting the tendency towards the musical standard of art.

Symons's evaluation of Beardsley's last works, however, accents the compromises which the works manifest, not their artistic purity alone; and this compromise is the same one that is referred to throughout Symons's writings:

> Beardsley has accepted the convention of nature itself, turning it to his own uses, extracting from it his own symbols, but no longer rejecting it for a convention entirely of his own making. And thus in his last work, done under the very shadow of death, we find new possibilities for an art, conceived as pure line, conducted through mere pattern, which, after many hesitations, has resolved finally upon the great compromise, that compromise which the greatest artists have made, between the mind's outline and the outline of visible things. (*Beardsley* 46–47)

Thus, by the conclusion of his study he has brought Beardsley to a stage at which he has managed to draw into correspondence aestheticism and a form of naturalism, for Symons the perfect artistic expression. As we have seen, the nature of this relationship forms the basis of his evaluation of various artists. Additionally, the line of mind in correspondence with the line of nature results in the artistic and spiritual illumination Symons values most. Whistler, about whom Symons had written very often, represents this type of artistic perfection. His description of Whistler's world, a description which turns up first of all in his essay, ''The Paintings of the Nineteenth Century,'' then in his review, ''Fantin-Latour and Whistler,'' and finally in his essay, ''Whistler and Manet,'' in *From Toulouse-Lautrec to Rodin*, closely parallels his final description of Beardsley's work:

> It is a world in which I, for one, find almost everything that I have ever cared to see, or to linger over, in what we call the real world. Here, at least, I see through a painter's vision the world which I have always lived in, a world which is full of beautiful appearances, and which, with all its fullness and satisfaction, is only a shadow and symbol of some supreme beauty, which we can see only through that shadow, but which is assuredly enough for one life. (*Studies in Modern Painters* 32–33)

Symons is identifying two related qualities of Whistler's paintings which appeal to him: Whistler creates a sense of beauty which reflects an even more ultimate, supreme beauty; and he accomplishes this beauty by depicting reality so that essentials, not details, are suggested. Artistic finish cannot create this quality; so what Symons admires is the suggestiveness, the sketchy quality which, nevertheless, captures a true sense of what is being depicted. The real secret of Whistler, Symons says, is that ''he does not try to catch the accident when an aspect becomes effective, but the instant when it becomes characteristically beautiful'' (*Works* 9:85). As Moore explains it, the sketchiness is an ideal derived from Japanese art.

By not particularizing nature the Japanese prints reveal more of the essential nature of the things we see: "With a line Utamaro expresses all that he deems it necessary to express of a face's contour. Three or four conventional markings stand for eyes, mouth, and ears; no desire to convey the illusion of a rounded surface disturbed his mind for a moment; the intention of the Japanese artists was merely to decorate a surface with line and colour" (*Modern Painting* 261). Like the Japanese, Whistler aims "to be taken at a hint, divined at a gesture or by telepathy" (*Works* 9:78). It is also for this reason that night figures so importantly in Whistler's work. The soft, outlined reality of the world predominates, while details recede: "As the light fades and the shadows deepen, all petty and exacting details vanish, everything trivial disappears, and I see things as they are in great strong masses: the buttons are lost, but the garment remains; the garment is lost, but the sitter remains; the sitter is lost, but the shadow remains; the shadow is lost, but the picture remains. And *that* night cannot efface from the painter's imagination" (qtd. in Spalding 66). Whistler's nocturnes are studies in the process of outlining for the sake of artistic and expressive perfection.

In line with the use of outline and silhouette, Symons values the expressiveness the paintings seem to project. As already seen in relation to impressionism, Symons states that the moment must become eternity. Monet seems limited in this respect; whereas Whistler, who was himself suspicious of the impressionists, turns the moment into a mysterious beauty which suggests a sense of artistic transcendence. Symons's description of Whistler's portrait of Connie Gilchrist dancing with a skipping-rope evokes this quality of transcendence: "He reveals to us a little, exquisite, pathetic creature, caught in a moment of harmonious movement, as the feet touch the floor between two turns of the skipping-rope" (*Studies in Modern Painters* 48). In line with the qualification of the impressionist ideal, which would only want to show a moment as a moment, Symons further evaluates Whistler, showing that he does much more. His analysis recalls the criticism of Monet in "The Painting of the Nineteenth Century." In reference to a Whistler seascape he comments: "And yet the picture is only a suggestion, a moment out of an unending series of moments; but the moment has been detached by art from that unending and unnoted series, and it gives you the soul of visible things in that miraculous retention of a moment" (*Works* 9:83).

The expressive and suggestive quality of Whistler's paintings is due, as we have seen, to a sense of strangeness implicit in them; the mysterious quality Whistler valued was, in part, the result of line used as expression rather than imitation. Symons learned to appreciate this technique through Baudelaire and Pater. But almost inherent in the belief in the necessity of a quality of strangeness in beauty is an interest in pathological strangeness. Baudelaire, in "The Universal Exhibition of 1855," had argued against strangeness as "a monstrous thing that had jumped the rails of life" (119). Pater, of course, begins to suggest a more pathological curiosity, "the charm which wrings it [beauty] even out of terrible things" (*Appreciations* 247). And he also draws in the grotesque. It is a short step from these ideas to a rather extreme interest in the pathological, and it is from this point of view that Symons's fascination with Toulouse-Lautrec is derived.

In *From Toulouse-Lautrec to Rodin* Symons constructs a long, rather oddly personal essay on Lautrec. As in his study of Baudelaire, the critical methodology is determined by personal identification with the artist. For Symons, as we would expect in much of this postbreakdown work, the sense of identification is very similar in all these cases. He states that Lautrec is the modern equivalent of the Charles Baudelaire. Symons also observes that these artists are always outside society, alienated from it: "Social rules are made by normal people for normal people, and the man of genius (there are limitations of course when one refers to men of genius) is fundamentally abnormal. Lautrec, like the majority of his pictures, was almost entirely abnormal, much more so than Verlaine" (50). At this stage, after his breakdown which left him intellectually shattered, Symons tries to identify abnormality and misfortune with artistic quality. In order to be a great artist one must be, in a sense, mad. Verlaine and Lautrec, through their pain, misfortunes, and calamities, became a great poet and a great painter, respectively.

In line with this thinking, he calls into play the belief in man as essentially corrupt and cruel, an idea which was emphasized during the late nineteenth century in opposition to the social faith in man's perfectability, which professed that all aspects of life, including human nature, were progressing. Symons sees Lautrec's life from a highly personal point of view: "In any case Lautrec possessed in the extreme, what I have always possessed, an unholy fascination for forms of evil, of cruelty, of horror; for abnormalities, for the exaggeration of things to a point in which one's nerves create their own visions" (69–70).

As Symons points out, he had met Lautrec in Paris in 1890, and his appreciation of him was long-standing; but what is interesting about this later evaluation of the artist is the fact that it carries to extremes some essentially sound critical insights. The passage just quoted, for example, makes the connection between the artistic exaggeration of things and mental abnormality. Perversity as a term defining expression and content dominates this essay. What Symons seems to have done is to carry the interest in strangeness to the level of artistic perversity. His discussion of Lautrec's lithographs, especially of the nude that decorates the cover of *Exposition du 20 Avril au 3 Mai, 1903*, is a case in point: "It is interesting to compare these versions of a subject which so many artists have treated, always in a spirit of perversity, from Hieronymus Bosch, with his swooping and crawling abortions, to Rops, with his woman of enticing flesh spread out mockingly upon the cross, from which she has cast off the divine body" (43). Here he sees the sense of perversity as defining artistic quality; his restrained and controlled interest in strangeness has, obviously, become completely pathological. So this rather wild list of artists finds its unity in their artistic abilities to depict and express the perversity of life. Later in the essay the same point is made in relation to some other figures: "Can one imagine a Duse, a Lautrec, a Rodin, a John, a Pachmann—to name five of the greatest artists I have known, all with their different kinds of genius—without

Perversity?'' (98). He also rates his top four visual artists, Degas, Lautrec, Beardsley, and Rops according to what amounts to their fascinating perversity.

Symons's interest in the perversity of line and content is also expressed in the serpent imagery that figures importantly throughout this essay and in other post-breakdown work. The exaggeration of line becomes tantamount to the depiction of a serpent: ''I have referred to the Serpent; perhaps Lautrec went on creating just as a serpent moves, which makes a fulcrum of its own body and seems forever twisting and untwisting its own strength'' (57). Even prior to this time, especially in his article on arts and crafts, he had used imagery associated with serpents to describe art in the industrial world, but here he carries the expressive quality of line, of exaggeration, to the point of perversity.

Elsewhere in the essay on Lautrec, however, there is a sense that this rather obsessive fascination with perversity is a continuation of his earlier interest in exaggeration. He compares Lautrec with Blake, quoting again his comment on the distinction between what is artistically right in painting and what is academically correct. In relation to Lautrec he says, ''he creates line, and the movement of figures—and the passion of gesture, with so unwearied an energy'' (94). He also alludes to Lautrec's interest in Spanish art, particularly Velasquez, Goya, and El Greco, for ''when he [Lautrec] was in Spain, that abnormal quality which in him was predominant, leapt like a flash of lightning'' to the odd and exaggerated qualities in these artists (64). But later he brings in a comment he made in the end of his essay, ''Domenico Theotocopuli: A Study at Toledo.'' In relation to the faces painted by El Greco, he says: ''And those faces, inconceivably more so than those painted by Lautrec,—in spite of the tormented imaginations both possessed, and in that exaggeration which has overtaken so many of those artists who have cared more for energy than for beauty—are all nerves, distinguished nerves, quieted by an effort, or intensely disquieted'' (64).

Embedded in his discussion of Lautrec is a more balanced consideration of his artistic qualities. The above quotation alludes to the problem of overly extensive exaggeration toward which Lautrec at times leaned. It is true, as Edward Lucie-Smith says, that ''like Degas, Lautrec seems to have regarded human beings as animals, creatures without any spiritual dimension worth considering'' (7). And Lautrec often tries to accent the animal quality. Denys Sutton has observed this aspect of Lautrec's work in his brothel paintings. His figures ''stretch themselves on divans like animals'' (8). The appeal on a sensual, animalistic level fascinated Symons, as did the music-hall and cafe world which figures so importantly in Lautrec's paintings; but Symons obviously values Lautrec on sounder, artistic grounds as well. There is, in fact, a dual aspect to the artistry: ''Yet these degraded beings, who endure callously enough their degradation, are not created by a man who hates them; he paints them as they are and not as they are. Their eyes and mouths thirst for they know not what; they have no other sense but that of flesh for flesh'' (*From Toulouse-Lautrec* 4). The point here, somewhat obscured by all the verbiage, is that Lautrec, like Degas, combines flesh with beauty, things as they are and things not as they are. The artist takes the chaos of the extensively corrupt and sinful world and translates it into "that wisdom which is the sorrowful desire of beauty" (69). Lautrec transfigures "things fearful and fervent into forms of pure Beauty" (69).

Much of this quality in Lautrec emerges because of his naturalistic use of scene with an antinaturalistic use of color. He makes us aware, as do many of the artists during this time, of the transforming power of art. An intense sense of life is always present in his paintings, but never without an equally intense imposition of art. Lucie-Smith makes this point in relation to Caravaggio, whose realistic paintings seem to correspond to Lautrec's but which do not. Lautrec wants us to witness the transformation, "the sea-change of life into art," which "implies a typically Symbolist attitude towards what he painted" (11). Symons, as well, appreciates this sense of transformation in Lautrec; for he "can produce beauty out of bestiality, and with pure perfection of Art" (48).

Once we have sifted through the oddly obsessive and personal aspects of Symons's postbreakdown criticism, we find that many of the same artistic principles which he developed years earlier still inform his work. In the later years of his life he simply carries to extremes his own artistic beliefs. In relation to Lautrec, we see that ideals derived from Degas, Baudelaire, and Pater form the backdrop of Symons's discussion.

Many of the same concepts which Symons uses to discuss the major artists of the older generation appear in his discussion of his contemporaries as well. Augustus John, who remained friendly with Symons throughout his life, is described in some ways as if he were Degas. In his review, "A New Painter," for *The Weekly Critical Review*, for instance, he shows his admiration for John by alluding to Degas's technique of painting the world through a keyhole: "He amuses himself by taking Nature always at a disadvantage; if he draws a child, it must be turning its toes in some disgraceful waddle; he waits on a woman's beauty until it sharpens or thickens into character; he waits on an abrupt gesture as other artists wait on a gesture which falls into some continuing curve" (2). Symons later incorporated this review in his longer essay, "Notes on the Genius of Augustus John" in *Studies on Modern Painters*. The title of the essay recalls his other essay, "On the Genius of Degas."

Symons continues this line of comparison elsewhere in the essay, particularly in relation to modes of perception. John does not rely on outmoded ways of seeing. He begins by destroying "some accepted pattern which men have come gradually to recognize as beautiful" (19). The issue of ugliness, of course, is part of what is intriguing in the work of various artists about whom Symons speaks. As he says about John, "we have only to look closely enough and we shall realize that life is never ugly. Beauty or ugliness is in our own eyes, and not on the object on which we look" (20). The sense of ugliness in relation to perception is connected to Symons's belief that strangeness is a part of perfect beauty. The quality of beauty in Degas, or in Lautrec, is due to new subjects, new ways of seeing, to the incorporation of strangeness in traditional notions of beauty.

In many ways, Rodin pulls together for Symons the various characteristics of the visual arts which he values. It may be because Rodin figures so importantly in his theory of the visual arts that Symons alters chronology so drastically in *From Toulouse-Lautrec to Rodin*; Rodin has to be seen as the culmination. His importance is especially strongly felt in relation to Symons's own chronology of artistic development. Symons's return to nature as an adjustment to his earlier aestheticism reflects, in part, his appreciation of Rodin. In *Cathedrals of France*, in fact, Rodin's comments on his own artistic development form a good parallel to Symons's growth as an artist. The change in his attitude toward his models shows a reorientation of purpose: "One must only observe, while intervening the least possible, in order not to disturb the actors of this drama and not to *denature* them. Formerly I chose my models and indicated their poses. I have long ago left that error behind. All models are infinitely beautiful, and their spontaneous gestures are those that one feels are the most divine" (94). The operative word here is "denature." Rodin seeks a more natural correspondence between the artist's mind and the world that he uses as his model. The point in Symons's early aestheticism, as well as in his continuing appreciation of artists like Charles Condor, is that this form of art self-consciously denatures everything it touches. Beardsley, too, is implicated. The beauty of art exists because it is different from nature.

Symons, however, is not abandoning this ideal; rather, he finds in Rodin a more balanced approach. Nature is taken for what it may yield, and an ideal artistic balance between it and the artist is sought. Symons's description of Rodin's methodology, particularly in relation to his use of models, unifies a number of issues which occur elsewhere in his writing about the visual arts: "There was a time, Rodin will tell you, when he sought for beautiful models; when he found himself disappointed, dissatisfied, before some body whose proportions did not please him." His view changes, however: "He has come to trust nature so implicitly that he will never pose a model, leaving nature to find its own way of doing what he wants of it. All depends on the way of seeing, on the seizure of the perfect moment, on the art of rendering, in the sculptor's relief, 'the instant made eternity'" (*Works* 9:2–3). The phrases that crop up throughout Symons's criticism, such as the quotation from Browning, "the instant made eternity," or "all depends on the way of seeing," seem to fall together quite nicely in his discussion of Rodin. We sense that he has found a figure who embodies the aesthetic theories he has been developing over the years.

One aspect of Rodin's art which Symons identifies in the above passage is the quality of life which he is able to express. Symons makes this point as well in his review article, "A Note on Rodin": "But it is above all of nature that he speaks, of the unfathomable beauty of life; and when he praises life it is like a priest who praises God. As Spinoza was drunk with divinity, so Rodin is drunk with the divinity of life" (107). The imagery of divinity connects Rodin's appreciation of life to the belief that it must be "the instant made eternity." Symons always takes the inclusion of nature in art out of the realm of the ordinary, but he nevertheless recognizes that the rather sensuous appreciation of the world is necessary. In "Rodin" in *Studies in Seven Arts* he accents the fact that Rodin's art is almost literally rooted in life: "His clay is part of the substance of the earth, and the earth still clings about it as it comes up and lives. It is at once the flower and the root; that of others is the flower only, and the plucked flower" (*Works* 9:1). The imagery of flower and earth corresponds with Symons's dual artistic aims, aims which Rodin seems to have realized. As Somerville Story points out, Rodin struggled with the same extremes: "For long he oscillated, as he himself said, between the influence of Michelangelo and that of Phidias, the Christian and the pagan—the expressive and the plastic" (15).

The delicate balance which Rodin's art seems to embody, which links his creation with nature's, also establishes certain relationships with the viewer. As we saw in the chapter on dramatic theory, Symons's sense of a perfect drama involves the spectator in the process of artistic transformation. Our ability to appreciate Rodin seems contingent upon the same process of participation. Rodin requires an active, not purely contemplative, response to his work: "He gives a twofold burden to the lines of his work: that which they express, and that which they suggest. The lines begin to whisper something to the soul, in a remote voice, and you must listen in order to hear it. The eyes have something more to do than see" (*Works* 9:7). Symons is trying to justify the ways of Rodin to man, but he is also stating what he considers to be the proper, active response to art. The art he enjoys requires that the imagination become actively involved in its completion. It is for this reason that he dislikes unlimited detail and realism, for it tires the eyes and mind. There is no room for the imagination. The active and imaginative involvement in art also mirrors, as well as influences, our engagement with life. We "divine over again" the mystery embodied in art: "The work is no longer a block cut sharply off from nature; it is part of ourselves, to be understood only as we understand one another" (*Works* 9:7–8).

As has been suggested already, Rodin also seems to project for Symons an interest in the modes of seeing. On an immediate level, our appreciation of Rodin's work is dependent upon our ability to see its quality. We need to forget any ready-made ways of seeing. This processes, however, is difficult. Ultimately, Rodin's way of seeing creates an insight that allows for an appreciation of the doctrine of correspondences. Symons, in this case, tends to describe art in terms of synecdoche; an instant or individual perception becomes emblematic of broader issues, vaster forces. In a very real way, the instant can be made eternity if we see in it its correspondence with the rest of nature. As does Rodin in his art, we have to break down ways of seeing which obscure life: "When a woman combs her hair, he will say to you, she thinks she is only combing her hair: no, she is making a gesture which flows into the eternal rhythm, which is beautiful because it lives, because it is part of that geometrical plan which nature is always weaving for us" (*Works* 9:2). The ability to see without preconceived frameworks is essential, life-giving, and out of this perception comes a sense of the pattern which art projects.

In a very real way, the points Symons makes in relation to Rodin could also have been derived from Ruskin, particularly in relation to our ability to see in nature the correspondence of all its parts. It is for this reason that Ruskin tries to balance the ideal of detail with the ideal of interpretation. He is concerned with revelation through the forms of the natural world, and this revelation requires a certain artistic ability. In terms of our sense of perspective, for example, he draws a balance Rodin would agree with as well: "And hence in art, every space or touch in which we can see everything, or in which we can see nothing, is false. Nothing can be true which is either complete or vacant; every touch is false which does not suggest more than it represents, and every space is false which represents nothing" (*Modern Painters* I:329–30). Ruskin, of course, did not appreciate the intense suggestiveness of Whistler; the fondness for unfinished works was contrary to all he valued in art. But Ruskin's point here in relation to the use of detail applies to Rodin's artistic methods and defines what Symons appreciated in Rodin's work.

Seeing is also related to the nature of beauty Rodin is able to create. Beauty cannot be defined by traditional modes of perception. Story, using Rodin's own words, elaborates this same point, and the issue of ugliness in nature is the same one that Symons describes often in his work: "He [Rodin] would not admit the existence of ugliness in nature. 'That which one commonly calls ugliness in nature may in art become great beauty,' he would say. 'As it is simply the power of character which makes beauty in art,' he explained on one occasion, 'it often happens that the more a creature is ugly in nature, the more it is beautiful in art'" (15). Rodin goes on to say that falsification and artificiality, line and decoration that do not correspond to line in realty, are what are truly ugly in art. As with Ruskin, this does not mean that he wants faithful realism. Details distract from the truth of line as well: "As to polishing nails and ringlets of hair, that has no interest for me; it distracts attention from the leading lines and the soul which I wish to interpret" (qtd. in Story 15).

In his sculptures and drawings, Rodin's use of lines as both suggestive and as corresponding with the reality which it depicts also brings to light his use of exaggeration, an important element in all artistic creation for Symons. In speaking about the relationship between Rodin and Michelangelo, Symons accents the fact that Michelangelo, for all his artistry, is still too rhetorical, too mannered in his expression: "His exaggeration is not the exaggeration of the Greeks, nor is it Rodin's, an attempt always at greater fidelity, at an essentially more precise exactitude; it deviates, for his own purposes, along ways of his own" (*Works* 9:6). Earlier in the essay he observes that "for the living representation of nature in movement, something more is needed than exact copy" (*Works* 9:4). At this point in the argument, he brings in Mérimée's comment: "All art is exaggeration à propos" (*Works* 9:4). As Symons observes, "it is on the perfection of this à propos that everything depends, and here Rodin's training as a draftsman gives him his safety in freedom" (*Works* 9:4). The paradox of artistic expression is that through appropriate exaggeration a more exact correspondence with the truth of nature can be achieved. Rodin's drawings accomplish this correspondence. Albert Elsen has observed that "we see in Rodin's work qualities of drawing that go beyond the mimetic to the poetic" (23). From Symons's point of view the poetic is also attached to life, to the mystery that moves through nature: "In these astonishing drawings from the nude we see woman carried to a further point of simplicity than even in Degas: woman the animal, woman in a strange sense, the idol. Not even the Japanese have simplified drawing to this illuminating scrawl of four lines, enclosing the whole mystery of the flesh" (*Works* 9:10).

5

Music and Musicians

Symons's interest in music began in his childhood. Several of his letters to Churchill Osborne ask questions about various composers and musical scores, as well as voice opinions on musicians and music criticism. In a letter dated November 24, 1880, for example, he mentions that he has been reading Roekstor's *History of Music*, which he thought was interesting but in which he found the text rather poor for instructional purposes. He was, at this stage, learning to play the piano and to appreciate the various forms of music. Later in the same letter, he thanks Osborne for his comments on Berlioz's work: "Thanks for your account of Berlioz—you have greatly interested me in him—has he much pianoforte music? I suppose his operas are published in England, are they not? I am much obliged for your advice in regard to editions of music—if it were not for your kind help I should be utterly at sea in such matters." Symons, during these early years, depended upon Churchill Osborne for artistic guidance in general, and his comments in this early letter show his relative ignorance of musical matters. But the questions he asks also show his intense interest in music, which is beginning to lead him to the study of various new composers and works: "Do you consider Schumann a very great musician, i.e., is he one of the *greatest*? I suppose his music is very difficult? I see Liszt referred to sometimes, he is not one of the greatest geniuses, is he? My notion may be very erroneous, but that is the idea I have of him" (letter, November 24, 1880).

As is usual with Symons, he wants to be exposed to and appreciate only the very best. He is a fifteen-year-old boy looking for the geniuses of the world. But as the letters to Osborne continue Symons becomes more confident; he is more fully able to rely on his own ideas about music and art.

"A Prelude to Life" also shows the importance music had in Symons's life. The picture of his early years that Symons paints is hardly idyllic; the imagery of prisons and prisoners defines his own sense of entrapment. The world to which he was exposed seemed insensitive and unfriendly. The pious, middle-class existence that his family led offered the growing, exploring Symons little stimulation. He turned inward, to his imagination, as a means of escape.

The description of his first real introduction to music is also developed to accent music as a form of escape. He had been taught musical scales and exercises, had tried to learn music, but with very little success. The problem, it seems, was the confinement he felt, the lack of individual expression. Scales and exercises had no meaning for him; they were part of the tedium from which he was trying to escape. Symons mentions that the headmaster of his grammar school had asked him to go into his drawing room to copy some work for him, again an activity of tedium and repetition. But the stage has been set for an alternative experience. A German music master comes in and begins to play the piano: "He played something which I had never heard before, something which seemed to me the most wonderful thing I had ever heard" (*Works* 5:17). He could not go on copying. The music seemed literally to envelop him. He finds out that he is listening to Chopin's Funeral March. He goes on to say, continuing the contrast of the sublime and the mundane, that he learned no more scales and exercises. Instead, he learned to play this and other pieces and to read music well; when he was not reading a book, he was "reading a piece of music at the piano" (*Works* 5:18).

This scene, it seems, is designed to show music as a means of transcendence and escape. Chopin, in fact, made a deep and lasting impression on Symons. His reaction to Chopin's music mirrors Baudelaire's response to Wagner's music, particularly as it is described in his essay, "Richard Wagner et *Tannhäuser* à Paris." In this essay, Baudelaire describes at great length the exhilarating sense of being freed from the bonds of gravity and the ecstasy of soaring above and beyond the natural world. These types of responses are not unusual in the literature of romanticism. E. T. A. Hoffmann, in writing about Beethoven in *Kreisleriana*, suggests that music opens to man a kingdom, a world which has nothing in common with the world of sense which surrounds him. This romantic vision is clearly in line with Symons's desire to rise above his limiting environment: "Books and music, then, together with my solitary walks, were the only means of escape which I was able to find from the tedium of things as they were" (*Works* 5:18).

Browning's various poems on music were undoubtedly influential as well. In *Introduction to the Study of Browning*, for example, Symons comments that " 'Abt Vogler' is an utterance on music which exceeds every attempt that has ever been made in verse to set forth the secret of the most sacred and illusive of the arts" (128).

Symons's short story, "Christian Trevalga," included in *Spiritual Adventures*, develops this same theme in its description of music as an ideal and transcendent form of expression. The opening sentence in the story makes clear that to the true musician music has very little in common with the world of the senses: "He had never known what it was to feel the earth solid under his feet" (*Works* 5:57). The music Christian plays never creates pictures. He could not understand music as the expression of pictures or as associated with any sensuous experience.

Symons's long-standing interest in music led to an extensive output of music criticism. *Plays, Acting, and Music* (1903) includes some of his essays on music from the *Academy*. *Studies in Seven Arts* (1906) contains some of his most substantial essays in music criticism, "Beethoven," "The Ideas of Richard Wagner," and "The Problem of Richard Strauss." The 1928 edition of *Plays, Acting, and Music* was considerably revised by Symons so as to become primarily a book of music criticism. He added to it many of the music reviews he wrote for *The Saturday Review* from 1907 up to his breakdown in 1908. "Music in Venice," which appeared in *The Saturday Review* on October 17, 1908, clearly shows the signs of his breakdown. The songs he hears in the Venice night are, to Symons, "instinctive and remote, melancholy and passionate, what strange and obscure secrets you conceal! Crimes and carnality of Doges . . ." (481).

Symons matured as a writer and critic during an era of articulate musicians. Schumann, Wagner, and Berlioz, among others, were writing about music as well as composing it. Berlioz actually earned his living as a reviewer. As David Cairns says in his introduction to Berlioz's *Evenings in the Orchestra*, "He was at least as renowned for his articles as he was for his music, and much more popular" (12).

Symons, like many of the writers he admired, did not devote his music criticism to a consideration of the technical aspects of the composition and performance; rather, he concentrated on the impressions the music created. It is undoubtedly true that his technical knowledge was limited, but his appreciation of music was certainly informed and articulate. Schumann's ideal of musical criticism is similar to the perspective Symons takes. Schumann did not want to approach his subject from the historical or technical viewpoint: "We confess, however, that for us the highest form of criticism is that which reflects most closely the impression made by the stimulating original itself" (*Musical World* 36). It was also Schumann who noted one of the difficulties in music criticism, the difficulty of critical proof. Paradoxically, the critical problem is the result of those aspects of music that late-nineteenth-century writers admired most:

> In no other field of criticism is it so difficult to offer proof as in music. Science can argue with mathematics and logic. To poetry belongs the golden, decisive word. Other arts have accepted nature herself as arbiter, from whom they have borrowed their forms. Music is the orphan whose father and mother no one can determine. And it may well be that precisely in this mystery lies the source of its beauty. (*Musical World* 36)

Symons's view of music is similar; its beauty is directly related to the fact that it is nonreferential.

In order to deal adequately with the wealth of Symons's writing on music, it is best to consider two areas of interest. The division, in relation to Symons's work, is natural. As we saw in the chapter on drama, Symons considered acting as much an art as playwriting. In his music criticism, he views performance again as an art. The best way, then, to organize a discussion of his music criticism seems, first of all, to consider his overall theory of music and, secondly, to evaluate his interest in individual performers.

Music Theory

Symons's abilities as a music critic were developed as much from reading about music as from listening to it. His letters to Osborne often speak of books on music, as well as of particular musical compositions. Symons makes clear whom he considers to be the important figures in music criticism and theory in a short essay, "On Musical Criticism," which appeared in *The Academy* on August 2, 1902 and which he reprinted in its entirety in *Plays, Acting, and Music* (1903). The essay is written in response to an objection that very little of interest had been written about the art of music. Symons begins his contrary view by stating that although "music is much more difficult to write about than any of the other arts, a great deal that is both interesting and valuable has been written about music, not only from a technical but from a general point of view" (177). Symons, of course, is mostly interested in nontechnical analysis of music and performance.

Symons then goes on to list those writers of music criticism he most admires, and it seems they are given to us in order of importance in Symons's own thinking about music. The top four are Richard Wagner, whose "prose writings present us with a body of theory concerning his art such as few poets or painters have given us"; Robert Schumann, "who wrote . . . with eager and watchful insight, which was rarely deceived, ready to discover a new genius before that genius had really discovered himself"; Franz Liszt, particularly in his study of Chopin; and Hector Berlioz, who "was a musical critic for thirty years, besides writing one of the most delightful and quite the most extraordinary of autobiographies" (177). He also mentions other writers-composers, including Gluck and Saint-Saëns, but it is apparent that the first four really formed the basis for Symons's ideas of music and music criticism.

Symons also identifies in this essay, without direct reference to other writers, aspects of music that he admires. Music, first of all, is difficult to write about, as Schumann had stated, "because music is the one absolutely disembodied art, when it is heard, and no more than a proposition of Euclid, when it is written" (179).

In comparison with the critical writing about the other arts, music suffers somewhat, primarily because music criticism is, at best, a compromise between what the programmes tell us about a piece, which often tell only which instruments are playing when, and a written "rhapsody which has nothing to do with the notes" and which is presented more "as an interpretation of what the notes have said in an unknown language" (179). As Schumann had said, and as Symons reiterates in this essay, poetry has words, painting has subject and handling, "but music has no subject outside its meaning as music" (*Musical World* 85). Symons believes in a transcendental theory of music. Music, as in "Christian Trevalga," transcends the human realm; it is a language spoken by immortals: "Music has indeed a language, but it is a language in which birds and other angels may talk, but out of which we cannot translate their meaning" (180).

Richard Wagner

Symons's general remarks about music and music criticism in "On Musical Criticism" give a clear sense of his belief in the transcendent quality of music, as well as elaborate the critical tradition he admires. Richard Wagner's prose writings had much to do with Symons's own work. He read William Ashton Ellis's complete translated edition, which began to appear in 1893, and he was somewhat familiar with the original prior to that, although his German was not really strong. He comments, however, in "The Ideas of Richard Wagner" that, with the permission of Ellis, he has modified a word of the translation here and there in his own quotations from it.

"The Ideas of Richard Wagner" is one of Symons's longest and most involved essays. In *Studies in Seven Arts* it runs for seventy-three pages and is the longest by far in that volume. His essay on Beethoven, which runs for thirty-one pages, should probably be included as well since it is as much an essay on Wagner's "Beethoven" as on Beethoven the composer. These two essays, both of which Symons reprinted in volume 9 of *Collected Works*, seem to function as one long essay on Wagner. By the conclusion of "The Ideas of Richard Wagner" Symons feels comfortable designating him the quintessential artist of the nineteenth century: "Of the future it is idle to speak; but, at the beginning of the twentieth century, may we not admit that the typical art of the nineteenth century, the art for which it is most likely to be remembered, has been the art, musical and dramatic, of Richard Wagner?" (*Works* 9:195).

Symons begins his essay on Wagner with autobiographical information. Wagner's *A Communication to My Friends* (1851) is, to Symons's mind, an autobiography of ideas. He feels that ideas which are based in life, in the living temperament of the artist, are the most vital and valid. Symons makes this belief clear in relation to Baudelaire's essay on Wagner. Baudelaire evaluates the artist-critic personality, of which Wagner was the supreme example, by stating that the artist must, in fact, become a critic. Artists must think about their art, must become critics. Symons reiterates this idea: "It would be prodigious for a critic to become a poet, and it is impossible for a poet not to contain a critic" (150). In his early sections of this essay, Symons evaluates Wagner as critic based on his estimation of his life: "The chief distinction and main valve of Wagner's theoretical writing lies in this fact, that it is wholly the personal expression of an artist engaged in creative work, finding out theories by the way, as he comes upon obstacles or aids in the nature of things" (151). He goes on to state explicitly that Wagner's work has substance and is vital because it comes from the very soil and substance of his life. In relation to this belief, Symons focuses on Wagner's distinction between two kinds of artist, "the feminine who absorbs only art, and the masculine who absorbs life itself, and from life derives the new material which he will turn into a new and living art" (151).

The major portions of the essay contain a detailed analysis of Wagner's two major critical works, *The Art-Work of the Future* (1849) and *Opera and Drama* (1851). In respect to *The Art-Work of the Future*, Symons is again intrigued by Wagner's interest in art as "an immediate vital act." He goes on to quote Wagner: "The first and truest fount of Art reveals itself in the impulse that surges from Life into the work of art; for it is the impulse to bring this unconscious, instinctive principle of Life to understanding and acknowledgement as Necessity" (qtd. 155). In relation to the vital, unconscious and instinctive principle of life, Symons admires the strong distinction Wagner makes between the value of the intuitive and the conscious mind. The conscious intellect exploits and splinters those direct impulses.

As Jack M. Stein shows in *Richard Wagner and the Synthesis of the Arts*, *The Art-Work of the Future* has two main themes: to proclaim an art work which would "appeal to the masses because it was an expression of their own thought, feelings and aspirations" and to portray "a work of art which is the product of a fusion of the separate phases of art" (61). These are both romantic ideals. Symons, too, associates the life impulse with primitive, folk life. This reasoning explains his interest in the folksong as an essential musical and poetic expression. To Symons, and to Wagner, the modern inability to understand the impulses that come directly from the people—perhaps because the industrial age is too much dominated by the scientific or intellectual mind—leads to what Wagner calls caprice, "the mother of all unnaturalness," and, as Symons says, to "the whole art-traffic of our shameless age" (155). Within the context of ideals, Symons admires Wagner's concern for the root of artistic expression, which seems lacking in the modern world, as an answer to the failings in current artistic expression. Art, as Wagner defines it, is not an artificial product, something manufactured by the mind as if it were a machine producing objects, mirroring the workings of the industrial landscape. As Symons says, art is "not a product of mind only, which produces science, but of that deeper impulse which is unconscious" (155). Yeats, who said he found Symons's essay on Wagner to be extremely helpful when it appeared in 1908, undoubtedly saw his own interests in the peasantry and their association with the Great Memory in Symons's discussion of Wagner.

As Munro says, Symons "believes that a great work of art is a composition of forces shaped by the artist into a 'harmony,' and possessed of an 'intensity,' [to quote Yeats] in which one discovers something supernatural, a stirring as it were at the roots of the hair" (30). This comment is certainly attuned to the imagery Symons derives from Wagner's prose. *Balance* and *harmony* are crucially important words. The folk song is emblematic of these qualities: "In the folksong words and tune had always grown together" (*Works* 9:162). Symons continues to describe Wagner's interest in the organic process by which all the arts may come together in opera. Music, dance, and poetry had then not yet been combined properly; they were still "a compact of three egoisms" (156). Wagner describes the development of drama and music to their individual perfections: "Where we see tragedy supreme in Shakespeare and music supreme in Beethoven we see two great halves of one universal whole" (*Works* 9:158). Words and music must come together:

"Just as the living folk-melody is inseparable from the living folk-poem, at pain of organic death, so can music's organism never bear the true, the living melody, except it first be fecundated by the poet's thought" (165). Wagner's point is based upon what he sees as the fundamental error of allowing music in opera to take precedence over words, "that a means of expression (music) has been made an end, while the end of expression (drama) has been made a means" (160). His discussion of the evolution of opera, of which Symons gives a rather detailed account, is based upon this belief.

Wagner's aim throughout, an aim which Symons greatly admires, is to allow music and drama to discover the ideal within us. In drama, "the unit man [must] expand to the essence of human species" (181); and we have to have "poetry carried to its utmost limits in drama; and music, carried to its utmost limits as the interpreter and deepener of dramatic action" (*Works* 9:181). In this way the artist has, indeed, created a "poetic figment of wonder" (171). This form of art also goes beyond the aestheticism whose sterility had concerned Symons earlier. Wagner's art is romantic and symbolist; it invokes a reality outside itself. The problems of modern art emanate from the lack of connection with life itself, Symons suggests: "The root of all evil in modern art, and especially in the art of drama, Wagner finds to be the fact that 'modern art is a mere product of culture, and not sprung from life itself'" (185). Wagner's "whole conception of art was unselfish, never in any narrow sense 'art for art's sake,' but art concealing art for the joy of the world" (180). Symons still admires the artistic ideals of aestheticism, but these ideals should ultimately point to a separate reality outside the work of art. His fascination with art's ability to conceal art, which he derived in part from Mérimée, seems related to his concern with true artistic principles combined with a symbolist reality. The ultimate unity as Wagner has outlined it, when the poet's intention and the musician's expression are so blended that neither can be distinguished from the other, leads to the artistic paradox: "Thus, at its height of realised achievement, 'art conceals art'" (175). Symons uses this classical concept often to define the perfect artistic achievement: *ars est celare artem*. The creation of art should not be obtrusively apparent. He sees Wagner and Coleridge as united in their artistic concerns: "Wagner and Coleridge, two great masters of technique, teach us equally that the greatest art can be produced only by the abandonment of art itself to that primal energy which works after its own laws, not conscious of anything but the need of exquisitely truthful speech" (191). Wagner's interest in hiding the mechanical means of production—that is, the orchestra—is part of his desire to express unobtrusively more important and intense truths. Gluck, who set out to reorganize the operatic tradition, had similar motives, as he states in his preface to *Alcestë*. He wanted music to support the emotional expression without interrupting the action.

Symons realizes, however, that the use of music in drama leads to an even more ideal form of expression. Drama, which is "the mirror image of life," becomes more significant "dipped in the magic spring of music," to quote Wagner, "which frees it from all the realism of matter" (184). Within this context,

Wagner's description of music as the test or touchstone for drama becomes extremely significant for Symons. Again, as in painting, music becomes the standard by which good drama is judged: "Could there be a more essential test of drama, or a test more easily applied by a moment's thought? Think of any given play, and imagine a musical accompaniment of the closest kind. I can hear a music as of Mozart coming up like an atmosphere about Congreve's *Way of the World*, as easily as I can hear Beethoven's *Coriolan* overture leading in Shakespeare's *Coriolanus*" (184).

The use of music as a standard for all art is based upon music's ability seemingly to transcend earthly matters. Symons had made this point earlier in his discussion of the combined arts in opera. Music as the orchestra presents it speaks with its own language, comes from an inarticulate realm. He quotes Wagner again: "The orchestra possesses a distinct faculty of speech, 'the faculty of uttering the unspeakable,' or rather that which, to our intellect, is unspeakable. This faculty it possesses in common with gesture, which expresses something that cannot be expressed in words" (174). Wagner, in *A Pilgrimage to Beethoven*, had also described the musical-orchestral quality of a work. In line with his belief that music and drama both express the inner nature of human life in action, he states that the instruments of the orchestra represent the primal organs of nature, capable of expressing only elemental emotions. The human voice, on the other hand, is more individual, speaks from the human heart. Combined, they speak from the most universal to the most individual.

As Symons rightly saw, such a notion of music could lead to some difficult contradictions. From 1854 Wagner was pervasively influenced by the work of Arthur Schopenhauer, which as Symons says, supplied him with "a complete theory, or what may be called a transcendental philosophy, of music" (173). Schopenhauer, indeed, glorified music as a super-art associated with the metaphysical will, the ultimate reality which exists behind the world of physical phenomena. Music is independent of the representational world: "Music is by no means, like the other arts, an image of the Ideas: but an image of the will itself, whose objectification the Ideas are. It is for this reason that the effect of music is so much mightier and more penetrating than that of the other arts; for these speak only of the shadow, music however of the essence" (qtd. in Stein 114). As Stein observes, Wagner found all of this theory irresistibly fascinating: "He not only accepted it fully, but it so affected his views on art and his creative faculties that one can say he was never again the same as an artist after having read it" (114). In his essay, "On Franz Liszt's Symphonic Poems" (1857), Wagner elaborates his Schopenhauerean creed, which sounds like a reevaluation of his music-drama theory: "Hear my creed: music can never, regardless of what it is combined with, cease being the highest, the redeeming art. Its nature is such that what all the other arts only hint at becomes in it the most indubitable of certainties, the most direct and definite of truths" (qtd. in Stein 116–17).

Symons notes this change in Wagner's writing; in particular he realizes that in *Opera and Drama* "nothing had been said of any such transcendental view of music, music being treated indeed almost wholly in regard to its dependence upon words and action" (172). It is Symons's belief, however, that Wagner's early theories of music are due to his primary concentration on music in relation to drama. Wagner's early newspaper writing shows that he saw music within an ideal framework during that period as well: "The language of music is eternal, infinite, ideal. It expresses nothing specific; not the passion, the love, the longing of this individual, but passion, love, longing themselves, in the abstract, and in the most universal terms" (qtd. in Stein 26).

Wagner's study of Beethoven, which Symons calls "the wonderful book," is the text in which Wagner goes deepest into music as music. It is, as Stein shows, "a new theory of the synthesis of the arts, a theory which succeeds, in Wagner's eyes at least, in justifying a *Gesamtkunstwerk* in terms of Schopenhauer's theories on art, which rules out synthesis in no uncertain terms" (157). Stein has it right, but Symons is more interested in the ideal realism. Music, Wagner shows, us, eliminates the outer world so that "we can dream, as it were, awake, redeemed from the strivings of the individual will, and at one with nature, with our inmost selves. Music, he shows us, blots out civilization as the daylight blots out lamplight" (189).

Although Symons spends a great deal of time discussing Wagner's *The Art-Work of the Future* and *Opera and Drama*, his real interests focus on the theory contained in *Beethoven*. His own essay, "Beethoven," shows that he felt Wagner had described both the artistic ideals of the artist and the art work. He asks in the end of his essay on Wagner whether or not we see music as Schopenhauer saw it, as an Idea of the world. The musician speaks the highest wisdom in a language his reason does not understand. Symons still shows that essentially he holds with the purely transcendental view.

Immediately, then, in his essay on Beethoven he quotes Wagner's study and alludes to a number of characteristics of artistic expression he finds valid: "The foundation of Beethoven's art is, as Wagner pointed out, a great innocence. It is the unconscious innocence of the child and the instructed innocence of the saint" (130). Wagner describes Beethoven in terms of the child's innocence. In his work the "world regains its childhood's innocence," and he "speaks but of the essence of things to him, and shows them in the tranquil light of Beauty" (V: 92). Symons follows the same line of thought: "There is, in every artist, a return toward childhood; he must be led by hand through the streets of the world, in which he wanders open-eyed and with heedless feet. Pious hands must rock him to sleep, comfort his tears, and labour with him in his playtime. He will speak the wisdom of the child, unconsciously, without translating it into the formal language of experience" (130). The saint and the child have access to inner visions, experiences which are denied to the worldly. Thus throughout this essay Symons mixes Wordsworthian imagery of childhood recollections with saintly visions of paradise. "Today shalt thou be with me in Paradise," Wagner quotes, "—who has not heard these words of the Redeemer, when listening to the 'Pastoral Symphony' " (V:92). Symons, in his article for *The Saturday Review*, "Wagner at Covent Garden," comments on the conditions at Bayreuth using the same imagery: "The conditions at Bayreuth are perfect, not only because of a theatre designed after Wagner's pattern, for that we have now got at Munich, but because Bayreuth is a little provincial place in the midst of pine-woods, where the religious-minded can go into retreat, and be disturbed by nothing in the world" (617). Wagner, indeed, compared Beethoven, the quintessential artist, to Tiresias, the blinded seer, "to whom the world of appearance has closed itself, and whose inner eye beholds instead the ground of all appearances" (V:92).

For Symons, the relationship of the artist to the world around him was extremely significant. In "Music and Social Flurry," for example, he argues with the premise that musical composition can in any substantial way be encouraged by society: "Great art is produced simply out of personal impulse, and has its birth for the most part in solitude. No external aiding, no social demand, no expectant public, can have anything but a bad effect, if it has any effect at all, on a sincere artist" (432). The child and the saint are emblematic artists. They are not, on the one hand, indoctrinated into the habits of the world, the stock responses, so to speak. As Symons says, recalling Wordsworth, "the child still remembers something of *that imperial palace whence he came*"; on the other hand, "the saint lives always in such a house not made with hands" (132).

What the child and the saint are able to discover is the reality which lies behind appearances. Symons again uses Schopenhauer as the source, a source which is focused for him in Wagner's study: "The musician, he tells us, 'reveals the innermost essential being of the world, and expresses the highest wisdom in a language his reason does not understand' " (131). Wagner, too, keeps coming back to the phrase, "expresses the highest wisdom in a language his reason does not understand."

The romantic opposition to reason made music as Schopenhauer had defined it even more significant. Symons here seems to be identifying himself with a line of thinkers and musicians who are essentially romanticists. The language issue, then, centers on what language is able to express. In *Opera and Drama* Wagner had suggested that there were two types of language, the modern, prosaic and the older, more emotionally vital. Symons suggests that music is "older and deeper and closer to us than our reason," whereas words are more definite and appeal to the mind. This opposition, as we have seen, relates to the other arts as well: "The musician, through what is active in his art, creates over again, translates for us, that whole essential part of things which is ended when we speak, and deformed when we begin labouring to make it visible in marble, or on canvas, or through any of the actual particles of earth" (132).

It is clear that Wagner's *Beethoven* reconciles his theories in *Opera and Drama* with Schopenhauer's transcendental theory of music. The dramatist and the composer, as Stein points out, may be combined: "Now, when the composer and the dramatist are one and the same person, his clairvoyant vision of the essence of the universe is the single impulse which is simultaneously transmitted to us in two complementary ways, in terms of visual drama and in terms of music" (163). Symons, however, abstracts from this study only those aspects of music theory which relate to its supreme status. Wagner's desire to combine the perfections of Shakespeare and Beethoven is finally irrelevant. The use of words in opera may be necessary, but Symons goes further to suggest a more absolute form of musical presentation using voices without words. He projects a purer art, perhaps the most universal, as also delineated in "Music Among the Arts," and he follows Schopenhauer in this ideal more than he does Wagner:

> Why need music, if it is the voice of something deeper than action, care to concern itself with drama, which is the ripple on the surface of a great depth? As it dispenses with the stage, or the conscious exercise of the eyes, so it will dispense with words, or the conscious exercise of the mind through the hearing, and, in an equal degree, with the intrusive reasonings of a programme, at best but misleading footnotes to a misinterpreted text. (144)

Wagner answers this question but Symons seems less interested in the answer than in a concept of absolute art which is based upon the views of Schopenhauer and Wagner. In the same vein, in "Wagner at Covent Garden," Symons objects to Wagner's realism. He wants to consider new possibilities of staging which are more in line with an ideal vision: "Might not the music be helped, rather than hindered, by a decor and by costumes in which only illusion, and the furthering of the mystery of music, should be aimed at?" (617). Symons's discussions of Gordon Craig's productions come to mind here.

Music, then, is more clearly allied with dream and remembrance. Wagner develops a very long argument for the connection among dreams, apparitions, and visual drama. In fact, he tries to show that music is associated with dreams and that drama is associated with apparition or vision. It is Wagner's point that they both originate in a single impulse and reflect the same inner reality. The elaborate dream theory is, as well, drawn from Schopenhauer's "On the Seeing of Spirits and Related Matters," in which he attempts an idealistic explanation of clairvoyance and the phenomenon of dreams. Symons takes the dream world as revelatory. Wagner says the same about Beethoven: "Must not his commune with the world resemble nothing but that state of the awakened out of deepest sleep, the toilsome effort to recall the blissful vision of his inner soul?" (V:95). Wagner, appropriately, also states that this situation is similar to the saint who is driven to try to regain the divine realm. As he goes on to say, Beethoven found this quality in various folk songs, and the same combined innocence and saintliness seems to apply: "Now it is a Scotch, now a Russian, now an old-French folk-tune, in which he recognizes the dreamt nobility of innocence, and at whose feet he laid his whole art in homage'' (V:99).

Music seems to recreate a dreamlike experience of religious devotion. Wagner had said, and Symons is fond of quoting, that ''music blots out civilization as daylight blots out lamplight.'' Symons goes on to suggest that ''it is the only art which renders us completely unconscious of everything else but the ecstasy at the root of life'' and it can be absorbed with our eyes closed, ''like an articulate perfume; it is the only divine drunkenness, the only Dionysiac art'' (133). Thus, music is also a remembrance, something akin to our more ideal childhood: ''To listen to music is a remembrance, and it is only of memory that men never grow weary'' (133). The refuge music creates is not individual, however; the memory is greater than individual memory. Music is ultimately impersonal: ''It is here that music is so different from literature, for instance, where the words mean things, and bring back emotions too clearly and in too personal a way'' (135).

Symons wants to see music as nonreferential in two ways. He feels that nothing in the music of Beethoven refers to anything specific in his life. Music comes from a deeper, more vital source. Additionally, music should not refer to anything specific in the world; it should not aim at some sort of realism. The Pastoral Symphony raises the issues most clearly because the sounds in it often seem to correspond to aspects of nature, to bird cries and storms, to country settings. Symons, however, views this realism as a form of humor, not an artistic policy. The implied realism should not be taken seriously. Feeling, rather than the representations associated with painting, is the true province of the musician and composer. Modern music, to Symons's mind most obviously practiced by Richard Strauss, is being misled. It is even more ironic that it is being misled by an aside of Beethoven's.

Music's ability to express impersonal emotions is also part of the development in Symons's short story, ''Christian Trevalga.'' At its most extreme a complete dedication to absolute music can lead to a divine madness. Christian is moved by this absolute: ''The emotion of music, the idea, the feeling there, that was what moved him; and his own personal feelings, apart from some form of music which might translate them into a region where he could recognize them with interest, came to mean less and less to him, until he seemed hardly to have any personal feelings at all'' (*Works* 5:60). The outside world comes to mean less and less to Christian. He takes a walk, but what he sees vanishes from his memory before he has returned to his house. For Christian, of course, music becomes a bit more than magic against the present.

By the end of the story, Christian has been confined to an asylum where he finally dies. The narrator has found some loose scraps of paper on which Christian has jotted down his thoughts on music. These show that Schopenhauer and Wagner are clearly the gods in his work; and individual emotion should ideally be eliminated, especially in modern music: ''Most modern music is a beggar for pity.'' The composer cannot limit himself to individual sufferings; he cannot set ''his toothache and his heartache to music'' (*Works* 5:74). In another setting, Christian comments on the various arts, still along the lines of Schopenhauer's theories which give to music an ideal status: "Music comes nearer than any other of the human languages to the sound of these angelic voices. But painting is also a language, and sculpture, and poetry; only these have more of the atmosphere of the earth about them, and are not so clear" (*Works* 5:73). Thus to adequately appreciate the development of Christian's character, we have to be familiar with Schopenhauer, Wagner, as well as Beethoven and with Symons's studies on these figures.

Richard Strauss and Programme Music

Symons's essay, "The Problem of Richard Strauss," could be retitled "The Problem of Modern Music." Symons felt, as we have seen, that music and musical composition had been misled, had, in fact, regressed. Modern music now takes "up again that old bondage from which music only had completely freed itself" (*Works* 9:196). In this essay, however, the theoretical emphasis comes first of all from Pater: "In that essay on *The School of Giorgione*, in which Walter Pater came perhaps nearer to a complete or final disentangling of the meanings and functions of the arts than any writer on aesthetics has yet done, we are told: '*All art constantly aspires towards the condition of music*'" (*Works* 9:196). Support for Pater's ideal comes from Symons's reading of Schopenhauer and Wagner. Pater's belief, for example, that "art, then, is thus always striving to be independent of the mere intelligence, to become a matter of pure perception, to get rid of its responsibilities to its subject or material" (*Renaissance* 138) is very similar to Schopenhauer's notion that music speaks in a language our reason cannot understand. Music should, therefore, not concern itself with the communication of ideas. Schopenhauer had suggested, in fact, that Idea is associated with the phenomenal world. Music, however, communicates on a rarer and more refined level. Symons suggests that music can not express or suggest an idea apart from emotion or sensation: "It cannot do so, not because of its limitations, but because of its infinite reach, because it speaks the language of a world which has not yet subdivided itself into finite ideas" (*Works* 9:197). Programme music, which attempts to express pure idea through our understanding, is contrary to the very qualities that make music unique, the supreme art form. He sees Strauss as the most guilty of the modern composers of this sin against the refined world of music and as emblematic of the trend towards idea and programme in music. In fact, a distinction can be made between programme music in general, with all its failings, and the music of Strauss, which, according to Symons, brings even more "thought" into music. Not only does the programme try to describe the music for us, the music itself tries to convey abstract thought.

Strauss is also important to Symons because he based many of his theories of musical composition on ideas he derived from Beethoven. Much of his correspondence with Hans von Bülow involves the discussion of his belief that further developments in instrumental music were only possible by emulating those works of

Beethoven with programmatic content. Music must be expressive, receiving meaning and purpose through a poetic idea. Strauss refused to recognize the difference between absolute and programme music.

Symons objects to Strauss's work finally because Strauss does not further the expressive power of music. The admirers of this type of music are intrigued by its philosophical content, by its ambition to convey idea, which is to Symons a fundamental fallacy. *Also sprach Zarathustra* is a case in point. The opening alludes to Wagner's *Ring*, to "the seven notes to which the priest officiating at the mass sings the 'Credo in unum Deum'." But what does this allusion really accomplish: "By the quotation of this easily, though not universally, recognized phrase he is able, it is true, to convey something approximating to an idea; but it is conveyed, after all, by association of ideas, not directly, and is dependent on something quite apart from the expressive power of music itself" (*Works* 9:200). Pater's statement that in music form and content are inseparable also informs Symons's objection. The content is overly intellectualized. The music is sacrificed to the expression of something which it can never express. Ironically, Symons finally accuses Strauss of being a decadent: "Strauss is the only decadent in music, and he has tried to debauch music, as Stuck has tried to debauch painting, and as Klinger has tried to debauch sculpture, for the satisfaction of a craving which is not 'simple, sensuous, and passionate,' but elaborate, intellectual and frigid" (*Works* 9:209). The elaborateness seems too artificial, to much a matter of brain rather than feeling. The music, therefore, "tries to express something which is not in itself but in the words of the text, never for a moment transcending those words, carrying them, as music can carry words, into new regions" (*Works* 9:203). Wagner, on the other hand, seems able to accomplish this transcendence: "Then I play a single page of *Parsifal* or of *Tristan*, and I am no longer in the same world" (*Works* 9:213).

Symons carries on his argument against programme music in favor of a transcendent and absolute theory of music elsewhere in his writings. In an essay for *The Saturday Review*, "Programme Music," he deals with many of the same issues. He is again concerned with the fact that the reliance on the programme undermines the qualities of music he admires: "But indeed the programme is a superfluity, for the reason that it can tell nothing of importance to the proper understanding of music which that music cannot say for itself, only in another language" (423). He does not want to involve the rational part of the mind, as Schopenhauer had said music should not. Nor does he wish to see music as in any way referential: "But what we have always to remember is what Wagner said so clearly in writing of Beethoven: that whatever may be the external cause which sets a mood in motion, that mood, at the moment of creative inspiration, will have already turned to music, and that which set it in motion will have been forgotten" (423). Symons does not want to see the art of music, which he feels is "as unbounded as sea or air," made "as solid as the earth." Programme music tends to limit: "It is because the doctrine of programme music is a degradation to music that it should be protested against as a heresy" (424). He concludes his arguments in this article with a statement against realism in musical expression. No art should merely imitate, especially not music: "Literature occupies itself with that region, and painting; though both can deal with rarer material. But it is the blessing and praise of music that it is shut out from the very possibility of communicating the non-essential things which go to the making of so much in the other arts" (424).

Another essay, "The New Art of the Black Board," written in 1908 in response to a music production at the Queens Hall, deals with the same problems but in a slightly different context. The stanzas to the songs performed were printed on a large blackboard so that the audience could follow along. The results were less that satisfactory: "So far from carrying out the claim of the programme, 'to enable the eye and intelligence to cooperate with the ear,' the result of this 'new art form,' as it was presumptuously called, was to baffle eye and ear alike, in a confusion of word and sound" (102). The folly of programme music, to Symons's mind, was never more fully demonstrated.

Other Writers and Composers

Wagner, and through him, Schopenhauer, had the most important influence on Symons's thinking about music. But as is clear in "On Musical Criticism," Symons read the work of other writer-composers. Schumann, for example, had an early fascination for Symons, as we have seen from Symons's letters to Churchill Osborne. Schumann was also a prolific writer on music. He founded the *Neue Zeitschrift für Musik* in 1834. Later, in 1854, he published *Music and Musicians*, a collection of essays and articles he assembled in 1852. Like Symons, Schumann's interest as a critic lies in the aesthetic rather than the technical aspect of music. He felt, as has been suggested, that an aesthetic appreciation of a composer's work served his art better:

> We confess, however, that for us the highest form of criticism is that which reflects most closely the impression made by the stimulating original itself. In this sense Jean Paul, for example, could contribute more to an understanding of a Beethoven symphony or fantasy by a poetical counterpart (without even mentioning the symphony or fantasy) than all those art critics who apply ladders to the colossus in order to measure it by ells. (*Musical World* 36)

Schumann was following the German romantic school and its ideals, many of which Symons held as well. His desire was to bring art to a place of honor in the world: "Let us not sit idly by, rather let us do something to improve matters, to restore the poetry of the art to its rightful place of honour!" (*Musical World* 13). The aims and aspirations he intended for *Neue Zeitschrift* were, first of all, to look to history for the pure sources of musical expression, "to recall old times and its works with great emphasis, thus to draw attention to the fact that fresh artistic beauties can be strengthened only at pure sources" (qtd. in Chissell 192). Secondly, he resolved "to attack as inartistic the works of the present generation, since they proceed from the praise of superficial virtues" (*On Music* 40). Symons deals with this issue extensively in such essays as "Technique and the Artist," as well as in most of his discussions of individual performances.

All of Schumann's writings, however, show his profound conviction that music is a language of emotions, articulate beyond words. He believed, as did Goethe, that "music begins where words end." As he says in "From Master Raro's, Florestan's and Eusebius' Journal of Poetry and Thought," "music speaks the most universal of languages, that through which the soul finds itself inspired in a free, indefinite manner, and yet feels itself at home" (*On Music* 40).

Schumann's belief in the transcendent power of music led him, as it did Symons, to be cautious about programme music. Symons's observations in "Beethoven" are strikingly similar to these given by Schumann: "Beethoven sensed the hazards to which he exposed himself in writing the Pastoral Symphony. In those few words, 'more an expression of sensations than a painting,' which he placed at the head of the score, lies a whole aesthetic for composers; and it is ludicrous to paint him, as many have done, seated by a brook, his head in his hand, listening to the ripple of the water" (*Musical World* 52). He also, at one point, argues against Berlioz's programme notes: "So let the artist keep his labour pains to himself" (*Musical World* 84). To paraphrase Mérimée again, as Symons often did, art should conceal art. Schumann objects to the conflict between the eye and the ear, especially in relation to Berlioz's *Symphonie fantastique*: "I confess that at the outset my familiarity with the programme spoiled my pleasure and inhibited my imagination. But as the written outline receded more and more into the background and my own imagination took over, I found it all there, and much more besides, almost always alive and warm" (*Musical World* 85). Music should maintain an ideal status associated with the full workings of the imagination. "Letters from a (Music-) Lover" shows that music finally appeals to the internal, not the external: "I know of nothing lovelier than a concert, unless it be the hour before one, when you go about on tip toe, humming eternal melodies and performing whole overtures on window-panes" (*Musical World* 64). He does not know which to prefer, the beauty of inflection or the beauty of innuendo.

Symons also admired the critical writings of Franz Liszt, particularly his study of Chopin, and the critical writings of Berlioz. In a letter to Rhoda, July 20, 1902, he mentions Berlioz's memoirs: "I have got Berlioz's autobiography (in English), a delightful book." We can safely assume he had read at least parts of it in French years before. Liszt's *Chopin*, as well, appealed to Symons on a number of levels. Chopin was the major early musical ideal of Symons, as "A Prelude to Life" shows. Liszt's book, as well, is an appreciation, often revelatory in tone. Again, the author is more concerned with aesthetic than with technical questions.

Liszt defined for Symons the perfect artistic situation. First of all, he was a struggling artist who was innovative and expressive but who was not entirely understood by the public. More importantly, he extended the boundaries of his art: "Since the many forms of art are only varied incantations destined to arouse sentiments and passions and make them, as it were, perceptible and tangible, since they communicate the quickenings of emotion, genius appears through the design of new shapes now and again adapted to feelings not yet embraced within the magic circle'' (29–30). Liszt's discussion of romanticism, as well as individuality and artistic integrity, relates to this artistic ability. Chopin championed the new and the expressive. Poetic inspiration and freedom of expression required individual styles. These composers ''accepted no other rule than that which springs from the direct relations of feeling and form so that the one would answer for the other'' (117). He felt that they followed Pater's ideal of musical expression, or perhaps leaned in the direction of poetic inspiration as the controller of musical form:

> Not stressing the excellence of form, they sought it only to the extent that its faultless perfection is indispensable to the full elevation of emotion, for they were aware that emotion is maimed as long as an imperfect form, like an opaque veil, intercepts its radiance. And so they subordinated professional craft to poetic inspiration, calling upon patience and genius to rejuvenate the form that would satisfy the demands of inspiration. (117)

Liszt observes often that it is the nontraditional and the expressive side of Chopin that appeals most. In a review of one of Chopin's performances, he comments that he chose those of his works farthest removed from classical forms. The choice shows the real quality of Chopin's music. He played preludes, études, nocturnes, and mazurkas, through which ''he could safely show himself as what he is—a poet, elegiac, profound, chaste and dreaming'' (14). Often, in fact, Liszt concentrates on the ethereal quality of Chopin's music, the qualities for which he is most famous and which Symons found most appealing. The language Liszt uses to describe Chopin's ballades, valses, and études is literary and expressive. He tries to approximate the appeal these have. Ultimately, Chopin's music ''brings closer the realm of fairies and unveils to us unguarded secrets of the Peri, of Titanias or Ariels or Queen Mabs, of all the genii of water, air, and fire, who are also the victims of the most bitter frustrations and the most intolerable aversions'' (77). At times, Liszt exaggerates, lets the literary qualities of his language overflow. The expressiveness, though, of his book on Chopin, which is used finally to celebrate the artistry of the composer, is part of the book's quality. It is a testimonial for Chopin and for a level of artistic expression of which he was emblematic. Liszt offers, in fact, a creed in honor of Chopin's death: ''Let us renounce, too, for ourselves, in the dreary time in which we live, all that is unworthy of art, all that lacks permanence, all that fails to shelter some grain of eternal and immaterial beauty which art must lighten gloriously in order to glow itself, and let us remember the ancient prayer of the Dorians, whose simple formula was so reverently poetic when they petitioned the gods: To give them good through Beauty!'' (87).

Liszt was also a great admirer of Berlioz. It is appropriate, then, that Symons would have identified the two as important to his thinking about music. Berlioz's journalistic output, of course, was extensive. Along with a great number of uncollected articles which he published over a thirty-year period when he wrote regularly for publication, there are the *Traité de l'instrumentation* (1844), its brief sequel, *Le Chef d'orchestre, théorie de son art* (1855), and the *Mémoires* (1870). The *Mémoires* consists mostly of reprints from earlier publications. Other books issued during the composer's lifetime, also containing reprinted matter, were *Les Soirées de l'orchestre* (1852), *Les Grotesques de la musique* (1859), and *A travers chants* (1862). Symons mentions specifically his admiration for the *Mémoires*, as well as a more general appreciation of all of Berlioz's writings. Symons responded to Berlioz's writing as a combination of precision and irresistible elan, but he reacted more generally to the overall aesthetic approach Berlioz presented, especially as the musical representative of a new movement for truth and freedom of expression in the arts. Berlioz felt, as did many of the writer-composers Symons admired, that he was involved in the same movement as poets and painters, championing the same causes and bound by the same obligation to preach by word as well as by example.

We get a sense of Berlioz's intense devotion to the ideal status of art in "The Story of the Wandering Harpist," which reads similarly to many of Symons's stories in *Spiritual Adventures*. Like Christian Trevalga, the harpist has discovered through his art a world removed from the ordinary: "I had discovered an ideal and sacred world, the mystery of which I would disclose to nobody" (57). A priest in the story identifies him as being a great saint.

The ideal status of music is fully expressed in Berlioz's desire to forge a new language of dramatic music. One of Berlioz's fictional characters, Alfonso della Viola (who really speaks for Berlioz's artistic ideals) believes that the poetic idea should always defer to the musical sense. Berlioz said that in Beethoven and Weber we find "a poetic idea everywhere manifest, but music is always in command" (322). He objects to operas that overdo the nonmusical aspects. The problem with opera, as he says in the "Ninth Evening," is the emphasis on "spectacle at the expense of the music" (321). Elsewhere in *Evenings in the Orchestra* he says, "Hence our final duty, to ensure that music which is independent of theatrical demands, free music, music pure and simple, should only be revealed in its most majestic beauty" (277).

In many sections of *Evenings in the Orchestra*, Berlioz describes the ideal society and contrasts it with the current world in which the social status of the artist is so poor: "We certainly find that misfortune has often dogged and opposed men of genius" (278). He mentions in particular Beethoven and Mozart. By contrast he gives a long description of "Euphonia" which is a "vast academy of music" in which "the practicing of this art is the sole object of its inhabitants' activities" (254). Later, we are given a speech on music and the future in which Berlioz outlines his sense of how music affects us and in what relation music works with the other arts. Music, of course, is compared to the other arts, some of which "are only intellectual in their appeal" and some of which "are static." These other arts cannot produce anything comparable to music: "Music, then, first appeals elegantly to a sense which communicates the thrill to the whole organism. This produces a feeling of delight now gentle and calm, now impetuous and violent, which must be experienced to be believed'' (279). And later in the same passage he describes music as the supreme art, a focused force which brings into harmony a number of elements:

> But when it brings all its resources to bear on the ear which it delights or cleverly irritates, on the nervous system which it excites, the circulation of the blood which it quickens, the brain which it fires, the heart which it fills with emotion and a throbbing beat, on thought which it sublimates immeasurably and launches into the regions of the infinite, then it is acting in its true sphere . . . then its power is vast, and can hardly be compared seriously to any other. Then, too, we are gods, and if the men who have been richly blessed by fortune could know our ecstasies and buy them, they would squander their gold to share them for a moment. (280)

Symons's discussion of individual composers in his music criticism for *The Saturday Review* follows in the tradition of this group of four: Berlioz, Liszt, Schumann, and Wagner. Many of the opinions he holds can be understood more fully in the light of these writer-composers. It is interesting, as well, to notice how he deals with contemporary composers. For example, it is not until the 1928 edition of *Plays, Acting, and Music* that Symons includes any essays specifically on Debussy's work. Many of the critics who have written on Symons have, in fact, not referred to this edition and are not familiar with it. Symons had referred to Debussy at various points and wrote for *The Saturday Review* several discussions of his music, "Debussy and Other Questions," "French Music in London," "Claude Debussy," and "On Some Modern Music." Debussy's impressionism, it would seem, would be very appealing to Symons, but his use of literary texts might raise some of the same problems Symons encountered with Wagner's theories. In "Debussy and Other Questions," which is a review of Debussy's symphonic prelude to Mallarmé's "Après-midi d'un faune," Symons immediately confronts this issue by describing his experience of the music in referential terms, but not in specific reference to the poem: "I listened, forgetting the poem" for the time being (746). But he does remember a line from the poem in response and hears crying voices in the music. Still, the final value of the music, as well as Symons's appreciation of it, is based upon the fact that the poem and the composition do not depend on one another. The music is ultimately nonreferential: "So much the music told me, and so much music, being a creative not an illustrative art, is able to tell without words. There is no scene-painting or word-painting, it is not programme music; music says over again in its own language the mental part of what has been said in the language of poetry" (746). The sins of programme music, of a poor marriage of spirits, is not here displayed. Rather, a legitimate interaction of the two arts emerges: "Here is no confusion between them, no conflict, neither asks the aid of the other. Mallarmé's poem is as beautiful without music, and Debussy's music as beautiful without the poem" (746). Only after settling this issue does Symons go on to consider the music as modern, as evocation: "Both [the music and the poem] have an equal magic of atmosphere, and belong equally to that most modern kind of art which aims only at evocation" (746).

To Symons the important characteristics of Debussy's music center on the necessary independence of music from any literary or referential context. Its ability to be evocative beyond words, which the words of Mallarmé's poem aspire to be, defines its quality and value. It is clear, however, at this point that though Symons is not terribly familiar with Debussy's music, he has been struck by something in it. In fact, he doubts that Debussy will become of the major composers. He admires, however, *Prélude à l'après-midi d'un faune* because it has the essential qualities of beauty according to his aesthetic, "a touch of that strangeness without which there is no exquisite beauty" (746). This piece had caused considerable controversy when it was first performed because it was perceived to be formless and strange.

By December 1907, however, Symons has a fully developed opinion of Debussy's superiority. In his review of the Parisian Quartet's concert, "French Music in London," he states, "Of the nine composers whose music was thus faithfully interpreted to us, two stood out from the others with a definite superiority. These were Ernest Chausson, who seems to close the past, and Claude Debussy, who seems to open the future" (723). Again, Debussy's music—like Verlaine's poetry—appears to be representative of the modern approach to art, of the evocative. Its content is lovely in a new and unfamiliar way, and the rather remote melody creeps in or just holds back "so that it may suggest the more" (723). Words, Symons finds, are too precise to describe this music, "which suggests nothing but music" (723).

Symons describes this music, then, as representative of the modern method. Finally, in line with Wagner and music which speaks from the heart, from the innermost recesses of the human soul, Symons identifies Debussy as the author of an important new music, new, it seems, because it is not like other recent music: "Here, if any, is a new kind of music, not merely showy nor wilfully eccentric, like too much that we heard at the two concerts, but filled with an instinctive quality of beauty, which can pass from mood to mood, surprise us, lead us astray, but end by leading us to the enchantment in the heart of what I have called the wood" (723).

Symons's discussion of Debussy's music is picked up again in February 1908, when he devotes an entire review, "Claude Debussy," to that composer. By now his music, which had scarcely been heard in England a year ago, was being performed everywhere. In fact, Debussy had now come to England himself to conduct *L'Après-midi* and *La Mer* at the Queens Hall. This "new music," as Symons observes, seems quite likely to become a fashion. The comparison Symons uses here is to Mallarmé and Verlaine, with Debussy more like Mallarmé. We know, of course, that of the two, Symons considered Verlaine the supreme poet. The grounds of comparison also show that Wagner is in the background: "Verlaine is a purely lyrical poet, quite simple, instinctively a singer: no effort is visible in his work, nothing is made, everything is born. He evokes, through sheer genius; Mallarmé suggests, through a genius which has something in it of the artificial" (170). In his essay, "Stéphane Mallarmé," Symons remarked that the poet had a too absolute vision, too removed from "the compromise by which, after all, literature is literature" (*Symbolist Movement* 62). But the ideal, it seems is correct: "Carry the theories of Mallarmé to a practical conclusion, multiply his powers in a direct ratio, and you have Wagner. It is his failure not to be Wagner" (*Symbolist Movement* 62). Here, however, Symons goes on to show that, finally, Debussy's art can be associated with nothing but music. He is not, as we have seen, guilty of the same sins as Strauss; but the fact that he is not a programme artist, not imitative in the pejorative sense of that word, needs to be justified somewhat:

> The music was still, in a sense, imitative, but again it was not programme music. What it aimed at was a representation, through the suggestion of sounds, of a mood of nature; and I can see no objection to the imitation on strings and harps of the swish and crying of waves, done as Debussy does it, in a subordination to what I have called a mood of nature. There is none of the crude realism of Strauss in "Don Quixote" or of his sensationalism in "Salome"; there is suggestion, which passes, fluid as water, with the cadence of wind. (170)

The suggestive quality of Debussy, which seems to speak of a world apart, Symons continually associates with a mythic woods, "a world of thin clouds, faint colours, a mysterious wood where birds sing and there is twilight at noonday. A magic circle surrounds the wood, and the wizard lives there, solitary with his phantoms" (170). Symons had said in "Christian Trevalga" that "music comes nearer than any other of the human languages to the sound of these angelic voices" (*Works* 5:147). Debussy's wood is inhabited by Merlin, "and no Vivien has taught him to be human" (170).

Appropriately, in "On Some Modern Music" Symons deals with Debussy's choral setting of Rossetti's "The Blessed Damozel." The suggestive and mythical world of Rossetti is, so to speak, a Merlin not yet human. But, as Symons says, the music serves us best when the words are forgotten and "strange mysterious combinations of sound float up out of the orchestra, tenuous, plaintive wailing of the strings, rich chords on the harp, all quite angelic and suitable" (298).

The angelic voice of the artist was nowhere more apparent for Symons than in the life and work of Mozart. Drawing from his own experience, as well as from the romantic tradition, Symons came to define the artist as a wandering outcast. This type of figure appears often in many of Wagner's operas. Morse Peckham identifies this pattern in romanticism:

> The Romantic experienced a sense of profound isolation within the world and an equally terrifying alienation from society. These two experiences, metaphysical isolation and social alienation—they are of course two different modes of the same perception—were the distinguishing signs of the Romantic, and they are to this day. To symbolize that isolation and alienation, and simultaneously to assert the self as the source of order, meaning, value, and identity, became one task of the Romantic personality. To find a ground for value, identity, meaning, order, became the other task. (40–41)

Symons's article, "The Martyrdom of Mozart," based upon his reading of Victor Wilder's two-volume biography, reads like a study in this type of romantic isolation, but the nature of the martyrdom is worked out within a context with which we are now very familiar. For example, Mozart's perfection is described by contrasting musical abilities with worldly ones:

> For Mozart was perfect, not only in his art, but in his life. Not a virtue, not a grace was lacking; he had a divine purity, which is seen expressing itself in the innocent letter to his father, in which he declares the necessity of his marrying. But he had no consciousness of outward things; his hands, swift and certain on the harpsichord, were idle things off the notes, so that he could not cut up his food at table without cutting his fingers. (624)

This description is reminiscent of Wagner's description of Beethoven which had such immediate appeal to Symons. The character, Christian Trevalga, in *Spiritual Adventures* is very much like the Mozart Symons describes in this review. Both "died of sound." In many ways this article mirrors Symons's story. Symons states that music was for Mozart even more intense than for Beethoven, more angelic: "Music was his heaven, and he lived in it through the whole course of his mortal life; and that divine world, in which he walked like one of the angels, never betrayed him" (624).

The final point of the essay is a familiar one, which is part of its tragedy: "It is the world's curse and foul crime, repeated age after age, that no divine being is to be allowed to share in this life the unearned portion of the average man: happiness" (624). The article begins, in fact, with a statement that "the cruelest martyrdom on record in the annals of art is the martyrdom of a faultless man and a faultless artist: Mozart" (623).

For Symons Berlioz falls just short of this ultimate artistic status. In a manner of speaking, he too was martyred: "He died of exhaustion, like a beggar by the wayside. Then the world saw, too late, and gave him a splendid funeral" ("The Genius of Berlioz" 110). In this case, the question centers on balance again. Compared to Beethoven, Mozart, Handel, and Wagner, "Berlioz just misses that supremacy" because his melodies, which are sublime, often seem lost among the "meaningless hubbub of the orchestra." Symons carries on the comparison with Wagner: "And there is something in his orchestra, 'à la fois colossal et vapoureux,' which, in its violence, lacks that depth of sound which Wagner could get out of fewer instruments" (110). The contrast between depth of sound, which Symons associates with Berlioz's melodies, and orchestral display, empty splendor, and surface rhetoric, is consistent with his discussion of Wagner, in whose music there is a harmonic focusing of forces.

This same issue, particularly the relation between pure music and life, dominated Symons's discussions of music up to his breakdown in 1908. In "Rameau: I.—The Man and His Art," for example, he discusses not Rameau's curious system of chord progression but the two basic sides of his music. In relation to dramatic music, "he was indifferent to words, only demanding good situations and expressive decors. His 'Hippolyte et Aricie' is written to the most inept verses; but the music conquered, and is immortal'' (414). On the other hand, Symons felt he did not believe in pure music: ''He denied the existence of 'pure music,' and declared that the end of music is not in itself'' (414).

Symons's two-part article on Moussorgsky continues this argument. The history of Russian culture during the years Moussorgsky was writing involves a steady growth of interest in the people and their life, and in the true-to-life, realistic methods of art. Many of his characteristic peasant songs follow this cultural development. Symons, as well, centers on this aspect of Moussorgsky's work. Echoing his comment about Rameau, Symons comments that Moussorgsky seeks truth first: ''And Moussorgsky, who never sought after music for its own sake, sought for truth at the expense of beauty'' (296). This statement, however, is not used by Symons to condemn him. He goes on to quote a passage from Moussorgsky's letters that actually makes a distinction between superficial and actual beauty:

> The artistic representation of mere beauty, from the material point of view, is puerile, a rudimentary form of art: the subtle traits of individuals and masses, the persistent exploration of this still unknown region: there is the real duty of the artist. Seek new shores! Fearless, through storms and reefs and deep waters, seek new shores! The crowd, like individuals, affords subtle traits, difficult to distinguish, not yet realized. To discover them, to learn to read them at sight, by observation and hypothesis, to study them to their lowest depths, to feed on human things as on a source of energy, not yet known, there is the duty, the supreme intoxication! (296)

In his review, ''The Genius of Berlioz,'' Symons uses Lamb's expression, ''the material sublime,'' to describe a similar situation. Clearly, he sees Moussorgsky's music as not mere realism, as some have called it. The composer looks beyond the surface of life for what is beneath it. In a very real sense, Wagner's belief that drama, in its own way, expressed the eternal Will, using Schopenhauer's concept, is echoed in Symons's discussion of Moussorgsky: ''Thus it came to be that the expressive value of the music is exactly of the same order as that of the text. He found his best inspirations in poems and incidents, of which he perceived instantly the inner meaning. The stronger the influence, the impulse, the easier he found it to create, and the atmosphere came with it'' (296).

The reality beneath the surface is also associated with the truth the peasants instinctively knew. Yeats again comes to mind, and Symons admires this quality in Moussorgsky's work: ''All these people are peasants. They speak in low, soft, swaying voices, as peasants do'' (362). As a result of this appeal to the deeper level associated with folk songs and peasant life, Moussorgsky has, in fact, avoided the pitfalls of much modern music: ''The vivid European music of Tschaikowsky, of Rimsky-Korsakow, with its accomplished technique, its showiness, its popular appeal, sounds trivial and meaningless beside this new, marvelous creation'' (362). His lack of association with this musical world, to Symons, proves to be one of his major assets. He was ''untouched by any of the ideas of his time, or the theories and practices of his contemporaries, though he lived, for long periods, in their company'' (362). The forest image Symons used to describe Debussy is, interestingly, used by Moussorgsky about his own work. He, too, talks about fantasy, peasant types, and the seclusion of the woods as a metaphor for the reality he wishes to evoke in his music. Realism is too limited a term to apply to this type of creation: "It is a true saying: the deeper one goes into the forest the more wood one finds there. And how subtle Gogol was in his fantasies. He observed the old women, the peasants, he found splendid types. All that will be useful to me, and the old women: an absolute treasure!" (qtd. in "Moussorgsky II" 362).

It seems that Symons has found the musical counterpart for his interest in gypsies and their ancient knowledge. He often associated their primeval sense with the Russian temperament and with the origins of dance. One of the rather long digressions in Liszt's *Frédéric Chopin*, indeed, deals with dance, "asserting that a whole aspect of a people's character is disclosed in their national dances" (55). Symons followed this line of thought in his study of Spanish dance and Russian ballets. His comments on Vasily Sergeyevitch Kalinnikoff, the little-known Russian composer who died at thirty-five of consumption, concern the Russian character of his music: "Nothing more Russian was ever written, nothing more youthful, more personal, more convincing. Clearly constructed, not modern in any bad sense, it was filled from beginning to end with vigour, the loadstar of all Russian music, the dance-music coming into it with its delirious cadences" ("Miss Smyth, Kalinnikoff, and Buhlig" 751).

In summary, Symons's discussions of various composers—written throughout his career, but particularly during the years just prior to his breakdown—are quite consistent in the musical theory they evidence and in the critical concerns with which they deal. They derive most clearly and forcefully from Wagner and, through him, Schopenhauer, with the nontechnical writings of such writer-composers as Schumann, Berlioz, and Liszt adding support.

Musical Performance as an Art

In "A Paradox on Art" in *Plays, Acting, and Music* (1903), Symons asks a series of questions which relate to his overall aesthetic, questions which focus on the fact or belief that art as a term should be used more broadly. Certainly, in the tradition of Pater, life should be considered an art; but other aspects of artistic expression, such as dance and musical performance, should also be included. Art, for Symons, "is the creation of beauty in form, visible or audible" (1). He does not distinguish between art and its material. The issue in terms of music is very clearly outlined:

And thus the old prejudice against the artist to whom interpretation in his own special form of creation is really based upon a misunderstanding. Take the art of music. Bach writes a composition for the violin: that composition exists, in the abstract, the moment it is written down upon paper, but, even to those trained musicians who are able to read at sight, it exists in a state at best but half alive; to all the rest of the world it is silent. Ysaÿe plays it on his violin, and the thing begins to breathe, has found a voice perhaps more exquisite than the sound which Bach heard in his brain when he wrote down the notes. Take the instrument out of Ysaÿe's hands, and put it into the hands of the first violin in the orchestra behind him; every note will be the same, the same general scheme of expression may be followed, but the thing that we shall hear will be another thing, just as much Bach, perhaps, but, because Ysaÿe is wanting, not the work of art, the creation, to which we have just listened. (3)

Symons believes that performance is as much an art as painting or writing, and he writes about performance in this way. He recognizes that all forms of the creation of beauty have an equal value. Certainly, he writes about dance as a separate art, and, in music, he writes about individual composers and compositions; but he also writes extensively about the nature of individual performances and performers, as well as about a number of related issues.

Central to Symons's discussion of performance is the relation between technique and art. In 1900, while he was writing for *The Academy*, he dealt with this issue fairly extensively in "Technique and the Artist." The article is loosely based on performances by Ferruccio Busoni, the world-famous pianist, and Eugène Ysaÿe, an equally famous violinist. The questions Symons raises in relation to these two musicians involve "the extent to which technique must go to the making of an artist, and the point at which something else must be superadded" (5). He gives us the answer, using the technique of acrobats as an example, performers who were important, as we have seen, to his music-hall world. Technique is crucial, "but the performance comes afterwards, and it is the performance with which we are concerned. Of two acrobats, each equally skillful, one will be individual and an artist, the other will remain consummately skillful and uninteresting; the one having begun where the other leaves off" (5–6). The problem, as Symons sees it, is that audiences have come to value technique too highly: "We have come to look upon technique as an end in itself, rather than as a means to an end" (7). Virtuosity seems to be dominating the stage.

In another article, "Music and Science," Symons associates the interest in technique as an end in itself with the scientific character of the century. Science is tending more and more to obliterate music, as it is art in general. Symons had been reading an interview with Joseph Holbrooke whose illuminated screen technique he had reviewed earlier. Holbrooke, however, is also bothered by the spread of shallow technique: "Apart from the men who feel deeply and who are few in number, I should unhesitatingly say that the advance is in technique. The great preponderance of composers of our time are spreading technique only; and true, deep feeling is absent. The result is that music is getting scientific, which I deprecate greatly, instead of being emotional" (232). Technique, like verbal rhetoric, inhibits true expression, particularly in music which expresses a depth of meaning which goes far beyond words; and for Symons this progress is part of the scientific spirit against which he protests: "Strauss is science. Elgar is science. César Franck is science. They are all cold, concerned with technique" (232). The essay continues with a description of those composers who use technique for the expression of deep feeling: Debussy, Dukes, and Moussorgsky. The ultimate aim is honest, sincere expression, not mere technical elegance or agility. Form raises a corollary problem. Liszt's discussion of romanticism in relation to Chopin's compositions made this point as well. Restriction, either as the result of using technique as an end or as the result of imposed forms, was to be avoided.

The issue of virtuoso performance, of course, was not a new one; and many of the writer-composers that Symons admired also examined this problem. Schumann, for example, comments that "virtuoso tricks change with the times; only where proficiency serves higher purposes has it value" (*On Music* 32). Berlioz's comments about Paganini are also important in this regard:

> Paganini is one of those artists of whom it must be said: they are because they are and not because others were before them. Unfortunately what he was unable to communicate to his successors was the spark which gave life and warmth to these shattering feats of technique. The idea can be set on paper, the form sketched, but the feeling which the performance needs escapes all definition: it is the spirit, the soul of the piece, the vital fire which, when it dies, leaves behind it darkness as black as the light was brilliant. (169)

The passage is strikingly similar to Symons's ideas in "Technique and the Artist." Both writers are concerned with what is beyond technique. As Berlioz says elsewhere, "the quality of the performance depends not only on the choice of the performers, but also on the spirit which animates them" (118). Symons, in these articles on individual performers, is also concerned with the spirit that animates them, or, as Liszt says, "the perfecting of technique can never rise to the level of creation" (117).

Two other articles in which Symons deals with this problem are "Piano-Playing as an 'Accomplishment' " and "Pianoforte-Playing as an Art." The intention of these companion essays is apparent in their titles. Part of the first essay deals with the distinction between male and female art: "Women's and men's art are two totally different things, and between them lies only a land of vague shadows" (166). Finally, Symons says that a woman artist can only produce vital work if she abandons "herself to her sex, to her instinct, to that which in her is nearest to the earth and to the beasts" (166). The distinction he is making seems to owe something to Wagner who, in *A Communication to My Friends*, makes a similar point. The problem Symons identifies in "Piano-Playing as an 'Accomplishment' " is that a deeper level of expression is missing. An accomplished player is a ladylike player: "Nowhere is there a sense of the music as it was meant by the composer, nowhere a new interpretation by an executant who gives a personal reading, which may or may not be the composer's but is at least alive" (166). Fanny Davis, although she was the first to play Debussy's *Préludes* in England, was a classicist and perhaps to Symons seemed somewhat cold because she lacked real expressiveness in her renditions. Maria Teresa Carreno, on the other hand, offered a bit more. Her Spanish temperament appealed to Symons, as did her interpretation, which combined great technical virtuosity with exceptional insight, dramatic intensity, and poetic feeling: "But what passion she can evoke out of passionate music, how her heart and senses, Spanish and a woman's, seem to cry and palpitate out of the ardent and resonant sounds!'' (166). Finally, the point of the contrast is made even more explicable: ''They [audiences] do not see that music is not a thing which can be made intelligible by a cold imitation of its sounds, but that it must be created over again by every player'' (166). Technical proficiency is not creation.

In ''Pianoforte-Playing as an Art'' Symons continues this argument, stating that ''technique is in danger of spoiling an instrument in developing a machine'' (417). Again, the style of play seems to be mirroring the industrial and scientific character of society. Individuality has disappeared, and machine reproduction has taken its place. Acrobatics have now become the prime audience interest: ''Acrobatics on the piano are more tangible, can be followed more easily by the uneducated ear, than acrobatics on the violin. And it is more and more for acrobatics that the public goes to its 'recital' '' (417). This interest in performance is tied to rhetoric, as in the case of Eugène d'Albert. His playing was noteworthy for power and poetic feeling. Symons compares him to Teresa Carreno, who was his second wife, in these qualities. But ''he seems to have lost the sense of how far rhetoric really is from truth, and is too ready to be content with a rhetoric which is oratory'' (419).

Symons's discussions of individual performances continue in his challenge that performers be expressive rather than just technically interesting. In ''On Some Violinists,'' for example, he comments about Fritz Kreisler: ''To hear Fritz Kreisler play the Chaconne, after hearing Jan Hambourg play it, is to realize all that music can gain or suffer at the hands of its interpreters'' (354). Later, he elaborates on the quality in Kreisler's playing which seems to reveal Beethoven's Violin Concerto. Kreisler plays as if Beethoven had revealed the music privately to him:

> This young athlete, who seems joyously ready to grapple with sound, has a quality which of all others is best suited to interpret Beethoven. His soul seems to confide in his fiddle, and the fiddle tells us the secret. His fingers, trained to swift accuracy like race-horses, play from the heart, with checked passion; the notes throb, and their shriek is withdrawn from the strings, they cry with veiled lovely voices. There is emotion in every note of the music, but the emotion mastered by art, as Beethoven mastered it. (554)

The combined quality of emotion and artistic control is what intrigues Symons about Kreisler, and it is a quality which he also sees in Beethoven's work. According to Symons, Kreisler does not just perform the work; he gives it to the audience in the same, animated spirit with which it was created.

Later in 1907 Symons wrote ''Kreisler: A Summing-Up,'' an article in which he brings together a number of familiar ideas to try to come to grips with Kreisler's musical performance. Here, the combined qualities of emotion and art are associated with Dionysian and Apollonian ideals Symons acquired from Nietzsche: ''Here was that romantic beauty which modern art has created out of stranger materials than the sufficient beauty of what may be called 'classical' art. The cadenza in Mozart seemed to give Kreisler all that he needed, but the first cadenza in Brahms had all Dionysus in it, with all Apollo'' (540). This duality represents a form of perfection: "He is without excess and without default; the perfection which he attains is that perfection of Giorgione's, beyond Titian's, because its level never falls below a certain divine height'' (539). As usual, Symons brings in another art form as an analogy for the quality he is trying to describe. But it is the combination of control and emotion which allows Kreisler to be himself and to become one with the music he is playing: "Throughout this concerto Kreisler was himself and Brahms, almost more potently than I have heard him be at once Beethoven and himself'' (540). And in this way he gives the audience the music because he has the power to be its voice: it "becomes audible through him, yet it is he who has the power to master inspiration, to translate the divine message'' (540).

The quality of restraint, of mastery of material, which in part defines Kreisler, is not, however, the most important aspect of his performance with which Symons wants to leave with us. His final summing-up of Kreisler involves the deepest level of his personality and temperament:

> For all his profound gravity, his breadth, his immense restraint, there is something which boils underneath, and is part of the motive power; and there are moments when I am reminded by some queer undercurrent, in his miraculous playing, of some thrilling and unexpected voice which one hears in Hungary, in a gipsy orchestra. Only, while with them this salt is scattered and falls loosely, with Kreisler it is a savour, and adds just that "strangeness" without which there can be no exquisite beauty. (540)

The strangeness of individual expression has to be present, even dominant at times, if the beauty is to be present as well.

Elsewhere in his essay on Kreisler, Symons compares him to a number of other musicians, including Ysaÿe, who "lulls us half asleep, that we may meet him halfway in a dream'' (539). Ysaÿe intrigued Symons profoundly. His style was unconventional and highly original, marked by fiery energy and *tempo rubato*. The expressiveness and intensity of his play were overwhelming. In "Technique and the Artist," in which Symons favorably compares Ysaÿe to Busoni, the violinist is described as if he had settled into a religious trance. Revelation in musical terms is spoken of as if it were the work of the gods, and the description recalls Symons's analysis of Duse as if she were being sculpted by a divine force:

> The face had been like a mass of clay, waiting the sculptor's thumb. As the music came, an invisible touch seemed to pass over it; the heavy mouth and chin remained firm, pressed down on the violin; but the eyelids and the eyebrows began to move, as if the eyes saw the sound, and were drawing it in luxuriously, with a kind of sleepy ecstasy, as one draws in perfume out of a flower. Then, in that instant, a beauty which had never been in the world came into the world; a new thing was created, lived, died, having revealed itself to all those who were capable of receiving it. (*Plays, Acting, and Music* 1903, 6–7)

All the operative qualities of music as a transcendental experience are given to us in relation to Ysaÿe. The great musician is the person who is able to expose us to the dream world Wagner had described in his study of Beethoven, the ideal, metaphysical world he had discovered in Schopenhauer. Ysaÿe, as well, hears and *sees* the music, as does Symons's Christian Trevelga. Duse, whose mystical acting Symons described as if the hands of God were forming her body, is also duplicated in his description of Ysaÿe—the music takes over the body as a sort of mystical experience.

Symons had first heard Ysaÿe play in May 1899, as he mentions in a letter to Rhoda dated May 30, 1899:

> Imagine, that this afternoon, by sheer chance, a man asked me to go with him to Ysaÿe's concert. I had never heard Ysaÿe: have you, I wonder? He played a Bach and a Mozart concerto. He was simply marvelous—different from anyone I had ever heard, with a tone like gold and like steel at once. He stood there, calmly possessed by the devil looking about him with a vague and wondering glance which saw nothing, a grotesque, impossible figure, with his vast white face and one long lock of black hair dangling into one eye, really as if he was not even conscious that he was playing—and what playing it was!

The fact that he is lost to the material world, transported, and in fact, transformed, by the music informs Symons's earliest descriptions. When he came to write a fuller evaluation, "Ysaÿe," for *The Saturday Review* in 1907, the same qualities are accented. His play is always a dream, an "unholy, a rapture, a fascination" (790). As with Moussorgsky, he is also without tradition, a characteristic which allows him full range of personal expression: "Ysaÿe's strange originality is not less evident in his technique than in his whole conception and treatment of music. It seems to be based on no tradition, to have found itself out for itself, to be something rarer and in a way vaguer than that of any other violinist, and as if the tone which he creates had some unfamiliar birth" (790). Ysaÿe's individual style allows Symons to discuss it in terms of personal revelation. It is a revelation of individual temperament.

Finally, however, Symons focuses on the earthy quality of Ysaÿe's playing. His fiery performance is a mystery of the flesh, a mystery which has a literary analogue: "The playing of Ysaÿe is a great mystery; it is the mystery of the flesh, in which beauty is almost sinful. Other violinists are grave, chaste, or passionate; but his is the voice of the unappeasable agony of the senses. What Swinburne once wrote, he plays; his whole art is the art of Swinburne, as Kreisler's, by comparison, is the art of Browning. Kreisler is greater, but Ysaÿe fascinates" (790).

The elements of Ysaÿe's playing, its fiery quality, for example, which appealed to Symons, also relate to his appreciation of Pablo de Sarasate, the Spanish violinist who often played Spanish music of his own composition and transcriptions of Spanish folk music. Symons reacts to "the Spanish fire which Sarasate was able to kindle. In "Sarasate: An Appreciation," which appeared in the *Illustrated London News* in 1891, Symons mistakenly assumes that "in the matter of execution there is apparently nothing that Sarasate cannot do" (658). Sarasate's hands were quite small and long stretches were difficult for him. He therefore avoided the works of Paganini and his school. But from Symons's point of view, virtuoso ability was not what was important, for "there never was a greater mistake than to suppose his mastery of his instrument to have in it any of the more doubtful qualities of the virtuoso" (658). Of course, in 1891 Symons sees Sarasate in terms of the age and the art that seems most allied to it: "Like the most typical modern art, Sarasate's playing is the art of *la nevrose*. Wagner in 'Tristan und Isolde,' Berlioz in 'La Damnation de Faust,' have written the typical music of the present age, music which appeals to us by its mysterious kinship with our vague distresses, its cry from we know not whence, its cry for we know not what" (658).

Symons's discussion of Joseph Joachim involves a completely different aspect of musical performance. Joachim used his extraordinary technique solely for the purpose of interpreting the music of the great masters with the utmost fidelity to their intentions. Symons, writing just after Joachim's death in an article about musical interpretation, "Joachim and the Interpretation of Music," describes him as "a great artist, the most disinterested artist of his time" (231). His value, and the value of his quartet, is that he is able to give the audience the music without allowing the personality to interfere. When he heard the Joachim Quartet play Beethoven's posthumous quartets, Symons states, "what I heard seemed suddenly to become clear; a voice that had never before been heard on earth began to speak in a tongue that was perhaps the speech of angels" (232). The Schopenhauerean qualities are revealed and nothing of Joachim interferes: "What Joachim taught us of most value was that only honest music is worth listening to, and that a complete honesty is the first requirement in the rendering of it" (232). This aspect of musical performance is probably not the most interesting to Symons, but it does tie in with his overall concerns for the presentation of music:

> And he taught us to look further than technique, to realize what there was under a technique not only sufficing but self-effacing. This kind of playing, it may well be thought, is the greatest of all kinds of playing, as it is the most reverent; it is certainly the most serviceable, to the composer and to the public alike. The fashion, in music as in all other matters, is turning towards a worship of virtuosity: the artist must now astonish, seem to overcome incredible difficulties at every moment, as if the dancer were to interrupt his rhythm by a saut périlleux. Let technique be all that it can, so long as its art conceals its art. (232)

Symons goes on in this article to deal with the issue of musical interpretation more fully, particularly in relation to the playing of Joachim, Kreisler, and Ysaÿe. Kreisler, who Symons feels may be a kind of successor to Joachim in his interpretation of music, has an important emotional level to his play. He has more to offer; his spirit is more animated and animating. Joachim gave music "as the unchanging ritual of the Catholic church is given, 'in the spirit,' yet with a strict adherence to the letter," and this distinction involves Ysaÿe, as well, who is perhaps too much lulled by sound, as was Christian Tevelga: "Music sometimes lulls Ysaÿe into almost the state of a medium, and he passes it on to you in a dream. But Kreisler is awake, joyous with the life that is in the music, and his ecstasy breaks from him like a divine strength, heroically self-content in action" (232).

Symons is most fascinated with musicians such as Ysaÿe, those who really do seem to abandon themselves to the dream world of music. As previously noted, Wagner describes Beethoven as one awakened from deepest sleep who in vain endeavours to recall his blissful dream (V:95).

This same quality Symons associated with conductors. In "Nikisch and Other Conductors," he speaks of Hans Richter as a sort of medium: "When Richter conducts Wagner we are in a new heaven and a new earth; he has but to turn his eyes gently and the players follow him as a subject follows a medium" (487). Arthur Nikisch does not, however, conduct with the same insight. He is faithful but not transfiguring: "Herr Nikisch has no magnetism, no magic; he renders music with a fine, close, sensitive fidelity, he does not transfigure it" (487). In "Wagner at Covent Garden" Symons compares Richter to Rodin. Both show that artistic control is extremely important, but they also show that the ideals of Apollo and Dionysus combine: "He has the immense quietude of the greatest men, in whom emotion is Caliban and Ariel at once, and both in servitude. He masters, and is never mastered, and it is with a thrill of surprise and pleasure that we see him as he unchains the elements in Wagner's universe, effortless in their midst, directing them, a more effectual Wotan" (617).

Symons was also a great appreciator of piano music, especially as it was performed by Vladimir de Pachmann, the Russian pianist who excelled as a painter of tonally beautiful miniatures. He was particularly suited for playing the works of Chopin, a composer Symons, as we have seen, admired greatly. Of all the musicians about whom Symons writes, Pachmann seems to satisfy him most. As he says in "Pachmann: With a Word on Godowsky," "Pachmann is the Verlaine or Whistler of the piano-forte" (681). And later in the article he states that his art is particularly modern: "Pachmann's art, like Chopin's, which it perpetuates, is of that peculiarly modern kind which aims at giving the essence of things in their fine shades: 'la nuance encor!'" (681). He is able to create music in its pure, inhuman form: "There is nothing human in him, and as music turns towards humanity it slips from between his hands. What he seeks and finds in music is the inarticulate, ultimate thing in sound: the music, in fact" (681). We recall that "music comes speaking the highest wisdom in a language which our reason does not understand." In relation to Pachmann, then, "to reduce music to terms of human intelligence or even human emotion is to lower it from its own region, where it is Ariel" (681). We cannot humanize pure musical expression: "In the attempt to humanize music, that attempt which almost every executant makes, knowing that he will be judged by his success or failure in it, what is most fatally lost is that sense of mystery which, to music, is atmosphere" (*Plays, Acting, and Music* 1909, 241). This mystery is music's native air. The conclusion becomes obvious. The musician has less difficulty evoking the divine than does the poet or painter: "With what an effort do we persuade words or colours back from their vulgar articulateness into at least some recollection of that mystery which is deeper than sight or speech. Music can never wholly be detached from mystery, can never wholly become articulate, and it is in our ignorance of its true nature that we would tame it to humanity and teach it to express human emotions, not its own'' (241).

Works Cited

Works by Symons

A complete bibliography of Symons's work, compiled by Karl Beckson, Ian Fletcher, Lawrence W. Markert, and John Stokes, will be published shortly by the Garland Press. A selection of Symons's letters, edited by Karl Beckson and John Munro, is also forthcoming from Iowa University Press. The following listing is of articles, texts, editions, letters, and manuscripts that pertain directly to this study. This list is organized alphabetically by title except where a work or article is about a specific author. The listing in those cases is given alphabetically by the subject's last name. *An Introduction to the Study of Browning*, for example, is listed under Browning, as are all reviews and articles by Symons on Browning. Unpublished letters are listed according to the last name of the recipient. Unpublished manuscripts are listed according to title, unless the manuscript is about a specific author.

Acrobatics and Mountebanks by Hugues Le Roux and Jules Garnier. Review in *Athenaeum* (22 Feb. 1890): 238–39.
"Acrobatics at the Empire." *Star* (6 Feb. 1892): 4.
"Amends to Nature." *Outlook* XVI (14 Oct. 1905): 516. (Poem, reprinted in *The Fool of the World*).
Amoris Victima. London: Leonard Smithers, 1897. New York: G. H. Richmond, 1897.
"The Arabs at the Empire." *Star* (12 March 1892): 4.
"Art and the Royal Academy." *Weekly Critical Review* I (4 May, 28 May 1903): 1–2, 10–11.
"An Art-Critic and Criticism." *Weekly Critical Review* I (9 April 1903): 1–2.
"The Art of Seeing." *Weekly Critical Review* I (16 April 1903): 13–14.
"At the Alhambra: Impressions and Sensations." *Savoy* I (Sept. 1896): 75–83.
"At the Empire." *Sketch* II (7 June 1893): 301.
"'Au Mirliton': A Visit to Aristide Bruant." *Black and White* IV (31 Dec. 1892): 774.
"An Autumn City." *Dome* n.s. II (Feb. 1899): 148–51. (Reprinted in "Arles II" in *Wanderings*).
"An Autumn City." *Weekly Critical Review* I & II (25 June, 2 July, 9 July, 1903): 78, 15–17, 8–9. (Reprinted in *Spiritual Adventures*)
"A Ballet Rehearsal." *St. James's Gazette* (16 Dec. 1892): 5.
Charles Baudelaire: A Study. London: Elkin Matthews, 1920.
Aubrey Beardsley. New edition, revised and enlarged. London: J. M. Dent, 1905.
"Beethoven." *Monthly Review* XIX (Apr. 1905): 31–47. (Reprinted in *Studies in Seven Arts*)
"Berlioz's 'Faust.'" *Illustrated London News* C (16 Jan. 1892): 86.
"The Genius and Failure of Berlioz." *Saturday Review* CVI (25 July 1908): 109–10.
"On a Sale of Blakes." *Weekly Critical Review* II (16 July 1903): 1–2.
William Blake: With Records from Contemporary Sources. London: Archibald Constable, 1907.
An Introduction to the Study of Robert Browning. 2nd. edition. Revised and enlarged. London: Cassell and Co., 1887.

Asolando by Robert Browning. Review in *Academy* XXXVII (11 Jan. 1890): 19–20.

"Robert Browning as a Religious Poet." *Wesleyan-Methodist Magazine* VI (Dec. 1882): 943–47.

"Robert Browning and George Meredith: A Note on Their Similarity." *Browning Society: Monthly Abstract of Proceedings* II (1884–85): 80–82.

"Browning's Women: Balaustion." *Browning Society: Monthly Abstract of Proceedings* II (1884–85): 121.

Ferishtah's Fancies by Robert Browning. Review in *London Quarterly Review* n.s. III (Jan. 1885): 370–71.

"Is Browning Dramatic?" *Browning Society's Papers* Part VII (1885–86): 1–12.

"Some Notes on Browning's Latest Volume." *Browning Society's Papers* Part IX (1887–88): 169–79.

Letter to Campbell, James Dykes. 4 Oct. 1886. Campbell Letters. British Museum.

———. 8 Jan. 1887. Campbell Letters. British Museum.

———. 8 Oct. 1887. Campbell Letters. British Museum.

———. 2 Jan. 1888. Campbell Letters. British Museum.

———. 21 Sept. 1888. Campbell Letters. British Museum.

———. 6 Oct. 1889. Campbell Letters. British Museum.

———. 1 Nov. 1889. Campbell Letters. British Museum.

———. 25 May 1890. Campbell letters. British Museum.

———. 3 July 1890. Campbell Letters. British Museum.

Introduction. *The Child of Pleasure* (*Il Piocere*) by D'Annunzio, Gabriele. London: William Heinemann, 1898. (Introduction reprinted as Part I of "Gabriele d'Annunzio" in *Studies in Prose and Verse*)

Cities. London: J. M. Dent, 1903.

Cities and Sea-Coasts and Islands. London: William Collins, 1918.

Cities of Italy. London: J. M. Dent, 1907.

The Collected Works of Arthur Symons. 9 vols. London: Martin Secker, 1924.

   1. *Poems: Days and Nights, Silhouettes, London Nights, Amoris Victima*.

   2. *Poems: Images of Good and Evil, The Loom of Dreams, The Fool of the World, Love's Cruelty*.

   3. *Poems: Knave of Hearts, Lesbia*.

   4. *William Blake*

   5. *Spiritual Adventures*

   6. *Tragedies: Tristan and Iseult, The Harvesters*.

   7. *Tragedies: The Death of Agrippina, Cleopatra in Judaea, The Toy Cart*.

   8. *Studies in Two Literatures*. [Incorporating *The Symbolist Movement in Literature*]

   9. *Studies in Seven Arts*. [Incorporating "Aubrey Beardsley"]

Colour Studies in Paris. London: Chapman and Hall, 1918.

Confessions: A Study in Pathology. New York: The Fountain Press, 1930.

Introduction. *Cymbeline* by William Shakespeare. Volume 14 of the Collected Works. London: Harrap, 1906. New York: George P. Sproul, 1906.

"'Cyrene' at the Alhambra." *Sketch* I (5 April 1893): 610.

"La Dame aux Camélias." *Star* (2 July 1901): 1.

"Debussy and Other Questions." *Saturday Review* CIII (15 June 1907): 746–47.

"Claude Debussy." *Saturday Review* CV (8 Feb. 1908): 170–71. (Reprinted in *Plays, Acting, and Music* [1928].)

"The Decadent Movement in Literature." *Harper's Monthly Magazine* European Edition XXVI (Nov. 1893): 858–67. (Reprinted with alterations in *Dramatis Personae* and *London Quarterly Review* CXXIX (Jan. 1918): 89–103.)

"The Decay of Craftsmanship in England." *Weekly Critical Review* I (19 March, 26 March 1903): 5–6, 17–18. (Reprinted in *Studies in Seven Arts*)

Letter to Dobson, Austin. n. d. Dobson Letters. University of London Library.

Dramatis Personae. Indianapolis: Bobbs-Merrill, 1923.

Eleonora Duse. London: Elkin Matthews, 1926.

"Duse in 'Magda.'" *Star* (11 May 1900): 1.
"Duse in 'The Second Mrs. Tanqueray.'" *Star* (14 May 1900): 1.
"Duse in 'La Gioconda.'" *Star* (15 May 1900): 1.
"Duse in 'Fedora.'" *Star* (17 May 1900): 1.
"Duse in 'La Princesse Georges.'" *Star* (19 May 1900): 1.
"Duse in 'La Dame aux Camélias.'" *Star* (5 June 1900): 1.
"Eleonora Duse." *Contemporary Review* LXXVII (Aug. 1900): 196–202.
"Duse at Zurich." *Weekly Critical Review* II (17 Sept., 24 Sept. 1903): 193–94, 227–28.
"The Failure of the Arts and Crafts." *Outlook* XVII (20 Jan. 1906): 90–91.
" 'Faust' at the Empire." *Sketch* X (15 May 1895): 121.
" 'Fidelia' at the Alhambra." *Sketch* II (28 June 1893): 461.
Letter to Field, Michael. 12 July 1988. Field Letters. British Museum.
———. 7 Sept. 1888. Field Letters. British Museum.
———. 11 Jan. 1893. Field Letters. British Museum.
Figures of Several Centuries. London: Archibald Constable, 1916.
"French Music in London." *Saturday Review* CIV (14 Dec. 1907): 723–24.
"From Stevens to Sargent." *The Outlook* XV (6 May 1905): 574.
From Toulouse-Lautrec to Rodin. London: John Lane, 1929.
Introduction. *The Golden Threshold* by Sarojini Naidu. New York: John Lane, 1905.
Letter to Gosse, Edmund. 9 May 1898. Gosse Letters. Brotherton Library. University of Leeds.
———. 28 Oct. 1901. Gosse Letters. Brotherton Library. University of Leeds.
———. 9 Jan. 1908. Gosse Letters. Brotherton Library. University of Leeds.
———. 5 April 1908. Gosse Letters. Brotherton Library. University of Leeds.
"Yvette Guilbert." *St. James's Gazette* XXV (2 July 1892): 5–6.
"Yvette Guilbert Last Night." *Star* (4 Dec. 1894): 2.
"Yvette Guilbert." *Saturday Review* LXXVIII (15 Dec. 1894): 656.
"Yvette Guilbert at the Empire." *Star* (15 May 1901): 1.
"Yvette Guilbert's Matinee." *Star* (8 June 1901): 1.
"Gymnastics on Stilts." *Star* (14 May 1892): 4.
"Gypsy Jane." *St. James's Gazette* XXIV (4 Feb. 1892): 5.
"In Praise of Gypsies." *Journal of the Gypsy Lore Society* n.s. I (April 1908): 294–99. (Reprinted in *Bookman's Journal* IV [22 July 1921]: 205–6.)
"Sir Thomas Browne on the Gypsies." *Journal of the Gypsy Lore Society* n.s. V (1911–12): 109–13.
"A Few Words on Gypsies." *Journal of the Gypsy Lore Society* n.s. VI (1912–13): 2–3.
"Two Portraits: Gypsy Jane, Gypsy Lee." *Journal of the Gypsy Lore Society* n.s. VII (1913–14): 1–4.
"Human Eels." *Star* (9 July 1892): 4.
"Hungarian Gypsy Music." *Illustrated London News* XCIX (5 Dec. 1891): 727.
"Mr. Holman Hunt's New Picture." *Academy* XXXVIII (6 Sept. 1890): 204–5.
Pre-Raphaelitism and the Pre-Raphaelite Brotherhood by W. Holman Hunt. Review in *Outlook* XVI (9 Dec. 1905): 822.
"Hymn to Earth." *Weekly Critical Review* III (22 Jan. 1904): 15. (Poem, reprinted in *The Fool of the World*)
"Henrik Ibsen." *The Universal Review* III (15 April 1889): 567–74.
"Ibsen on the Stage." *Scottish Art Review* II (July 1889): 40.
"Ibsen's 'Ghosts' at the Théâtre-Libre." *Pall Mall Gazette* (5 June 1890): 3.
"A Note on Ibsen's Technique." *Star* (15 May 1901): 1.
"Joachim and the Interpretation of Music." *Saturday Review* CIV (24 Aug. 1907): 231–32.
"Kreisler: A Summing-Up." *Saturday Review* CIV (2 Nov. 1907): 539–40.
"Galuppi—Vernon Lee." *Browning Society: Monthly Abstract of Proceedings* II (1884–85): 69.
"Vernon Lee on 'The Ring and the Book.'" *Browning Society: Monthly Abstract of Proceedings* II (1884–85): 102–3.

Letter to Lee, Sydney. 7 March 1902. Walpole Collection. Bodleian Library.

London: A Book of Aspects. London and Minneapolis: Privately printed, Edmund D. Brooks, 1908. With twenty photogravures by Alvin Langdon Coburn. London: Privately printed, Edmund D. Brooks, 1914. (Two copies only.)

The Memoirs of Arthur Symons: Life and Art in the 1890s. Ed. Karl Beckson. University Park and London: Pennsylvania State University Press, 1977.

"Mr. Meredith's Latest Novel." *Time* n.s. I (May 1885): 632–36.

"Meredith's 'Evan Harrington.'" *Time* n.s. II (Nov. 1885): 631–33.

"Meredith's 'Richard Feverel.'" *Time* n.s. II (Dec. 1885): 751–52.

Henry Richmond by George Meredith. Review in *Time* n.s. III (Feb. 1886): 247–48.

Sandra Belloni by George Meredith. Review in *Time* n.s. III (March 1886): 379–80.

Beauchamp's Career by George Meredith. Review in *Time* n.s. IV (Oct. 1886): 508–9.

The Egoist by George Meredith. Review in *Time* n.s. IV (Dec. 1886): 755.

"George Meredith's Poetry." *Westminster Review* CXXVIII (Sept. 1887): 692–97.

Mes Souvenirs. Chapelle-Reauville, Eure, France: The Hours Press, n.d. [1929].

"The Miracle Plays and the Puritan Attack." Unpublished essay. Walpole Collection. Bodleian Library.

"Miss Smith, Kalinnikoff and Buhlig." *Saturday Review* CV (13 June 1908): 751–52.

"Frédéric Mistral." *National Review* VI (Jan. 1886): 659–70.

"Moussorgsky: His Songs and Piano Forte Music—I." *Saturday Review* CVI (5 Sept. 1908): 295–96.

"Moussorgsky: His Songs and Piano Forte Music—II." *Saturday Review* CVI (19 Sept. 1908): 362–63.

"The Martyrdom of Mozart." *Saturday Review* CV (16 May 1908): 623–24. (Reprinted in *Plays, Acting and Music* [1928])

Introduction. *My Life* by Josiah Flynt [Frank Willard]. New York: The Outing Press, 1908.

"Music Among the Arts." *Saturday Review* CIII (23 March 1907): 360–61.

"Music and Science." *Saturday Review* CVI (22 Aug. 1908): 232.

"Music and Social Flurry." *Saturday Review* CV (21 March 1908): 367–68.

"Music in Venice." *Saturday Review* CVI (17 Oct. 1908): 480–81.

"The Music-Hall of the Future." *Pall Mall Gazette* LIV (13 April 1892): 1–2.

"The New Art of the Black Board." *Saturday Review* CV (25 Jan. 1908): 101–2.

"The New Ballet at the Empire." *Sketch* III (4 Oct. 1893): 488.

"The New Ballet at the Alhambra." *Sketch* VII (3 Oct. 1894): 557.

"New English Art Club." *Saturday Review* XCVII (23 April 1904): 518–20.

"The New English Art Club." *Outlook* XVI (21 Oct. 1905): 550–51. (Last section incorporated in the Appendix to *Studies in Seven Arts*)

"A New Painter." *The Weekly Critical Review* I (2 April 1903): 2.

"Nikisch and Other Conductors." *Saturday Review* CIII (29 April 1907): 487–88.

"Notes on My Poems." *Athenaeum* (March 1916): 111–12.

"On Musical Criticism." *Academy* LXIII (2 Aug. 1902): 139–40. (Reprinted in *Plays, Acting, and Music*)

"On Crossing Stage to Right." *Academy* LXIII (9 Aug. 1902): 161–62. (Reprinted in *Plays, Acting, and Music*)

"On Some Modern Music." *Saturday Review* CV (7 March 1908): 297–98.

"On Some Violinists." *Saturday Review* CIII (4 May 1907): 554.

"An Original Dancer." *Star* (20 Feb.1892): 4.

Letter to Osborne, Churchill. 24 November 1880. Arthur Symons Collection. Princeton University Library.

———. 14 July 1883. Arthur Symons Collection. Princeton University Library.

———. 19 Mar. 1885. Arthur Symons Collection. Princeton University Library.

"Pachmann and Paderewski." *Saturday Review* CVI (11 July 1908): 44–45.

"Pachmann: With a Word on Godowsky." *Saturday Review* CIII (1 June 1907): 681.

"The Painting of the Nineteenth Century." *Fortnightly Review* n.s. LXXIII (March 1903): 520–34. (Reprinted in *Studies in Seven Arts* and in *Studies in Modern Painters*)

A Study of Walter Pater. London: Charles J. Sawyer, 1932.

"Walter Pater, 'Imaginary Portraits.'" *Time* n.s. VI (Aug. 1887): 157–62.

"Pianoforte—Playing as an Art." *Saturday Review* CIV (5 Oct. 1907): 417–18. (Reprinted in *Plays, Acting, and Music* [1928])

"Piano-Playing as an 'Accomplishment.'" *Saturday Review* CIV (10 Aug. 1907): 166–67. (Reprinted in *Plays, Acting, and Music* [1928])

Plays, Acting, and Music. London: Duckworth, 1903.

Plays, Acting, and Music. New edition, revised. London: Archibald Constable, 1909.

Plays, Acting, and Music. New edition, revised. London: Jonathan Cape (Traveler's Library): 1928.

"A Prince of Court Painters." *Weekly Critical Review* II (10 Sept. 1903): 183–84. (Reprinted in *Colour Studies in Paris.*)

"The Pre-Raphaelites at Whitechapel." *The Outlook* XV (1 April 1905): 450.

"Programme Music." *Saturday Review* CIII (6 April 1907): 423–24.

"Rameau I: The Man and His Art." *Saturday Review* CVI (3 Oct. 1908): 414–15.

"A French Blake: Odilon Redon." *Art Review* I (July 1890): 206–7. (Reprinted in *Colour Studies in Paris* and in *From Toulouse-Lautrec to Rodin.*)

"A Note on Rodin." *The Weekly Critical Review* II (20 August 1903): 107.

The Romantic Movement in English Poetry. London: Archibald Constable, 1909.

Dante Gabriel Rossetti. International Art Publishing Company, 1909. Issued without the author's permission.

"Sarasate: An Appreciation." *Illustrated London News* XCIX (21 Nov. 1891): 658.

"She Walks on Her Hands." *Star* (5 March 1892): 4.

Spiritual Adventures. London: Archibald Constable, 1905.

Studies in Elizabethan Drama. London: William Heinemann, 1919.

Studies in Modern Painters. New York: William Edwin Rudge, 1925.

Studies in Prose and Verse. London: J. M. Dent, 1904.

Studies in Seven Arts. London: Archibald Constable, 1906. New York: E. P. Dutton, 1906.

Studies in Two Literatures. London: Leonard Smithers, 1897.

"Swinburne as Dramatist." *Saturday Review* CI (24 Feb. 1906): 238–39.

The Symbolist Movement in Literature. Enlarged edition. 1919. Introduction by Richard Ellmann. New York: E. P. Dutton, 1958.

"A Study of John Addington Symonds." Unpublished manuscript. Arthur Symons Collection. Princeton University Library.

Carlo Gozzi by John Addington Symonds. Review in *Pall Mall Gazette* (21 Dec. 1889): 530.

Our Life in the Swiss Highlands by John Addington Symonds. Review in *St. James's Gazette* XXIV (17 May 1892): 6.

In the Key of Blue and Other Prose by John Addington Symonds. Review in *Athenaeum* (12 May 1893): 598.

Letter to Rhoda Symons. 30 May 1899. Arthur Symons Collection. Butler Library. Columbia University.

———. 20 July 1902. Arthur Symons Collection. Butler Library. Columbia University.

"Three Contemporary Poets." *London Quarterly Review* n.s. V (Jan. 1886): 238–50.

"Two Stage Societies." *Academy* LXII (29 March 1902): 343.

"The Training of the Contortionist." *Pall Mall Gazette* LIV (13 April 1892): 1–2.

Introduction. *Venus and Adonis* by William Shakespeare. London: W. Griggs, 1885.

"Wagner at Covent Garden." *Saturday Review* CIII (18 May 1907): 617–18.

"The Ideas of Richard Wagner." *Quarterly Review* CCIII (July 1905): 73–108. (Reprinted in *Studies in Seven Arts*)

Wanderings. London: J. M. Dent, 1931.

"Water Colours and Toys." *The Outlook* XV (18 Feb. 1905): 225.

"Watteau in Piccadilly." *Black and White* II (5 Dec. 1891): 757.

"Ysaÿe and Others." *Saturday Review* CV (30 May 1908): 689–90.

"Ysaÿe." *Saturday Review* CIV (28 Dec. 1907): 790–91. (Reprinted in *Plays, Acting and Music* [1928].)

Secondary Sources

For the most complete bibliography of writings on Symons see Stern, Carol Simpson, "Arthur Symons: An Annotated Bibliography About Him" *English Literature in Transition* XVII (1974): 77–133.

Arnold, Matthew. *On the Classical Tradition*. Vol. I of *The Complete Prose Works of Matthew Arnold*. Ed. R. H. Super. Ann Arbor: The University of Michigan Press, 1960.

Bablet, Denis. *Edward Gordon Craig*. London: William Heinemann, 1966.

Batten, Charles L. *Pleasurable Instruction*. Berkeley: University of California Press, 1978.

Baudelaire, Charles. *Selected Writings on Art and Artists*. Trans. P. E. Charvet. Harmondsworth: Penguin Books, 1972.

Beckson, Karl. "The Critic and the Actress: The Troubled Lives of Arthur and Rhoda Symons." *Columbia Library Columns* XXXIII (Nov. 1983): 3–10.

———. "Symons' 'A Prelude to Life,' Joyce's *A Portrait*, and the Religion of Art." *James Joyce Quarterly* XV (Spring 1978): 222–28.

Beckson, Karl and Munro, John M. "Arthur Symons, Browning, and the Development of the Modern Aesthetic." *Studies in English* X (Autumn 1970): 687–99.

Berlioz, Hector. *Evenings in the Orchestra*. Trans. C. R. Fortescoe. Baltimore: Penguin Books, 1964.

Bordeux, Jeanne. *Eleonora Duse*. London: Hutchinson, 1924.

Borrow, George. *Lavengro*. 3 Vols. London: John Murry, 1851.

Byron, Lord George Gordon. *The Poetical Works of Lord Byron*. Ed. Ernest Hartley Coleridge. London: John Murry, 1905.

Cairns, David. Introduction to *Evenings in the Orchestra* by Hector Berlioz. Baltimore: Penguin Books, 1967.

Campbell, Mrs. Patrick. *My Life and Some Letters*. London: Hutchinson, 1922.

Cox, Edward Godfrey. *A Reference Guide to the Literature of Travel*. Seattle: University of Washington Press, 1935.

Craig, Edward Gordon. *The Art of the Theatre*. London: T. N. Fowlis, 1905.

———. *Gordon Craig on Movement and Dance*. Ed. Arnold Rood. London: Dance Books, 1977.

———. "A Note on the Proceeding Essay." *The Mask* (March 1914): 189.

———. *On the Art of the Theatre*. London: William Heinemann, 1911.

C. S. C. "A Reminiscence." *The Sketch* (23 May 1894): 173–74.

Dunlop, Ian. *Degas*. London: Thames Hudson, 1979.

"Duse in *Camille*." *The Stage* 1 June 1893: 10–15.

Ellis, Havelock. *From Rousseau to Proust*. London: Archibald Constable, 1936.

———. *The New Spirit*. London: Walter Scott, 1892.

———. *The Soul of Spain*. London: Archibald Constable, 1908.

Ellmann, Richard. Introduction to *The Symbolist Movement in Literature* by Arthur Symons. New York: E. P. Dutton, 1958.

Elsen, Albert. "Rodin's Drawings and the Mystery of Abundance." In *The Drawings of Rodin*. Ed. Albert Elsen and Varnedoe, J. Kirk. London: Elek Books, 1972.

Fitzgerald, Percy. *The Art of Acting*. London: Swan Sonnenschein, 1892.

———. *The Art of the Stage as Set Out in Lamb's Dramatic Essays*. London: Remington, 1885.

Fletcher, Ian. "Explorations and Recoveries—II: Symons, Yeats and Demonic Dance." *London Magazine* VII (June 1960): 46–60.

Gilcher, Edwin. *A Bibliography of George Moore*. Illinois: Northern Illinois University Press, 1970.

Gordon, Jan. B. "The Dance Macabre of Arthur Symons' *London Nights*," *Victorian Poetry* IX (Winter 1971): 429–43.

Gourmont, Remy de. *Selected Writings*. Ed. Glen S. Burn. Ann Arbor: The University of Michigan Press, 1966.

Guilbert, Yvette. *The Song of My Life*. Trans. Beatrice de Holthoir. London: George G. Harrap, 1929.

H. N. "An Appreciation." *The Sketch* (23 May 1894): 137–38.

Halls, W. D. *Maurice Maeterlinck: A Study of His Life and Thought*. Oxford: The Clarendon Press, 1966.

Heine, Heinrich. *The Works of Heinrick Heine*. 12 Vols. Trans. Charles Godfrey Leland. London: William Heinemann, 1891.

Hoffmann, E. T. A. *Kreisleriana*. Trans. Albert Benguin. Paris: Editions Fourcade, 1931.

Hough, Graham. *The Last Romantics*. London: Gerald Duckworth, 1949.

Houghton, Philip. "The Marguerite Gautier of Eleonora Duse." *The Theatre* XXIII (1 June 1894): 303–5.

Houghton, Walter E. *The Victorian Frame of Mind*. New Haven: Yale University Press, 1957.

Hutton, Edward. *Italy and the Italians*. Edinburgh and London: William Blackwood and Sons, 1902.

Huxley, Aldous. *Letters of Aldous Huxley*. Ed. Grover Smith. London: Chatto and Windus, 1969.

James, Henry. *English Hours*. London: William Heinemann, 1905.

——. *Portraits of Places*. London: Macmillan, 1883.

Jenkyns, Richard. *The Victorians and Ancient Greece*. Oxford: Basil Blackwell, 1980.

Joyce, James. *A Portrait of the Artist as a Young Man*. Definitive Edition. Ed. Richard Ellmann. London: Jonathan Cape, 1964.

Kermode, Frank. "Poet and Dancer Before Diaghilev," *Partisan Review* XXVIII (Jan.–Feb. 1961): 48–75.

——. *The Romantic Image* London: Routledge and Kegan Paul, 1957.

Kirkpatrick, F. A. "The Literature of Travel, 1700–1900." In *The Cambridge History of English Literature*. Vol. XIV. Ed. A. W. Ward and A. R. Waller. Cambridge: Cambridge University Press, 1916.

Knapp, Bettina and Myra Chieman. *That Was Yvette*. London: Fredrick Muller, 1966.

Lamb, Charles. *Charles Lamb: Prose and Poetry*. Ed. George Gordon. Oxford: Oxford University Press, 1921.

——. *The Works of Charles Lamb*. 6 Vols. Ed. E. V. Lucas. London: Methuen, 1912.

Le Gallienne, Eva. *The Mystic of the Theatre*. London: Bodley Head, 1966.

Lee, Vernon [Violet Paget]. *The Enchanted Woods*, London: John Lane, 1905.

——. *Genius Loci*. London: Grant Richards, 1899.

——. *Limbo*. London: Grant Richards, 1897.

Lhombreaud, Roger. *Arthur Symons: A Critical Biography*. London: Unicorn Press, 1963.

Liszt, Franz. *Frédéric Chopin*. Trans. Edward N. Waters. New York: Macmillan, 1963.

Lucas, E. V. *A Wanderer in Florence*. London: Methuen, 1912.

——. *A Wanderer in Venice*. London: Methuen, 1914.

Lucie-Smith, Edward. *Toulouse-Lautrec*. London: Phaidon Press, 1977.

MacColl, D. S. *Confessions of a Keeper*. London: Alexander Maclenose, 1931.

——. *The Life, Work, and Setting of Philip Wilson Steer*. London: Faber and Faber, 1945.

——. *Nineteenth Century Art*. Glasgow: James Maclehose and Sons, 1902.

"Madame Réjane: A Chat During an Entr'acte." *The Sketch* VI (4 July 1894): 520.

Moore, George. *Impressions and Opinions*. London: David Nutt, 1891.

——. *Modern Painting*. Enlarged Edition. London: Walter Scott, 1897.

Morris, William. *William Morris, Artist Writer Socialist*. 2 Vols. Ed. May Morris. Oxford: Basil Blackwell, 1934.

Muehlig, Linda P. *Degas and Dance*. Northhampton: Smith College Museum of Art, 1979.

Munro, John M. *Arthur Symons*. New York: Twayne Publishers, 1969.

Pater, Walter. *The Letters of Walter Pater*. Ed. Lawrence Evlans. London: Oxford University Press, 1970.

——. *The Works of Walter Pater*. 10 Vols. London: Macmillan, 1910.

Peckham, Morse. *The Triumph of Romanticism*. Columbia, South Carolina: University of South Carolina Press, 1970.

Peters, Robert L. *The Crown of Apollo: Swinburne's Principles of Literature and Art.* Detroit: Wayne State University Press, 1965.

———. "Whistler and the English Poets of the 1890's." *Modern Language Quarterly* XVIII (Sept. 1957): 251–61.

Pritchett, V. S. "The Writer as Traveller." *The New Statesman and Nation* LI (16 June 1956): 692–3.

Redfern, B. A. "Some Notes of Borrow: His Books and Personality." *Manchester Quarterly* CXXV (Jan. 1913): 55–63.

Reff, Theodore. *Degas: The Artist's Mind.* London: Thames and Hudson, 1976.

Roberts, Keith. *Degas.* Oxford: Phaidon Press, 1976.

Rodin, Auguste. *Cathedrals of France.* Trans. Elisabeth Chase Geissbuhler. London: Country Life Books, 1965.

Rowell, George, editor. *Victorian Dramatic Criticism.* London: Methuen, 1971.

Ruskin, John. *The Works of John Ruskin.* 25 Vols. Ed. E. F. Cook and Alexander Wedderburn. London: George Allan, 1903.

Savage, Henry. "Richard Middleton (1881–1911)." *English Review* II (July 1912): 549–68.

Schumann, Robert. *The Musical World of Robert Schumann: A Selection from Schumann's Own Writings.* Trans. and Ed. Henry Pleasants. New York: St. Martin's Pres, 1965.

———. *On Music and Musicians.* Trans. Paul Rosenfeld. Ed. Krond Wolff. New York: Pantheon Books, 1946.

Scott, Clement. "Madame Réjane." *The Sketch* VI (27 June 1894): 475–59.

Shaw, George Bernard. *The Works of George Bernard Shaw.* 33 Vols. London:

Shelley, Percy Bysshe. *The Letters of Percy Bysshe Shelley.* 2 Vols. Ed. Frederick L. Jones. Oxford: Oxford University Press, 1964.

Sickert, Walter. "French Pictures at Knoedler's Gallery." *The Burlington Magazine* XLIII (July 1923): 34–43.

———. Introduction to the Catalogue of the *London Impressionists' Exhibition.* Reprinted in D. S. Mac-Coll. *The Life, Work, and Setting of Philip Wilson Steer.* London: Faber and Faber, 1945. pp. 175–76.

———. "Modern Realism in Painting." In Andre Theuriet, *Jules Bastien-Lepage and His Art.* London: T. Fisher Unwin, 1892. pp. 140–41.

Spalding, Frances. *Whistler.* London: Oxford: Phaidon Press, 1979.

Stein, Jack M. *Richard Wagner and the Synthesis of the Arts.* Detroit: Wayne State University Press, 1960.

Stevenson, R. A. M. *Velasquez.* London: George Bell and Sons, 1895.

Stokes, John. "The Legend of Duse." In *Decadence and the 1890s.* Ed. Ian Fletcher and Malcolm Bradbury. London: Edward Arnold, 1979.

———. *Resistible Theatres.* London: Paul Elek, 1972.

Story, Sommerville. *Rodin.* Oxford: Phaidon Press, 1979.

Strauss, Richard. *Hans von Bülow and Richard Strauss: Correspondence.* Ed. Willi Schuh and Franz Trenner. Trans. Anthony Gishford. London: Bogsegand Hawkes, 1913.

Styan, J. L. *Drama, Stage, and Audience.* Cambridge: Cambridge University Press, 1975.

Sutton, Denys. *The Complete Paintings of Toulouse-Lautrec.* London: Weidenfeld and Nicholson, 1973.

Swinburne, Algernon Charles. *The Complete Works of Swinburne.* 20 Vols. Ed. Edmund Gosse and Thomas James Wise. London: William Heinemann, 1926.

Swinglehurst, Edmund. *The Romantic Journey.* London: Pica Editions, 1974.

Symonds, John Addington. *Essays Speculative and Suggestive.* 2 Vols. London: Chapman and Hall, 1890.

———. *Italian Byways.* London: Smith, Elder, 1883.

———. *The Letters of John Addington Symonds.* 3 Vols. Ed. Herbert M. Schueller and Robert L. Peters. Detroit: Wayne State University Press, 1969.

——. "May in Umbria." *Cornhill Magazine* XLIV (Oct. 1881): 444–60.

——. *Our Life in the Swiss Highlands*. London: Adam and Charles Black, 1892.

——. *Sketches and Studies in Italy*. London: Smith, Elder, 1879.

——. *Sketches and Studies in Italy and Greece*. London: Smith, Elder, 1874.

——. "Spring Wanderings." *Cornhill Magazine* XLI (June 1881): 672–83.

Sypher, Wylie. *Rococo to Cubism*. New York: Random House, 1963.

Temple, Ruth Z. *The Critic's Alchemy*. New York: Twayne Publishers, 1953.

Wagner, Richard. *Richard Wagner's Prose Works*. 10 Vols. Trans. William Ashton Ellis. London: Kegan Paul, 1896.

Warner, Eric and Hough, Graham. *Strangeness and Beauty*. 2 Vols. Cambridge: Cambridge University Press, 1983.

Waters, Edward N. Introduction to *Frédéric Chopin* by Franz Liszt. New York: Macmillan, 1963.

Werner, Alfred. *The Graphic Works of Odilon Redon*. New York: Dover Publications, 1969.

Whistler, James McNeill. *The Gentle Art of Making Enemies*. London: William Heinemann, 1890.

——. *Mr. Whistler's Ten O'Clock*. London: Chatto and Windus, 1888.

——. *"Notes"—"Harmonies"—"Nocturnes."* London: Tite Street, Chelsea, 1884.

——. *Whistler v. Ruskin. Art and Art Critics*. London: Chatto and Windus, 1878.

Willard, Frank. *Tramping with Tramps*. London: T. Fisher Unwin, 1908.

Yeats, William Butler. *Essays and Introductions*. London: Macmillan, 1966.

——. Letter to Rhoda Symons. 13 Oct. 1908. Arthur Symons Collection. Butler Library. Columbia University.

Zabel, Morton D. Introduction to *The Art of Travel: Scenes and Journeys in America, England, France, and Italy from the Travel Writings of Henry James*. New York: Doubleday, 1958.

Index